Coghlan and Quo

Coghlan and Quo

Steven Myatt

Aureus

First Published in hardback 2004
This paperback edition published 2020

ISBN 978 1 899750 47 4

Printed in Great Britain.

A catalogue record for this book is available from the British Library.

Aureus Publishing Limited
Castle Court
Castle-upon-Alun
St. Bride's Major
Vale of Glamorgan
CF32 0TN

Tel: (01656) 880033 Fax: (01656) 880033
Int. tel: +44 1656 880033 Int. fax: +44 1656 880033

E-mail: sales@aureus.co.uk
Web site: www.aureus.co.uk

for

MPH
TJQ
PJZ

Photographs

The author would like to thank the following for their permission to use photographs in the book.

From John Coghlan's collection:
Page No.s 20, 25, 45, 91, 137, 141, 147, 152, 163, 181, 183, 189, 193, 213

From Colin Johnson's collection:
Front cover and inside front flap; Page No.s 2 (Chalkie Davies), 15, 36, 40, 85, 129, 135, 198, 206, 223 (Chalkie Davies)

From Steven Myatt's collection:
Page No. 214

From Lilian Rodd's collection:
Page No. 126

From Bob Young's collection:
Page No.s 74, 131, 145, 157, 171

From Dieter Zill's collection:
Page No.s 48, 54, 57, 66, 77, 80, 166

Acknowledgements

For their assistance, enthusiasm and patience, particular thanks go to:

Maartin Allcock
Keith Altham
Trevor Baines
Richard Beddall
Paul Brett
Andy Bown
Charlotte Coghlan
Gillie Coghlan
Jess Jaworksi
Colin Johnson
Kenney Jones
Alan Lancaster
Roy Lynes
Phil May
John Peel
Don Powell
Chris Tarrant
Bob Young

and State Of Quo

Preface

In 1967 I bought the 45rpm single of *Pictures Of Matchstick Men*; not on my own account, but on behalf of the Saint Andrew's Church Youth Club in Timperley – though curiously I did hang on to it, and even now it's on the juke box in my kitchen. After that there was Ice In The Sun, which made some impression on me, but then the band sort of disappeared and I gave them no more thoughts.

I next came across the band in the early seventies; I went to any number of biker events - shows, runs and rallies - and Quo music was as fundamental to that scene as beer, unspeakable burgers and 'Born to Be Wild'. By then they had made a huge sea-change and evolved into a blues-tinges boogie band, and one thing I recognised was that they knew their audience, and what that audience wanted, as well as any other band on the planet. As I was working on this book, just about everyone I spoke to mentioned the fact that they have the most loyal fan-base imaginable; their fans simply adore them. And would walk a hundred miles over hot coals to catch one of their songs.

This isn't the story of the band though; this is the story of John Coghlan, yet one Quo fact leaves me bemused. Since their renaissance in the early Seventies, Quo have been a massively successful band. They have sold many millions of records and have toured tirelessly. However, no-one – not even Francis Rossi, who either wrote or co-wrote a very large number of their songs – is truly wealthy.

They spent a lot of money, of course they did; but no more than most Premier League bands – and a lot less than some. The amount of money they have turned over in the last four decades must be enormous, while what they actually hung onto was a pittance. Very curious – but that's a different book, I guess.

John's is one hell of a story. As a youngster growing up in South London not long after the Second World War had finished, it looked as if his future would be far from distinguished. He didn't excel at school, and didn't stand out from his friends and colleagues in any obvious way. His only advantage in life was that he was supported by a loving and encouraging family. He was very lucky, in conventional thinking, when his father secured him a white collar job on leaving school, which meant that he would have clean hands and smarter than average clothes all his working life. When most of his school chums would be looking at fifty years bashing sheet metal or welding pipes, John's prospects looked good. Right now he might still be living in those Victorian suburbs, might drink in the same pubs around where he grew up, and might be looking forward to his retirement – and thinking of moving to a little bungalow on the coast.

John was that one in a thousand that broke out though, and for him it wasn't sport or 'academic suburban kid makes it to Oxbridge', but music, which in the early Sixties was just becoming one of the very few routes which talented youngsters could take – if they dared – to revolutionise their lives and bring them fame and fortune. By the late Seventies his lifestyle could hardly have been more different from that of his parents and his school chums, and yet everyone who knew him then says that he remained a very approachable and down to earth bloke. Or at least, when he was away from the pressures of rock 'n roll he was ...

What has utterly frustrated me, as his biographer, is that at no time, through many long conversations (sober and not entirely sober) have I managed to get him to say a bad word about anyone in, or involved in, Status Quo. He's not angry, he's not bitter – he's proud, and that's all. That's not what I expected. No matter how I dug, I couldn't find any resentment; no personal or professional grudges, no snide comparisons between himself and 'them'. That's truly remarkable.

Steven Myatt
Cheshire, May 2004

1

Christmas Eve 1975; John Coghlan booked into the Holiday Inn in central London. He had a few personal things in a small bag, and in the hotel car park he'd left his new Range Rover. He had no cash in his pockets but he did have a credit card, which had the sort of credit limit which would allow him to buy just about anything and everything he could possibly want or need. He was on his own however, and he wasn't in the best of moods.

He was the drummer with the rock band Status Quo; already highly recognisable, and with his long straight, centre-parted hair, his droopy moustache and his faded, low-waisted blue jeans he looked every inch the rock star. The band had enjoyed a handful of hits up to that point, and 1975 had been their best ever year – indeed at the beginning of the year they had seen their first number one in the UK singles charts, with *Down Down*. They had toured almost endlessly, made any number of TV and radio appearances, and been in studio recording new material. They had survived very lean times earlier in the decade but were undeniably back on top.

Known for his tendency to moodiness at best, and his temper at worst, the shutters were definitely down, and you'd have been well advised to keep your distance. Any fan who had spotted him in reception and dared ask for an autograph at that point would have had a tale to tell their grand-children.

It looked as if he was going to spend Christmas alone, in an anonymous hotel room. His wife had kicked him out. She didn't understand the rock 'n roll world, and the glamour had faded from their marriage all too quickly. John's seemingly incessant touring, and his habit of turning on the charm for almost any woman who crossed his path, had probably meant that the marriage was in fact never going to last.

Now though, with festive lights sparkling all through the city and the radio churning out that season's Christmas hit, he was on his own. The rest of the band were with their families; heaven knows, everyone's with their families at Christmas. Except John; he was in a hotel room on his own, with little more than a toothbrush and a fully-stocked mini bar. He wasn't feeling hugely rock 'n roll.

Having paced up and down for an hour or so, and exhausted the contents of the mini-bar, John picked up the phone and called Trevor Baines at his home on the Isle of Man. He wanted to share his woes with someone. Trevor was an acquaintance rather than a friend – but would in time turn out to be a very good friend - and John poured out his troubles. Trevor simply told John to get on a plane and fly over immediately. He's the sort of man who would know exactly when the flights left – and how to hold them for half an hour so that a friend wouldn't miss one.

He didn't need to repeat the invitation. John drove straight to Heathrow, abandoned the Range Rover there, and boarded a scheduled flight - which would have him on the island in less than an hour, where Trevor would have a car waiting for him.

Ronaldsway airport is at the southern end of the island, so for the majority of flights, as you fly in you've seen nothing of its landscape. You might spot the waves of the cold, dark-grey Irish Sea hitting the rocks, and see flat, featureless fields stretching out to the north. It's a barren landscape, with few trees, and what there are, are no more than twenty or so feet high. Seen through an aircraft window, it's not a heart-warming sight, even on a bright day, and in the early Seventies the airport buildings gave the impression that you'd arrived in a Third World country.

However, this was how the rich and famous came and went, and in the Seventies they did so in ever-increasing numbers. Personal taxation was rising to crippling heights in the UK, but just a few miles away, this tiny bump in the sea had its own parliament, its own laws and its own tax regime. Over here things were very different.

Less than three hours after walking out of the Holiday Inn, John was in Trevor's more than palatial home, with a drink in his hand. He and Trevor were very different; John was ten years younger and was a south London boy who had made good, and had never lost the accent. He was very much the rock musician from central casting, and in that sense wasn't entirely of this world. He's the same today, in fact. Trevor was sophisticated, well educated, and moved effortlessly on an international stage. He looked, sounded and acted like the banking magnate he was. Still does.

There was one other crucial difference; John was the musician and Trevor was a fan. Those who can, do. Those who can't, buy the records.

On the other hand they had a lot in common. The two could giggle together for hours when the rest of the company didn't even know that there was a joke hanging in the ether. And they had two great interests in common, which they pursued with unfailing energy and dedication; alcohol and women.

Trevor had warned John that he would 'have to rough it'. That was a relative term. In this case it meant that John had the lodge at the end of the drive to himself. He says that late afternoon on Christmas Eve he remembers lying down on the bed, and at some point someone came in and pulled the covers up over him – tucking him in almost, as if he was a child. He might have been dreaming, it might have been true, but the effect was the same. He drifted back into sleep knowing that he had found sanctuary.

1974 had been quite a year. The itinerary of live shows had run into three figures, and as well as twice touring what were then Britain's biggest venues, the band had toured Sweden, the USA, Australia, France, Germany – also twice - and played in Norway, Finland, Canada. Then there had been the recording sessions, the TV appearances, the press interviews and the unavoidable glad-handing with record company executive and their families, their friends and, it often seemed, their friends' friends' friends.

It was a very gruelling schedule, and although many musicians seemed oblivious to the fatigue and pressure, John was starting to see the downside of the success that the band had been looking for, for so long. In that, it was the shape of things to come.

That first night, in Trevor's lodge, he slept, he says, better than he had done for years. When he awoke though the skies were leaden and there were hints of sunlight very low on the horizon. He guessed it was dawn, but feeling hungry he made his way up to the house. The door was unlocked so he went in and set off for the kitchen. On his way he glanced through the door of the dining room. The table was set for a large number of people, and it was dominated by what was left of a huge turkey. It had been stripped of its flesh, and looked, he thought at the time, like the bones of a dinosaur in a museum. The crockery and cutlery were all used, the glasses and bottles were all empty. He began to realise that it wasn't dawn, it was twilight, and Christmas Day had just about been and gone.

He wasn't unhappy on his own in the huge house – in the way that he had been disconsolate in the hotel bedroom – but having sat for a while, helped himself to a drink and made himself a sandwich, he had a brain-wave and phoned The Palace casino in Douglas. Yes, they told, Mr Baines and party were there and yes, of course he would be more than welcome to join them. A car would be sent for him.

He had had his moments of peace and solitude. From the moment he walked through the door of the casino he was pitched head first into a world-class party. In a land where the party never stopped. John didn't spend Christmas '74 in a hotel room. Instead, it was a riot. He was with people in whose company he felt comfortable, and the booze was unlimited; endless.

Life on the Isle of Man was very different from what he was used to. For ten years he had been playing in the band; a period which had seen him move from adolescence to adulthood with hardly any exposure to the real world. He had been in the company of the same very small group of people for a decade, living first in draughty, rattling vans, then in limousines; first in bed and breakfast accommodation with Formica on the dining tables and 40-watt light bulbs in the bathrooms, and then in luxurious hotels. He'd been in the band since he was fifteen, and had been professional since he was seventeen. It had been a very long, very hard slog. They had seen success, then failure, but they had stuck at it. Now they were becoming very well established and were now seeing the rewards of their work.

Life in the Baines household was leisured and effortless. It was a long way from everything that had gone before. That Christmas – despite the endless alcohol – was an eye-opener.

Trevor nicknamed him 'The Lost John': Most days lunch was served at one, but John didn't get out of bed until six. That was typical. By then, as a rock star, he did whatever he wanted to do, and whenever he wanted to do it.

The festive season came and went and he was still in residence three months later. He paid for his bed and board by presenting his host with a full professional drum kit (which Trevor still has), but John didn't leave it at that; every so often he would add to it or update it.

On one occasion Trevor came home to find that John had quaffed two

Blue denim, white baseball shoes, lots of energy – and all ending together.

bottles of very rare, very expensive wine, which he had set aside for a special occasion. He let John know his feelings in no uncertain terms, and John crept off sheepishly – and returned with a case of the very best champagne by way of an apology.

John was in his element on the island. Here there was lots of space, endless amounts to drink, and innumerable new women to get to know. As Trevor says, 'When it came to the girls over here, John certainly did the business'. Trevor's marriage to Carole had ended, and there's no doubt that he was up for his share of the good times too. They were quite a pair. They believed that every night should be party night, but then that's what both rock 'n roll stars and jet-setting playboys are supposed to do.

There was also a discothèque in the basement of Trevor's home. This was decorated as a medieval dungeon, and was fully equipped; very fully equipped, by all accounts. It was the setting for many of their parties. These events became legendary – spoken of in whispers by outsiders - and as Trevor puts it, more than slightly obliquely, 'Some of the performances were pretty grand ...'

John had first been to the island in June '74, when Quo were booked to play at The Palace casino – which was on of the, admittedly few, big venues which catered for holiday-makers. Even in high summer, flying into Ronaldsway wouldn't have inspired delight. They weren't greeted by a rock 'n roll sight, and the band must have wondered what on earth they were doing there. First on a bleak, wind-swept airstrip which was only one notch up from a landing strip, and then in Douglas, a resort that looked, felt and smelt as if it had been preserved in formaldehyde since the Thirties. The Isle of Man was where your gran went for her holidays; where the elderly, who found the modern world just far too fast, retired to – and died.

Trevor was the promoter of the Quo gig in that he had put the money up; 'More for fun that for business' he says, and he recalls that the band played for £400 plus expenses. That wasn't a huge amount of money for the band; after they'd paid the roadies and the management had seen their cut the four got maybe £60 each; the equivalent of perhaps a reasonable week's wages for a working man. Three years earlier though – despite having had two top ten records at the end of the previous decade - they might have been performing just for their expenses. Or their management might even have had to pay the venue to get them in front of an audience.

Their particular rock 'n roll roller-coaster had taken a long time climbing them up, but had then dropped them back down far more quickly. In recent times though it had started to take them upwards once again; much further up. A year previously they had been back in the top ten, with a number eight, and then in the autumn one of their singles had gone to number five – the highest-placed single they had ever had in the UK. Now people knew their name, and as importantly, recognised their sound. Pretty well instantly.

Status Quo's manager, Colin Johnson, remembers a moment of great embarrassment at the party after that first Manx gig; 'Trevor had a very beautiful wife, Carole, and she was sat in the casino with her feet up on a coffee table. John wanted to get past her, and he would never say excuse me to anyone, so he deliberately fell over her legs – which was more usually a Rick Parfitt trick. I said to him 'John! That's the promoter's wife!' And he said 'She shouldn't have her legs on the table; I wanted to get past'.' That was the way John did things.

It had been a great gig though, and Trevor had enjoyed it enormously. He recalls bringing the band back to his home after the gig – despite John's behaviour - and that Rick Parfitt tuned his guitar to make Trevor's admittedly very amateur playing much easier.

So far as being party boys went, Status Quo had met their match – even though he did look and sound an unlikely candidate for the job. Trevor's house was designed for having good times, and as the evening wore on, the party got livelier. And livelier still. Much drink was taken, before it was decided that they would play tag in the garden. No-one can remember whose idea it was – or more likely, no-one is owning up.

Tag is the schoolyard game where everyone runs around like daft things, and one person is 'it', but if that person touches you then you're 'it'. The only difference was that Trevor and Quo played their game in Trevor's collection of cars. The rich are different, as the saying goes, and they certainly don't drive the same cars as the rest of us. In the mid-Seventies Trevor wasn't seen behind the wheel of an Allegro or a Cortina.

In the morning there were seven badly damaged cars scattered over the garden – the previously immaculate garden. It was chaos. It looked like the set of The Blues Brothers after they had filmed the end sequence. A car nut would have wept. There were cars on their sides. There were cars nose-first through the hedge. And boot-first through a wall. At least one was on its roof. Trevor thought it was a hoot - and he didn't go looking for his insurance documents.

It was about right for one of his parties. A year or so later Status Quo played a return gig on the island, and again they all piled back to Trevor's house after the show. The following morning Trevor woke to see a certain amount of destruction – but also nine donkeys peacefully grazing in the garden on windfall apples. He remembers that there were nine because he counted them several times. He doubted his sanity, or sobriety, until he discovered that they were refugees from a donkey sanctuary some way away. How they got there remains a mystery to him to this day.

Trevor - whose main interest is his family's private bank - had moved to the island in 1972 to avoid swingeing UK death duties, and tended to be described in the press as a millionaire playboy. Certainly he has always taken his pleasures very seriously, and believes that the good things in life are there to be enjoyed. He's also known as a very dedicated racing driver. On his first visit to his home John was greatly impressed by the fact that Trevor had a cinema beneath the house.

Within a few years the island was to become home to both John and the girl who would join him there, and in turn become his second wife, Gillie West. On the Isle of Man they would immerse themselves in a life of leisured extravagance and endless partying. They had a glorious life, with every luxury they could want or imagine. As a high-profile rock 'n roll star John was a big celebrity on the island. Everyone wanted to know him, everyone wanted to be his friend, and he and Gillie were welcome everywhere.

It wasn't to last forever though. When the band was at the height of its powers, when they had achieved everything they set out to do – and more - John simply walked away. He walked away from the glory, the private jets, the gold records, and the seemingly-endless cash. And at that point, pretty well everything froze. He had spent nearly twenty years climbing up the steep slopes. He was to have a short time sitting on the summit before he realised that in fact the ground beneath him was sloping away. Over the next twenty years the gradient was to get steeper and steeper.

2

John Coghlan was born in Dulwich Hospital on 19 September 1946. He was very much of the generation which became known as the 'baby boomers'. Soldiers, sailors and fliers returning after demobilisation were re-establishing their lives, their careers and their marriages, and of course this latter part often involved fathering children. A large number of babies who went on to become rock and pop stars were conceived soon after the end of hostilities, indeed 1946 was a good year for London-born rockers; they include Keith Moon, Peter Green, Roxy Music saxophonist Andy Mackay, Joe Cocker's drummer Pete Gavin, Faces/Small Faces bassist Ronnie Lane, Marianne Faithfull, punkmeister Malcolm McLaren and steel-lunged teen queen Helen Shapiro.

The young John Coghlan was no rebel. He was never part of that strand of pop and rock which only made its way forward by forcefully, and often nihilistically, turning its back on everything that had gone before. As a youngster, John had nothing he needed to rebel against. He disliked school, but there was compensation enough in a loving and supportive home life. It was lively and colourful too; John was brought up in packed home, surrounded by three generations of his family, including, exotically for 1950s south London, a French grandmother.

He was an only child, so the age range at his house was sharply tipped away from him, but – again there's another side - he was the focus of all the affection. In the days before effective contraception was freely available it was unusual to be an only child; as John says, 'Other kids used to

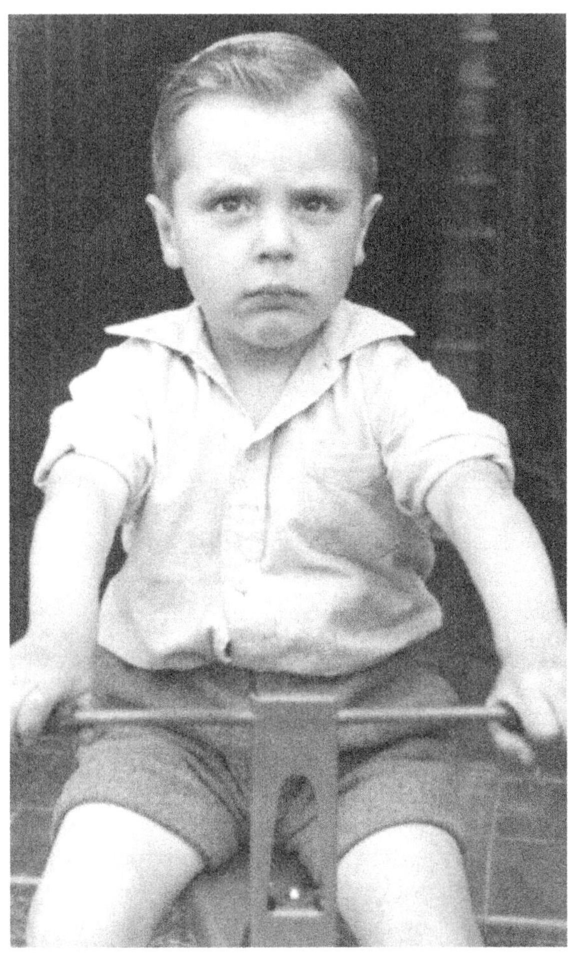

John Coghlan aged three, and already practising mean and moody - and the perfect quiff.

ask me, 'What's up with your mum and dad? How come you haven't got any brothers and sisters?' I always told them that it was nothing to do with me, and that they'd have to ask my parents. That tended to shut them up.'

John's father, Jack, a Glaswegian, was a furniture salesman in a local store. He had spent his war in the Middlesex regiment, driving a Bren gun carrier, and eventually taking part in the D-Day invasion and the subsequent push into Germany itself.

His mother, Ann, was a local girl from South Norwood, but of French descent. They lived with her parents and John's aunt and uncle; all in a three-bedroom semi-detached; 'My granny come over from France with her husband, my granddad, and she always said that the crossing was so rough she was never tempted to go back. As a kid I thought that was very strange. She was a typical little old French grandmother; she was a wonderful cook and made great stews. I reckon it's because of her that I love France to this day.'

Jack and Ann's passion was dancing, and there was rarely a weekend through the Fifties when they weren't sparkling at the local dance halls, dressed to thrill and dancing to the very best of the big bands.

They weren't musicians, but of course, as skilled dancers, they had natural rhythm. As a special treat John was allowed to tag along with them when they went to the local ballrooms. 'That's where his sense of rhythm came from, he reckons; 'In later years my dad always said that all I ever wanted to do in the dance halls was watch the drummer. He reckons that one day, during a break, I crept round behind the drum kit, got settled in and started playing. I don't remember that! The drummer would have been bloody annoyed.

'My parents danced to live bands, and I do remember enjoying the music, and in particular watching the drummers in whichever dance band it was. Actually, it was often more of an orchestra rather than a band; lots of musicians up on the stage – I loved it. They played either swing jazz the more straight-laced ballroom stuff.'

The Coghlan home was in the rather drab Victorian suburb of Upper Norwood in south London; part of the huge brick-built expansion of the city that was made both possible and necessary by the growth of the railways in the Nineteenth century. They lived in Sainsbury Road – at number 48 - just off the romantic-sounding Gypsy Hill (with its very handy railway station). At the back of the house was an allotment where John's grandfather grew their vegetables and a few flowers. Across the road was a timber yard, Davies's.

John's earliest memories include buying sweets at Cowie's shop down the road, and the endless shunting of coal and timber wagons on the railway. A couple of hundred yards down Sainsbury Road, into Bristow Road and turn right into Whiteley Road, was the pleasant open space of Norwood Park with its playground.

In the other direction, up the hill, was Crystal Palace. Joseph Paxton's great glasshouse, built in Hyde Park for The Great Exhibition of 1851, was re-erected here after the exhibition, and gave both the summit of this steep hill and the surrounding area its name. The building was destroyed by fire in 1936, but the park was an extensive pleasure garden in the Fifties, and indeed still is – with acres of well-mown grass, boating lakes, tennis courts, tea rooms and a large sports arena made famous by the athletics events held there.

Crystal Palace was also nationally and internationally famous for having what was then the tallest structure in London; its own Eiffel Tower. The Crystal Palace radio and TV transmitting tower is over 900 feet high and is a landmark for most of south London. It is unique in being a self-supporting lattice structure, rather than being held up by steel guys, and it still relays entertainment to one-fifth of British viewers and listeners,

For any young boy an afternoon at the Crystal Palace Park was an adventure and a great treat; a ten minute walk up the hill and into another world, where there was endless space, acres of green grass, fresh air, and ice lollies.

The Coghlan family took their annual holidays at the coast – along with most of the British population. Ramsgate was a favourite, as was Margate or Brighton. Winchelsea made a bit of a change. 'We usually stayed in caravans – probably because it didn't cost much. I suppose I enjoyed that when I was little … but I so hate them now! I hate them on the road; I hate the things. To be fair, they served their purpose in those days. I loved the seaside. They were great holidays.'

Jack Coghlan had a rare passion for Hillman Huskys; a shorter, load-carrying version of a Hillman Minx, but more of a van with side windows than an estate car. The first was crimson and cream, and the second one blue and cream – smart two-tone paint jobs. One of these became John's first car in time (once he'd passed his test – he failed first time on account of going straight through a red light); a tricky thing to drive, with no synchromesh on first gear, but great for lugging a drum kit around.

John attended Kingswood Primary School from the age of five to eleven, which was just round the corner, and then went to Kingsdale Comprehensive. This much larger school was a mile or so to the north, between Alleyn Park and Dulwich. He was an undistinguished pupil.

'I don't like looking back to my school days, primary or secondary. I hated school; it terrified me. I enjoyed Physical Training as they called it, English, Geography and Woodwork – and hated the rest. I absolutely *hated* Mathematics.

'Some people enjoy school and are keen to go on to college or university, but I just wanted to get out of the system as soon as I could. I could have had a better education, but I just hated the whole process.

'I had no idea what I wanted to do for a living. I had friends who seemed to know what they wanted to do, but I had no idea at all.'

Like many boys of his generation, one of John's passions was Airfix models of war machinery. He says that he didn't go for tanks and the other military vehicles (which were to become a great passion later in his life), but he adored RAF planes of all kinds. The most famous names, Spitfires, Hurricanes and Lancasters, were his special favourites.

'I also had the model of HMS Victorious, but only because that had lots of tiny plastic planes on it. You were supposed to paint them once you'd put them together, but I never did. Too fiddly. Too technical. Too time-consuming. I wanted to get on and play with them so I just left them grey. My mum was always on at me about them; she said they gathered dust.'

School aside, John has nothing but happy memories of his childhood; 'It's funny how you remember little scenes from when you were young. I can remember one Christmas, when I was really young, the whole family walking down Gypsy Hill to The Two Towers pub in West Norwood, through thick snow. Great memories.

'Actually, years later, that was the first place I played the drums in public. There was a back room in The Two Towers, and there was a woman who played the piano for the customers as they drank. I talked to her one day, told her I played drums, and she invited me to bring my kit down and accompany her. So I did! With just the two of us and no bass guitar or anything it probably sounded dreadful. My parents' friends used to congregate there at weekends; it was like 'Come and see John play the drums!' and they seemed to think it was brilliant.

As a teenager the biggest thing in John's life was the Air Training Corps, the Royal Air Force's cadet arm.'A guy in my class at school, Stephen Ainsworth, had this little badge on the lapel of his jacket. I asked him what it what and he told me it was the ATC. He said, 'You'd like that – you like aeroplanes', which was true. He took me along to the local squadron, in Lordship Lane in Dulwich. It was based at the Territorial Army building there; Stephen introduced me to the CO and I joined up straight away.

John cycled there every week from home; 'I was issued with a uniform, which was great, and we were taught things like Morse Code, foot drill, and rifle drill. We had a little flight simulator, which taught you how to fly an aeroplane – sort of. I was 15 and I absolutely loved it.'

The Air Training Corp gave John his first taste of life away from his family. He went flying at RAF White Waltham, on the other side of London, near Heathrow. Then there was summer camp – at Colerne, down the A4, almost in Bath. At the World War Two fighter base of RAF Tangmere, near Chichester in West Sussex, John actually got to do some flying – in small trainer aircraft like Chipmunks, Hastings and Vikings; 'The first time I went up in a plane was at White Waltham, in a Chipmunk. I touched the wing and it was soft, just fabric. I wondered if it was really going to fly. I was terrified.'

John recalls that the professional RAF pilots, who took the ATC lads up, did their best to make them sick – rolling the plane, diving and generally not being content until they'd throw up. For a teenage boy though this was bliss; a great adventure.

With two other ATC recruits, Johnny Bush – who played bass, and Wally Rogers – who played guitar, John formed a band. No fuss; they just got together and started playing. It was 1962, it was what everyone was doing, and they played all The Shadows hits they could master. They rehearsed every Sunday afternoon in the front sitting rooms of their parents' homes.

'One Sunday two guys just turned up – Francis Rossi and Alan Lancaster. They asked if they could just watch and listen, and we said yes. They came two or three times and just sat around. On the third occasion they asked me if I would go and play with their band. I don't know if that was meant to be 'as well' or 'instead' but I said yes.

Alan Lancaster had been a member of the orchestra at Sedgehill School in Lewisham and was something of a musical protégé; 'I used to run the music class and had my own music room. I used to transpose the hymns for assembly every morning', Alan says. He played trumpet and trombone, but gradually came to the realisation that he wanted to make a significant, seismic shift - and decided to form a band.

Alan says that his major influences were Jerry Lee Lewis, James Brown and The Everly Brothers – anything that could be described as soul or

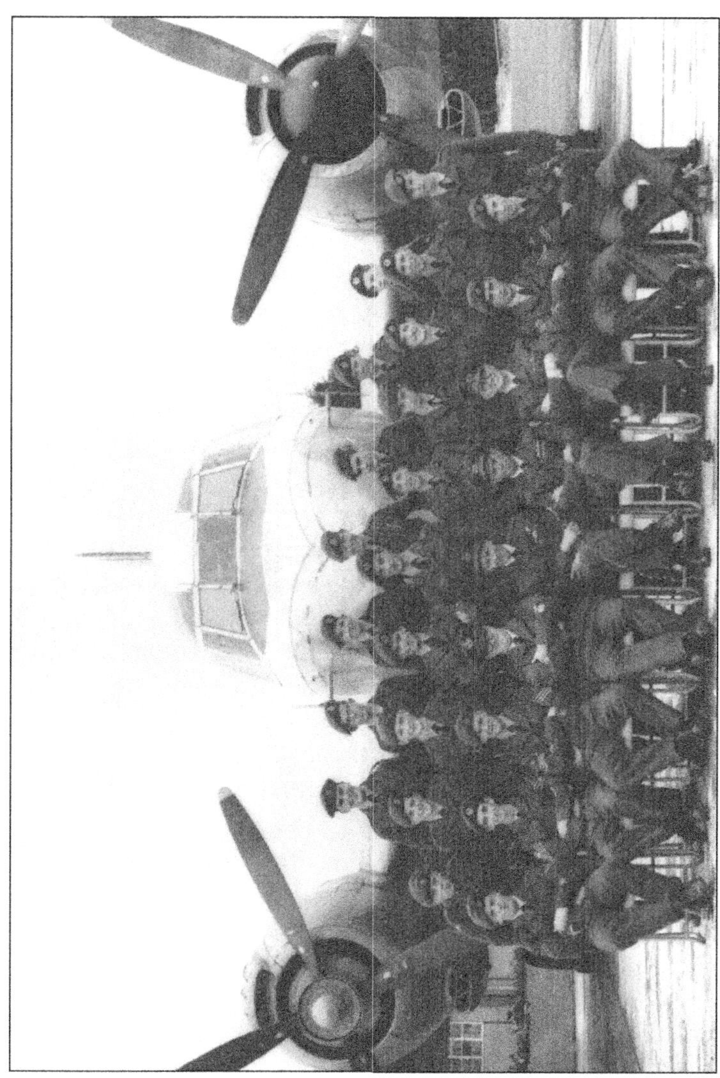

ATC cadet John Coghlan; back row, third from the right.

rock 'n roll. 'I didn't actually understand that music because I was classically trained. I first had to teach myself to play guitar, but I found the music confusing at first: It was a very different format, it was like playing in a minor key and a major key at the same time'.

Alan first recruited Alan Key, who was in the same class at school, and then Francis Rossi, whom he also knew from school ('I was in the grammar school stream', Alan says, 'He was in the dunces class'). Alan says that both Key and Rossi were only learning to play as well; 'That was good because we needed people that couldn't play but were willing to learn.'

Michael Lancaster, Alan's elder brother, was crucial to the band's development because being a rock 'n roll fan too – one with money – he bought all the records, which Alan was allowed to borrow so he could start to play along with them. Alan's parents were persuaded to buy him a bass – which rather dwarfed him. He wasn't a big lad.

They played as a trio for a while but Alan Key left, reducing them to a duo. Alan Lancaster had gone to Butlin's holiday camp in Bognor Regis with his parents earlier that summer and had seen a band playing Tornadoes' songs. What struck Alan was the strength of the organist, and he decided that was what his embryonic band needed.

In the same year at Sedgehill was Jess Jaworski, the son of Polish émigrés. He played piano accordion, which was hardly the most rock 'n roll of instruments. Jess knew Alan because they were both in the school rugby team, and he, he says, knew Francis because he was 'a bit of a character – he had that lively, jokey personality. Everyone knew him'.

Francis Rossi was a similar age to Jess and Alan. He was born May 29 1949, so in the summer of 1962 he was still only 13. Alan Lancaster wasn't much older, having been born on February 7 1949. At that age a difference like that really mattered.

Francis used the name Mike – his fourth christian name (Francis Dominic Nicholas Michael Rossi, in full) – as Francis was too girlie by half for a teenager in south London. He came from a devout Roman Catholic family and had an Italian father and an Irish mother. His parents, in partnership with his grandparents, ran a café and an ice cream business. He was musical from a very early age, and got his first guitar as a Christmas present when he was seven. By the time he joined up with Alan, John and Jess he was playing a large semi-acoustic, with violin-style 'f' sound holes, and ' M R' on it in stick-on gold letters.

One day, walking past the school music room, Jess Jaworski saw, and heard, Alan and Francis playing their guitars. Intrigued, he went in and they started talking; 'I mentioned that I played the piano accordion', Jess says, 'And they immediately suggested that I abandon that, take up the guitar, and join them.'

Jess's parents, who come out of this story with immense credit, part-exchanged the accordion for a guitar, and he tried to learn to play it. That wasn't a success, and he realised that his strength lay in playing keyboards, so it was decided that what was needed was for his parents to now part-ex the guitar for an electric organ.

So it was a trip, which Jess remembers to this day, to Larry Macari's Musical Exchange in Charing Cross Road. It was where all the best-known musicians of the time bought their instruments, and for star-spotters and autograph hunters it was paradise. 'I used to love hanging about there, trying out instruments', Jess says, 'And I'd see Mike Smith from the Dave Clarke Five, Manfred Mann, John Lennon and Paul McCartney, and loads of other famous musicians.' It was one of the very few places in Britain where you could buy a Vox Continental, which was one of the best electric organs on the market.

Jess's parents had fled from Eastern Poland when the Germans invaded, and his father enlisted in the Polish Free Forces, serving in North Africa, Italy and Montecassino. After the war he was offered free passage to America, Australia or Britain, and chose the latter simply because it was geographically closest to his native land.

Having come to this country with almost nothing, they were determined that they were going to provide the greatest opportunities for the next generation. By the early Sixties, Jess's brother – older by eight years – had left home, and Jess was the sole object of Edward and Nadia Jaworski's affection and optimistic hopes for the future. Jess says that explains why they were so happy to encourage his interests; 'They encouraged me in anything and everything I wanted to do', Jess says. 'The organ cost a lot of money, but they were behind me 100%. There was a lot of competition within the Polish community for children to do well.'

Jess says, 'We needed a place to practise and that was difficult because of the noise. Someone had suggested the Territorial Army range up at the top of Forest Hill, towards Dulwich.'

They rehearsed frequently up at the TA centre, and eventually the son of the caretaker, Barry Smith, asked if he could join as drummer. He was also thirteen and had been playing in a band which called itself The Debutantes – despite them all being boys. 'We knew that we needed a drummer', Jess says – and there he was. More to the point, he had the one crucial qualification;

he owned a drum kit. So he was in.

Barry wasn't to last though; 'One day we saw a band made up of members of the Air Cadets, and when we saw the guy on the drums we just went 'Blimey!' He was much better than Barry.' John's Air Cadets band was perhaps unimaginatively called The Cadets.

'We'd had a tip-off about a guy named John Coghlan', Alan says, 'He was playing with his ATC friends and it became clear that he was the guy to have on drums. We went down to see him, and he was playing all The Shadows' numbers and we just stood around and watched and listened. I think he saw us, and we were auditioning him and he was auditioning us.

'He was a much better musician than we were. We were way below his class, but we asked him to come and rehearse with us.'

Older than the others, John was all of fifteen. 'They other guys lived in Forest Hill, on the far side of Crystal Palace hill and down Dartmouth Road', he remembers. 'My dad took me over there in a taxi – which was a really big deal in itself – and delivered me at the house of this guy called Jess Jaworski. He had his Vox Continental – which was seriously impressive.

'In this little front room, the Jaworski's front lounge, there was all this amazing gear; a Vox amp, professional microphones, shiny new guitars and leads going everywhere. It looked amazing. I thought 'this is a serious, professional outfit'. Alan doesn't remember the kit as being anything like as glossy, 'We had Jess's Vox AC30 amplifier. It had six inputs and we plugged the organ in – which took up a hell of a lot of power – as well as the bass, which took even more power than the organ, and Rossi's guitar and two mikes. We used a tape recorder microphone when he started doing more vocals – when we started covering Beatles' songs.'

The Jaworski's home was larger than average, and the family tended to live upstairs. Jess's father wasn't just happy to turn the downstairs lounge over to this embryonic rock 'n roll band, but had bought a roll of linoleum to cover the carpet, so that the boys had a more solid and resonant surface to put their instruments and amplifier on. Perhaps one day there'll be a blue plaque on the front of 83, Devonshire Road, Forest Hill, London, SE23.

The first song the quartet played together, as Alan recalls, was 'a rocked-up version of Swan Lake'.

Alan says that as soon as John started playing drums with them it immediately felt like a real band. John agrees, 'We just started playing and it gelled together immediately. It was really good. They asked me to come and practise the next week, but no-one ever said 'Yeah, you've passed the audition; do you want to join the band?' No-one ever asked me that. We just kept practising, just started playing together. Soon we were rehearsing just about every night. It was that simple – that's how the band was formed.'

'John was just brilliant', Jess recalls, 'We tried *Wipeout*, which was the theme music to Six Five Special and he was really good. We played just a couple of numbers and we thought 'Right, you're in'.'

Alan adds, 'As soon as John came in, he put the beat to it, and what we were doing locked together. He was key to the development of the band.'

A short while later Barry arrived at the house, expecting to join the other three in one of their regular rehearsals. The guys informed him in no uncertain terms, and without any diplomatic niceties, that he wasn't up to the job and they had taken on a new drummer. So poor Barry Smith dropped into obscurity and became Status Quo's Pete Best.

By the time they played their first public, professional gig – professional in the sense that they got paid for it - in October 1962, the band hadn't actually thought of a name. The venue was the Samuel Jones Sports Club – which was part of a local engineering company. Alan's dad got them the gig and they played covers of Shadows' and Tornadoes' instrumentals to, as Alan remembers it, fifty or sixty people. The hat was passed round and when the assorted change was totted up the band came away with £5 between them.

When a name was finally decided upon they called themselves The Palladins, and under that name they played wedding receptions and the like. After just three or four gigs the band was re-named The Scorpions – or not, depending on who's telling the tale - but that soon became The Spectres.

The band got themselves and their equipment to these gigs as best they could, which usually meant scrounging lifts. When it was Mike Rossi's dad's turn to drive him he took them in his ice cream van, with all four youngsters and the instruments jammed in the back next to the refrigerator.

On stage all four wore smart casual trousers with a sharp crease front and back - 'slacks' as they were known - and smart pullovers over white shirts and black ties. Mike and Jess looked older than their true ages, but Alan, shorter than the others and with a snub nose, always looked like the baby of the band.

John started his drumming career with just a snare drum and a hi-hat, but soon acquired a Broadway kit; 'It wasn't very good, to say the least. It was adequate – the starter kit. I remember getting a tom-tom to add to the kit, and then I thought I'd really got a proper drum kit. It was very precious to me.' By now John had 'The Spectres' written across the bass drum, with 'John, Mike, Alan, Jess' running round the outside.

That was followed by a Ludwig Super Classic kit, which John still has somewhere in the attic; exactly the same kit that Ringo played in The Beatles' early days; 'They're quite rare now, and worth a lot of money.' Soon after Status Quo became famous Premier offered him 'a deal' and he stayed with their drums for many years. 'I've had a lot of different kits though. I had a Slingerland kit which had belonged to Louis Bellson, who played with Duke Ellington. That kit had two bass drums, which of course he was famous for. He introduced the two-bass kit in the Fifties and both Ginger Baker and Keith Moon picked up on that. That was a fantastic kit.

'I had a WFL, a really old kit; the initials stood for William F Ludwig and of course they were just called Ludwig later on. I had that for many years but eventually sold it. A kit like that will go for $3,000 in the States now; there are specialists who deal in classic drums. It was a long way on from that first Broadway kit. Heavens, you don't see those anymore.'

John remembers his teenage years with as much affection as his childhood (schooling not included); 'It was fun, and exciting. Rock 'n roll was young, and was life revolved round beer and girls and rock 'n roll. I loved every minute of it.'

In terms of that music, what mattered to John and his new colleagues was what was going on in England rather than what was coming across the Atlantic. He was never an Elvis fan, he says, though most of friends were. His band was Cliff Richard & The Shadows; a softer, more socially acceptable English imitation. Cliff's first single, *Move* It, was a fast, hard-edged, raunchy rock 'n roll track with a very exciting guitar intro. Soon though more conservative, old-fashioned influences began to assert themselves, and he moved away from American rock 'n roll and closer to Tin Pan Alley. His first number one, in the summer of 1959, was the soppy ballad *Living Doll.*

The Shadows weren't only Cliff's backing band; they had a huge string of instrumental hits without him. Between 1960 and '64 they had an incredible total of thirteen top ten hits (and five number ones, to Cliff's seven), and these were faster, rockier and harder-edged than Cliff's singles; perfect juke box records, distinguished by Hank Marvin's unmatched lead guitar. Somehow it seemed that The Shadows kept faith with gutsy rock 'n roll, while Cliff went after the mummsie market.

Cliff, who is six years older than John, was seen as belonging to the older, pre-Beatles generation of pop stars, and his star waned through the Sixties. From late 1962 on the British music scene was hit by an unprecedented tidal wave of new talent, who brought with them new and very exciting sounds and images – and washed away a huge amount of what had gone before. Although, by 1964, The Animals had arrived from Newcastle-upon-Tyne and Freddie And The Dreamers, The Hollies and Herman's Hermits had emerged from Manchester, all the first wave of this new music came from either London or Liverpool.

London made sense; music had always originated in the capital, and all the business side was based there; record companies, studios, publishers, everything. The Kinks, The Dave Clark Five and The Rolling Stones were the southern heroes, but the Liverpudlian contingent was larger still – and utterly unexpected. The rise of the north – well, primarily of Liverpool, came as a huge shock to the London-based music establishment. Huge numbers of bands and a smaller number of solo singers erupted from what was that a very provincial, very grimy seaport which had emerged to fuel the mills and factories of Victorian Lancashire and the Midlands. They also emerged with amazing speed; in a matter of a few months the charts were successfully assaulted by the likes Brian Poole and The Tremeloes, Gerry And The Pacemakers, Cilla Black, The Merseybeats, Billy J Kramer And The Dakotas, The Searchers, and of course – bigger than all the rest put together – The Beatles.

For London lads like John and his band, what was happening in Liverpool in the early Sixties was as remote as if it had been Memphis or Nashville; 'Liverpool seemed a million miles away. At first we thought we'd never go up there, but after a while we did – and it was a great city for rock 'n roll. We got on well there, but it seemed like a foreign country to us at first.

'It had always been that London was the place. If you didn't have an office in London you weren't on the scene; you were nobody. They changed all that too, and it was nothing but a good thing.'

Rock 'n roll PR man and former music journalist Keith Altham says that Londoners such as himself related much more easily to London-based bands, 'It was just because you were a Londoner. You were more comfortable with London bands, and the way you reacted to them was different. You had similar backgrounds, supported the same football teams.'

Between the two biggest bands, the Liverpudlian Beatles and the London-based Rolling Stones, it was the southern band that had the bigger impact on John; 'The Beatles made great records and at their peak were bigger than anyone had ever been, but The Stones were raw and real. Their songs were better. What a combination; Jagger and Richards. The ultimate rock duo.'

Having left school at fifteen that summer John got a job – thanks to his father - who got his son a salaried position, doing what he did, in the Times Furnishing shop in Brixton. It was the ethos of the time – your dad, your uncle, whoever 'got you in'; put in a good word with the boss and eased you into a good job, regular hours, clean hands, a decent pay packet every Friday.

It was his responsibility to dress the shop windows; 'I had to make it look like a real room in a dream house. I hated it. The shop was opposite the Town Hall and I used to watch the clock on the front of the Town Hall, just counting the minutes until I could go home.

'Quite often we'd have played a gig or been rehearsing the night before and might not have got home until one o'clock in the morning. Going to work on the bus I'd be feeling like death.

'The manager was always telling me off for drumming my fingers on the pieces of furniture which were for sale. I always had a rhythm going through my head and I'd just tap it out. He said, 'You're annoying everybody. Why are you doing that?' I told him that my real vocation was to be a drummer, and he said 'You'll never get anywhere doing that'. He was really unpleasant about it.

John's father worked at that branch of Times Furnishing after he'd left, and when he'd had his first hit record Jack Coghlan proudly told the manager. John adds, 'He was all smiles of course then, and told my dad to get me to pop in and see them again. I thought "Sod off", and never did.'

John did consider going into the RAF full-time, but had no idea which discipline within the Force would be right from him; 'I'd had quite a bit of flying experience, though whether or not I'd have been able to become a pilot, I don't know. Being in the band clashed with the ATC however, so I gave up the cadets, and any thoughts of joining the RAF went out with that. From that moment on I just wanted to be a drummer; there was nothing else.'

Like most of his generation, the music he was exposed to was what came out of the family's wireless: 'Dad always had the radio on at home', John says. 'He listened to jazz a lot, or the big bands. I always used to listen out for the middle section, where the drummer might do a solo. I loved that; absolutely loved it.

'No-one ever taught me to play drums. I don't think I ever read any books or anything. I learned by listening to drummers, and, when I could, simply watching what they did. Listening to records was easier than listening to the radio because I could play the song again and again, and try and copy whatever the drummer was doing.

'It's what would-be drummers did in those days. It sounds very crude, but it worked for a lot of us. The first record I could really keep up with was *FBI* by The Shadows. Tony Meehan was their drummer then. I suspect it influenced my playing enormously because it's a shuffle, and that's what I ended up doing with Status Quo. That 'four to the bar' shuffle became the mainstay of my drumming with Quo. Drumming with Quo didn't require any great technique. It was 'four on the floor', straight forward and in your face. The important thing was to keep time and hold it all together.

'The big difference back then was that in the Fifties and Sixties there were hundreds of places where musicians could play. Every town had its dance halls, and there was much more live music in pubs. You could always go along on Friday, Saturday, Sunday night and watch a band. I'd go along just to watch the drummer. It was very easy and very cheap. Nowadays there are far fewer venues; so many dance halls have been knocked down for development and now there are flats or offices in their place. And publicans don't want to give over space for a band. They want people drinking – and especially eating – in every square inch of their pub. Where do young people play music these days? How do they get started? It's one thing to practise in your bedroom or in the garage, but where can you go to find an audience?'By late '63, early '64 The Spectres were playing regularly in pubs and clubs around south London; mostly within a few miles of home. One early residency was at the social club of a local printing company. The band got that because Alan Lancaster's dad worked there and had put in a good word or two.

They were, as Jess remembers, very different characters, 'Alan was always serious. He didn't have the jokey streak that the rest of us had. He took himself too seriously. Francis and I used to do all the joking and laughing. I can't really compare it with the banter that there is now between Francis and Rick Parfitt, but it was *like* that. We got on really well, and we were the light-hearted end of the band.

'John was somewhere in between. Being older made a difference - it showed. For example, we did a gig at our school after a drama evening. The drama bit only had a few parents in attendance, but by the time we came on the room was packed out. Having not been to that school, and having left school anyway, John didn't kow-tow to the teachers. In fact he was really lippy! We thought we were going to get detention because of him.

'The four of us actually got on very well most of the time. There was one big argument with Alan, and he left the band ... for about three hours.'

At their second gig at the sports club they had gained a manager; Pat Barlow, a local plumber who also owned a heating business. The band were flattered by his interest and felt, understandably, that this development was, in itself, a real break-through

His presence was a reassurance for the parents of the younger band members, and he was constantly hustling for gigs for the band. He got them a regular slot at the Café Des Artistes in Brompton Road between Chelsea and Knightsbridge. This was up in the West End, and was to be taken far more seriously than gigs at the local social club. The Café Des Artistes didn't have an alcohol license – which reassured the band's parents, but served 'ice cold coke and smelly hamburgers for ageing beatniks' as Alan remembers, 'And there was one underground entrance and no other way out. If there was a fire you were dead.'

They played four half-hour slots between 10pm and 4am and were paid £1 each, with the rest of the fee going towards equipment. Pat had invested a fortune in a professional PA system; it was only 100 watts, which wasn't really powerful enough but it looked and sounded terrific.

The band was starting to get around; they played a small club in Lewisham in a regular basis. Alan recalls that though it was a struggle to get up for school the following mornings, on a good week he was actually earning as much as his father.

The band was offered the chance to play a residency in Hamburg, as The Beatles had done, famously. When they came to apply for their passports though the truth about their ages was revealed, and as Jess says, 'We looked quite mature for our ages, but in Hamburg we would have been playing strip joints and God-knows-what-else. We were told we couldn't go and we were heart-broken.'

At this stage the band was still playing covers – a couple of Billy Fury songs, maybe something by The Beatles and a handful of American rock 'n roll numbers - and there was no thought of going for the big break-through and writing their own songs.

'We played some brilliant cover versions when we put our minds to it, and I especially liked the ones that had good organ parts – of course', Jess says. 'We did a great *House Of The Rising Sun,* with that very difficult keyboards solo. Another was *Gimme Some Lovin'.* We were okay'

'Pat Barlow saw a sort of quirky, naïve passion', Alan Lancaster says, 'And I think he thought we had time on our side because we were so young. More than talent, we had time.' He had no previous experience in the music business, but was prepared to put his broader business experience – and crucially, some cash – behind the band.

They were certain that the big recording contract and the inevitable hit records were just around the corner. It wasn't going to be quite like that. The band did any number of audition nights, where there was a line-up of bands and the promise of the once-over from a record company A&R man – but these often turned out to be a small scale promoter's way of getting bands to perform for free. They had a lot to learn.

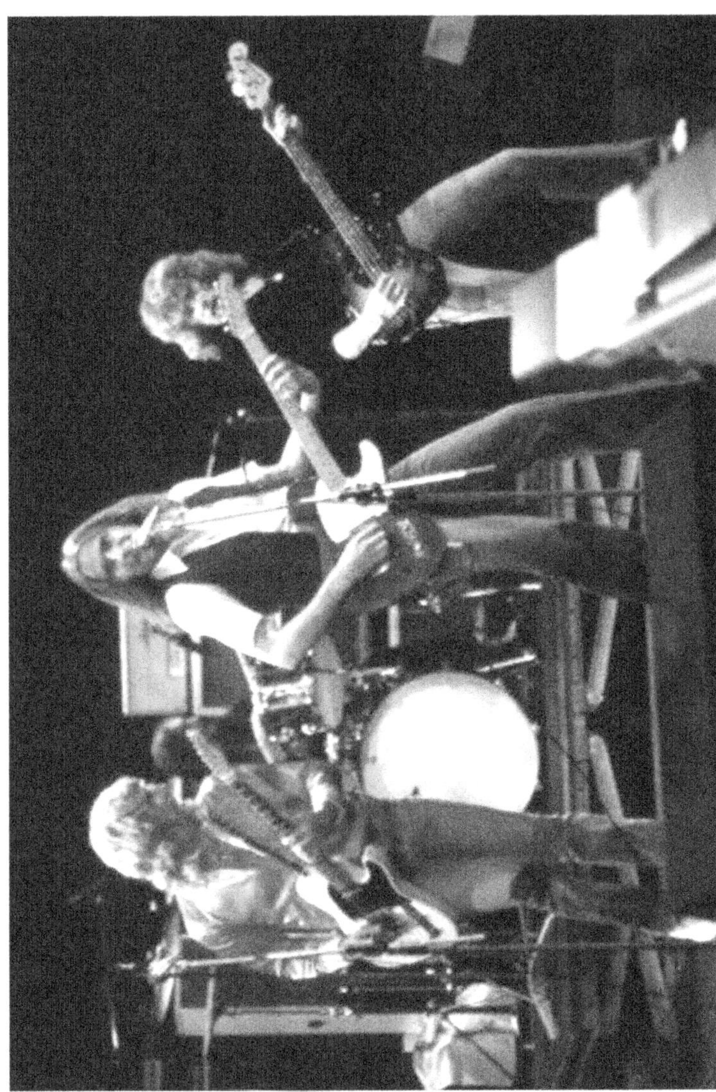

Francis tells Rick that his guitar's neck is five degree off parallel with his and Alan's.

3

Pat Barlow wasn't to know that he was making one of the most crucial moves in the creation of what would become a massive rock 'n roll band when he got them a residency with the holiday camp group Butlin's, at their Minehead camp in North Somerset. They auditioned at an office in the Tottenham Court Road in late '64, and were immediately offered four months work the following season.

The younger members of the band were coming up to the point where they had to make decisions about the subjects for their A-level exams – or, more pertinently, whether they were going to stay on at school for those qualifications or jump out into the big world. John needed no further prompting to leave his job at the furniture store, and both Alan and Francis were entirely happy to more or less go straight from school to being professional musicians. On his last report the Headmaster of Sedgehill noted that all the young Rossi did was dream of being a pop star. How right he was, and how right Francis was to do so.

Jess decided he was going to stay on at school and then go on to university. 'It was a hard decision for me', Jess says, 'Francis and I were really good mates and I felt I was letting the band down'. Doubtless his parents would have supported him if his decision had gone the other way, but it's not hard to imagine that they were relieved that their younger son was going to concentrate on academic qualifications and tread a more conventional career path.

Once the band had become Status Quo and were enjoying chart success,

Jess was, he admits, very slightly envious. 'I was very pleased for them. They had pursued my own career and achieved what I wanted to achieve for me, and they were enjoying their achievements. I'm proud to be able to say that I was a member of that founding four, and I've got very fond memories. As a band made up of young teenagers we did very well; we played as warm-up to big names, like The Who, Jerry Lee Lewis, Screaming Lord Sutch. We had our own sound.

'Once I had finished at university though, if they had asked me to re-join I'd have done so in a flash.'

For the less-academic Alan and Francis there was no decision to be made. John was already a working man, and for all three of them the band was their future.

Holiday camps were essentially a 1930s idea which enjoyed their heyday in the Sixties, but went out of fashion as people began to holiday abroad in larger numbers, and sought greater individuality.

Thousands of working class families would descend on a holiday camp on a Saturday, to sleep in tiny cabins, and have their every moment catered for within the camp's high fences. All meals were included in the cost, as were group competitions of the most hideously embarrassing kind and unself-conscious cringe-making jollity. The highlight of the day was the evening's entertainment, which would be the traditional post-music hall mix of comedians, ventriloquists, illusionists, dancing girls and live musicians.

The holiday camp bookers, keen to gain and keep the attention of the younger guests – the paying customers of tomorrow – latched onto pop music as soon as it emerged, and added rock 'n roll and pop acts to their line-ups. They had to be family-friendly, guaranteed not to offend, and cheap. Many British musicians who went on to pop and rock fame gained early experience in holiday camps, of which the ever-smiling Billy Butlin's chain was the largest and the best known.

Just before leaving for Butlin's they had the task of replacing Jess. Pat took Alan and John to see an organist playing in Redhill in Surrey.

Roy Lynes was a very different sort of guy from the members of The Spectres. He was a country boy, from a farming background, and had first started played keyboards on his aunt's wheezy, pedal-powered harmonium; 'It really was about a hundred years old, and you used to pedal away to get the air through it, and pull the stops out to get the different tones. I loved it, and always wanted to play keyboards.'

Eventually his mother bought a piano and paid for Roy to have piano lessons, but he admits that he couldn't stand the discipline, and used to 'accidentally' lose his sheet music on the way home from his lessons. He was better off teaching himself, he thought.

The little local band he was playing with were gigging in and around Redhill and Guildford; 'We weren't much cop', he says, disarmingly.

He hadn't been told that these city boys were coming down to see him play, but he soon spotted them: 'I couldn't help spotting them. They were staring at me. They were all there apart from Francis; for some reason he didn't come down.'

Pat opened the conversation by offering to book the Surrey band to support The Spectres at a gig in London. Pat really had the gift of the gab, Roy remembers, and the story was very credible – but in fact it was only him they were interested in, and not his colleagues.

Roy was offered the job on the spot, especially as he could sing too. As Alan says, 'It was perfect; he had a Vox Continental, which he could play, he could sing, and he could drive and had his own car – even if it was a tiny Goggomobil! Great, we had a new organist and, at last, a driver.' Roy was born in 1943, so at 22 he was the oldest member of the group by far.

Roy was very nervous about his ability to fit in with the team; 'I saw them play after I'd agreed to join, and they were great. And they really had charisma. Francis played very good lead guitar; I thought he played like Chuck Berry. They could put things together, musically, and they certainly knew where they wanted to be going.'

Prior to their arrival at the Redhill gig he had had no thoughts about becoming professional, let alone aiming for the big time, but Pat Barlow built up the prospects for Roy's benefit, promising lots of gigs and a record contract sooner rather than later. Roy felt a bit awed, but the notion was irresistible.

The new line-up started emergency rehearsals in the basement of Pat Barlow's heating showroom in Lambeth. One immediate problem was that the band had an audition for Phillips Records, and Roy wasn't completely on top of the keyboard parts. They phoned Jess and persuaded him to play at the audition, which delighted him and made him feel less bad about leaving.

The Butlin's contract was a big deal for the still-young members of The Spectres, being away from their homes and their parents. It was only really John who had experienced that before, thanks to his ATC excursions. Communicating with home – other than by letter or postcard – was very difficult. They were kids in a very grown-up situation. They weren't to be

The Spectres at Butlin's in Minehead in the summer of 1965.
Beneath the assorted animal heads, from left: Alan, John, Mike (Francis) and Roy.

completely out on a limb there; Alan's parents made a point of booking their summer holidays at Butlin's Minehead establishment. Perhaps so that they could see their son and his band playing to a ballroom full of happy campers, or perhaps so that they could reassure themselves about his physical and moral health.

They arrived at the holiday camp on Mike Rossi's sixteenth birthday – April 29 1965 - and were contracted to play from three until five every afternoon, and then from seven until midnight. They earned £20 a week each, but, says Alan, only ended up with a fiver each to pay their way. They didn't live in the holiday camp, but lodged in a guest house down the road – sharing two rooms in Mrs Fitch's Bed &Breakfast rooms.

Alan shared with Francis, and Roy with John. Roy remembers being closer to John than to the others; 'He introduced me to beer. Until I met him I was a good boy. I didn't swear and I certainly didn't drink. All that changed very soon after meeting John. He was a great guy; I could talk to him.

'I was the serious one in the band, but I got on with John because he was so down to earth. Francis was always the joker. I couldn't get much sense out of him. I could have a serious conversation with John. We talked for ages about our other interests apart from music.'

As well as being the serious one, for a long time Roy was the elder statesman; the sage. Because he was older - he was two years older than John and had nearly five years on Alan and Francis - he was regarded as the *eminence gris*, and his opinions were received with gravity.

It was at Butlin's in Minehead that the band's paths crossed with one Rick Parfitt, who was quite a show biz veteran despite being only fifteen. He was very good looking, with a charming smile and golden blond hair – but he was about as rock 'n roll as a teapot though. As John says, 'He had a completely different act from us. He wore a gold lamé jacket and played an acoustic guitar and sang with twin girls who danced. They were aimed at the mums and dads rather than the kids and were on in the posh bit of the holiday camp, in the ballroom.' Sometimes he wore a white tuxedo and a bow tie; at other times, it has to be said, he also wore a cravat.

Rick Parfitt was born Richard Harrison on October 12 1948 in Woking in Surrey, where he was brought up. Even as a young teenager he'd been something of a teddy boy, and was greatly influenced by the early rock 'n roll records he heard on the radio. He had a natural talent for musical instruments and took up the guitar at a young age. His family didn't have a showbiz background, indeed his father was a Navy man, but they recognised his abilities and pushed him in that direction. His father entered him for talent contests, and before he was thirteen years old he was playing and singing in clubs. By the time he met The Spectres at Butlin's he had attended drama school and already appeared on TV. Since the age of fourteen he had been performing professionally.

Rick and the twins – two years his senior – had their own agent and worked as The Highlights, but he knew that his act was old-style and, frankly, somewhat cheesy. When he heard The Spectres it was a revelation, though he was nervous of making contact with the band, afraid that they'd take the mickey out of him for the sort of songs he was performing. The Spectres though had seen Rick walking around with the twin girls, dressed to kill, and thought that was the hippest thing they had ever seen.

He got on particularly well with Mike (Francis) and kept in touch with both him and Alan Lancaster after both groups had finished their residencies at the holiday camp. Eighteen months later The Highlights imploded during a show at Skegness, and he ended up getting straight jobs – first as a baker and then as a clerk. And that was very nearly that for Rick.

'In those days we played wherever we could get in front of an audience', John recalls. 'We played all over. We did a tour backing the American girl band The Dixie Cups; that was good fun. Another time we were backing Guy Darrell, who was a big American star in the Fifties. Not necessarily our sort of music but very good experience for us.

'For some reason there was a gig in France at some stage. We got hold of a Commer van, and drove down to Avignon, taking turns to drive. I don't know how we got a gig down there, but it was amazing how many English bands were offered work there – and were quite prepared to drive all the way there just for the gig.

'So, having got there, we started playing in this French club and there was absolutely no-one there. No-one at all. So we stopped playing. The owner came over and told us that he was expecting a party of ten people, so we started again. He was right. Eventually they turned up; until they did we were playing to an empty room. We played all night to exactly ten people. Needless to say, the van broke down on the way home, of course.

'I went back to the town years later, with my wife, but couldn't find the club, which was a shame. I did find a wonky church that we'd been in though. It leaned to one side, and getting on for thirty years later it was still leaning over.'

Covers bands don't become superstars though, and as The Beatles and The Stones had shown, you have to write your own material. It was Alan more than anyone else who was starting to write songs, though he describes his efforts as 'a load of rubbish'. Pat Barlow trotted them round the music publishers in Soho, but he did attract the attention of Ronnie Scott (not the jazz musician and club owner), who was an A&R man with Valley Music, which was a subsidiary of what became MCA.

Scott took the material to John Schroeder, who was a producer with Pye records. Schroeder – who, with his immaculate hair and his droopy moustache, looked like the prototype for Jason King - had signed the then very young singer Helen Shapiro to Columbia at the very beginning of the Sixties, and in '61 she had seen two huge-selling number one hits. Now he was at Pye's Piccadilly label and his roster of signings wasn't nearly so impressive. He was very much on the look out for a band that would give him hits.

Shroeder said that if The Spectres could come up with an original take on an existing song and one original number he would think seriously about signing them.

Alan wrote a song called *When He Passes You By*, and this was teamed with a rocky version of Shirley Bassey's hit *I (Who Have Nothing)* and Pat took the band back to Pye's West End offices within days. Shroeder was impressed by how quickly the band came back to him with both the original song and the new take on the Bassey song, and agreed to record them. Pat Barlow had pulled a recording contract out of absolutely nowhere, and the band recorded their first single. It was July 1966.

The single came out on the Piccadilly label that September. It had an incredibly chunky backing track, a strong, echoing vocal from Francis and a thunderous beat provided by Alan and John. It had a real epic feel; a bit like Barry Ryan's *Eloise* of 1968. Francis's singing grated at times and sounded harsh on the higher notes, but it was an impressive performance for an immature voice. Roy's organ playing opened the song but then rather got devoured by the big production itself. Shirley Bassey had taken the song to number six in the autumn of 1963, but it wasn't to be as successful for The Spectres as it had been for La Bassey, and it failed to either get significant airplay, or to chart. It was backed by their version of the rhythm 'n blues standard *Neighbour, Neighbour*. That was distinguished by a high-pitched, slightly tinny opening – which sounds eerily like *Pictures Of Matchstick Men*.

Similarly, *Hurdy Gurdy Man* (not the song by Donovan, which came out in November 1966) flopped. The Spectres performed both songs on Saturday Club on BBC radio in September 1966 however, plus an impressive cut of Van Morrison's *Gloria*. That was a prestigious airing for the band; the show was one of the very few outlets for new music on the mainstream media. The presenter, Brian Matthew, interviewed Francis – who was introduced as Ross, which was apparently his nickname at the time.

In early 1967 The Spectres released *(We Ain't Got) Nothin' Yet*, a cover of a song which had been a hit for the American band The Blue Magoos, which doesn't seem to have been released in the UK. It was a very competent single; really quite distinguished - fast, heavy and rocky – with a great Lancaster bass line and some great, very fast Rossi guitar work. Listening to it now it's seems a great shame it wasn't a hit. It is certainly the best thing that The Spectres recorded, but it failed to make any impact. A couple of years ago it re-appeared on a compilation ... of 1965 singles.

Things were looking discouraging; they were a good live band but chart success seemed like another thing altogether. More often than not they were working as a backing group – for The Dixie Cups still, for infamous trouser-splitter P J Proby or for the Mancunian Wayne Fontana. Financial success depended on being in the charts; you didn't get rich by simply gigging, no matter how busy you were.

'We were living hand to mouth, really', John says; 'Though we weren't motivated by the money, and when we did earn a few bob we'd buy better equipment with it. It was all so new, it was an adventure, and people were always going 'Oh, you're in a band. Wow, that must be great. You lucky bastards'. It was exciting, we never knew where we were going next - and being in a band seemed to attract women, which was really nice. Money didn't really ever come into it.'

In the publicity photographs organised by Pye the four still look like nice, clean-cut lads. The ties had long gone, the shirts were now patterned and the trousers were hipsters with broad belts, but they still look like the sort of guys a girl could take him to meet her parents with some confidence. In some of the shots Alan looks as if he's about to poke a finger in your chest, while Roy looks least at ease. Francis looks like a lippy Mod. John smiles out of the pictures; which wasn't to last.

To a large degree the band was now being financed by a friend of Pat Barlow's, the appropriately named Joe Bunce. He owned a waste paper business and was intrigued by Pat's side-line in music management. He became a partner, and his principal role was writing cheques. With hindsight he is an unsung hero in the Status Quo story.

By this point the name The Spectres was starting to sound a bit old-fashioned; a bit too much like an old-style rock 'n roll group or someone

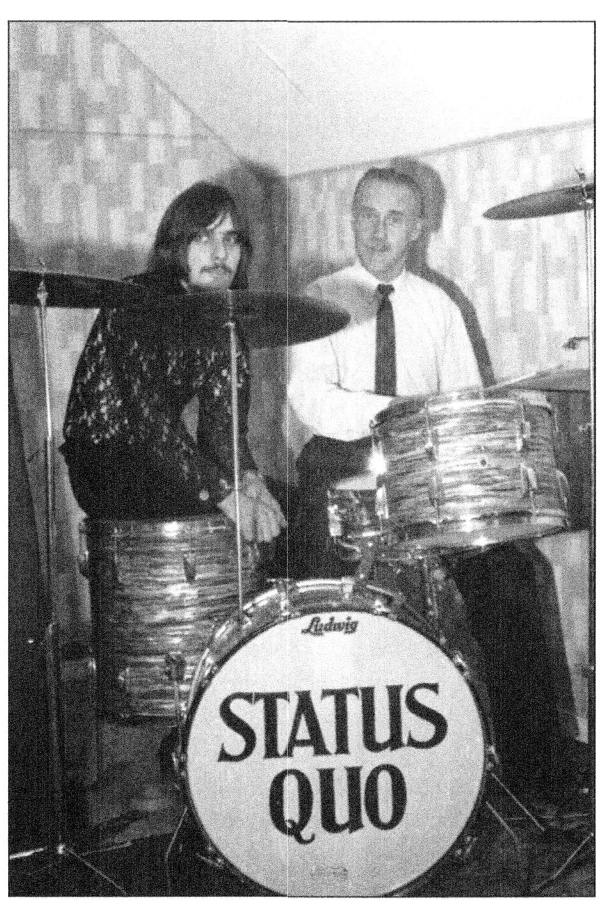

John's dad, Jack Coghlan, sits proudly at John's Ludwig kit.
John wonders if the pubs are open yet.

else's backing band. It hadn't brought them too much in the way of success or glory, and their was no great pedigree to be lost by trying something else. It was time for a change.

Naming a pop band was a tricky, hit or miss business. No-one called themselves Thingie Wossname and the Whatdoyoucallits anymore, and to be honest, once a band had seen considerable success despite the ludicrous name of Dave Dee, Dozy, Beaky, Mick and Titch it was obvious that the name mattered hugely – but also didn't matter. Both 'The Queers' and 'The Muhammad Alis' were briefly considered and mercifully discarded.

Dropping the definite article was becoming fashionable, so someone came up with the idea of 'Traffic'. It was a great idea except for the fact that Stevie Winwood had recently left The Spencer Davis Group, which he had fronted successfully 1963 (when he had been just 15) and formed a new group with Dave Mason, Jim Capaldi and Chris Wood – called Traffic. His profile was much higher than theirs, so that idea was dropped; or rather amended to Traffic Jam.

Only one single was released by Traffic Jam; the very poppy *Almost But Not Quite There.* Written by Francis and Pat Barlow (a rare writing contribution from the manager), it sounded like a heavier Herman's Hermits. Although it was allegedly banned by BBC radio for its sexual innuendoes, it was one of three songs performed on Brian Matthew's Saturday Club radio show in June '67.

There was still some confusion with Stevie Winwood's band though, and threats of legal action. There are obviously only so many names to go round; in 1965 a band came out of Northern Ireland calling themselves The Spectres. They released a single called *The Facts Of Life*, before disappearing.

Time for another change. Pat Barlow finally set everyone on the right track by suggesting Quo Vardis, which eventually emerged from discussions as The Status Quo. Eventually it became Status Quo. It was, it turned out, a damn good decision.

4

By late 1967 the band was working as Madeleine Bell's backing band and with Pat Barlow only as a part-time manager. Later that year they went into the studio to record a new single for Pye, but this one was to be quite different from what they had recorded as The Spectres.

Pictures Of Matchstick Men became their first single as Status Quo, and was a huge departure from everything they had done beforehand. John says that he has absolutely no idea where the shift to psychedelia came from; 'It just happened'.

In February 1967 The Beatles had released a double-A-sided single. One side was the catchy, Tin Pan Alley schoolyard ditty *Penny Lane* – which has always seemed to sum up the best that Paul McCartney brought to the group. The other side was utterly original, and made the music world catch its breath. There had never been anything quite like *Strawberry Fields Forever*. It was a masterpiece, and a dark invitation from John Lennon to join him in a drug-fuelled fantasy, deep in the Gothic heart of Victorian Liverpool. Both songs were set in real places in their native Liverpudlian suburbs, but whereas Penny Lane was bright and breezy, cheery and carefree, the landscape of Strawberry Fields was crazed, intoxicated and Hadean.

Strawberry Fields Forever was, and perhaps remains, British pop's most potent drug song. It owed nothing to the American West Coast culture, but it did drag the psychedelic into the forefront in the UK. It left its fans shell-shocked, their parents confused, and the mainstream media outraged.

Through the sea of blue denim John keeps his eye on the blonde in the front row.

The loveable mop-tops had moved a long way from *I Wanna Hold Your Hand* and *She Loves You.*

In June of that year The Beatles showed that *Strawberry Fields* wasn't a one-off, and confirmed their position as the music industry's most stunning innovators, here or in the USA, with the release of the album 'Sgt Pepper's Lonely Hearts Club Band'. This was psychedelia on an awesome scale; the result of the then unheard-of total of 700 hours of studio time and a recording budget of £25,000. The BBC, ever at the cutting edge, banned its final track *A Day In The Life.*

Apart from The Beatles though, the British were never very good at producing psychedelic pop. That's not to say that the Americans were either; what the likes of The Grateful Dead and The Doors were doing in southern California in the mid-Sixties was actually light years away from folkie Scott McKenzie's embarrassing single *San Francisco (Be Sure To Wear Some Flowers In Your Hair)* and the unspeakably awful *Let's Go To San Francisco* by The Flowerpot Men. In July '67, to the record-buying public's endless shame, the former went to number one in the UK charts, while the latter crept guiltily to number four the following month.

If Donovan can be seen as a celtic druggie rather than an ersatz Dylan, then a good case can be made for him writing some of the UK's best psychedelic songs, of which *Sunshine Superman,* released in late 1966, and *Mellow Yellow* (entered the charts in February '67) are the best. Watching him on television it wasn't hard to believe that he was utterly spaced out – whatever that meant.

At the poppy end of pop, The Move's *I Can Hear The Grass Grow* (April '67) and *Flowers In The Rain* (September '67) were standard-issue happy singalong songs spiced up very slightly with very cautious drug allusions – and matching, flower-pattern shirts and ties. About as threatening to the fabric of society - and stylistically-challenged - as the opening titles of the Simon Dee show.

Procul Harem took *A Whiter Shade Of Pale* to number one in June 1967, but was that a drug song? Or a sub-operatic anthem? Whatever, mums and dads rather liked it – which robbed it completely of any subversive edge it might have had.

In the early summer of 1967 The Small Faces – a truly great London-based beer, birds 'n a bit of a punch up band – released *Here Comes The Nice,* the drug references within which were lost on just about all their fans. It prepared the ground for *Itchycoo Park,* which went to number three in August and is one of their greatest singles. It was a very good showcase for lead singer Steve Marriott's vocal abilities, and it used the electronic effect of 'phasing' which was the must-have recording fashion for that year. It was also far from coy; a guy is trying to coax a girl to the park. She asks, quite reasonably, 'What will we do there?' Steve doesn't tell her that they'll dive behind the bushes and shag like crazy – which would have been the ambition in any pop song up to that moment – but, 'We'll get high' he says. And then, doubtless, shag like crazy.

Itchycoo Park and *Strawberry Fields Forever* aside (and how interesting that they were both set in the traditional suburban boys-meet-girls no-man's land – is the best British psychedelic pop sing of its generation. It worked because you believed it. The Small Faces' interest in drugs wouldn't be because they wanted to change the world. More likely because it made a change from pints of bitter, and it helped get impressionable girls out of their underwear. That was *exactly* what these dirty-minded working class lads would get up to.

John, Alan, Francis and Roy actually went into the studio to record *Gentleman Joe's Sidewalk Café* as the A-side of the single. It was a song which publisher Ronnie Scott had suggested to them. Alan Lancaster says, 'In those days you didn't realise that publishers were palming songs off on you. We thought that people were taking interest in us by giving us their songs to record. They rather coerced you to do things, and we were flattered by being asked – but in fact you were being used.' Alan admits that it was a very poppy song and he wasn't terribly keen on it.

Pictures Of Matchstick Men, written by Francis Rossi, was to have been the B-side. As a psychedelic song it could have been seen as a fairly obvious exercise in bandwagon jumping. The lyrics were obscure, even for a pop song, with the verses seeming to come from a different thought process from the chorus.

'It was originally a rather insipid song, with four-part harmonies filling the gaps – but we weren't four-part harmonists. It wasn't that great and we didn't know what to do with it,' says Alan.

It was Roy that came up with a new gadget – a wah-wah pedal. He attached it to his organ and demonstrated the sound to the other guys. John Shroeder's engineer, Alan Jones, added the phasing effect – having heard it on The Small Faces' singles. By the time Alan had finished with it, it was obvious that it ought to be the A-side, so *Gentleman Joe* was relegated to the flip side.

It was a very well-produced, professional song, and very much of its time. It hardly broke new ground in any sense, but it did everything that a mid-Sixties teenage audience required. It had a very high, catchy lead riff which opened the single and re-appeared in the bridge, and a particularly attractive bass line supplied by Alan Lancaster, who also sang. It was perfect for radio, juke boxes and hissing, scratchy transistor radios – and just the right length. For a psychedelic single it came out six months too late though, at the end of '67, and didn't chart until January 1968.

Rick Parfitt was still in his 'straight' job at this point, but the band hadn't forgotten him. Alan says that he knew that they needed another voice; 'I had a rockier, bass voice, Francis was very poppy and Roy was a crooner. I remembered Rick from Butlin's, but though he was really a cabaret artiste I knew he wanted to be in a rock band, and he could sing. And he was a very good-looking bloke, ideal for a front man.'

It hadn't been hard for Alan to keep in touch with Rick; he was going out with one of the twins in The Highlights and Rick was going out with the other. Even when both relationships collapsed the guys remained friends. Alan says that no-one else in the band was particularly keen on Rick joining them; he thinks that Francis was slightly jealous, and Roy wasn't keen on the money being split five ways instead of four. Alan says that he convinced both Pat Barlow and John Shroeder of Rick's merits, and left them to sell the idea to the rest of the band. Just when it looked as if Rick's showbiz career was over and he was doomed to a life of far from exciting, conventional jobs, Pat Barlow phoned him and invited him to join the band as vocalist and co-guitarist. He couldn't say 'yes' quickly enough.

Roy Lynes says, 'Rick and Francis just clicked. They were on their own wavelength straight away.'

What Rick actually joined was Traffic Jam, indeed that was still their name when they recorded *Pictures Of Matchstick Men*, but by the time it was released they were The Status Quo.

Matchstick Men was the only record that the band ever got into the Billboard charts in the USA. It entered the chart at the end of 1968 – very late – and stayed around for eleven weeks, topping out at number twelve (when *Hello, I Love You* by The Doors was at number one). Unfortunately neither the band, their manager nor their record company was in any position to follow up on that incursion into the American top ten.

The band didn't have a particularly strong image, but Pat Barlow now dressed them to match their single. It was time for another change of shirts.

The uniform was satin trousers, velvet jackets, ruched shirts with frilly fronts, ballooning shoulders and collars shaped like the wings on a DC10 (but larger). It actually had nothing to do with psychedelia; it was post-Mod, a bloated and decadent version of everything that Mod had actually held dear; and everything to do with the emergence of Carnaby Street as a massive force in teenage (and, sadly, not so teenage) fashion. Their hair stretched down over their collars, and all but Alan had centre partings; Alan was more the sweet-looking, low-dried Peter Noone, with a low-swept fringe that covered his eyebrows. Francis and John had grown dropping moustaches – Zapata style, the press called it.

Pat Barlow had issued John with a maroon jacket made of velvet, probably bought from one of John Stephens' shops in Carnaby Street. It was very much a jacket of its time, and he loathed it; 'We were round at Pat's house one night, and I was standing with my back to an electric fire in his front room. Someone said 'Can you smell something?' and as he said it my jacket burst into flames. I was panicking to get it off and the other guys were trying to help me. When I finally got it off we were all jumping on it, trying to put the flames out. I don't know what it was made of but it went up like a fuel dump. But I was secretly delighted; it was the best thing that could have happened to it.'

'The *Matchstick Men* thing put me off them', says Keith Altham, 'They were obviously trying to be something which they weren't, and they were doing *anything* to get a hit. It smacked of desperation. I understood it but it rang false. And they certainly came to it too late. But I suppose it got them their foot in the door.'

Francis's dad made it into the London newspaper The Evening News when *Matchstick Men* was released. He had re-recorded the jingle tape on his ice cream van so that he could drive down the streets of South London and announce his presence, and the availability of cones, choc-ices and lollies, with his son's record. Great publicity.

The sleeves for all these singles show the band in all their satin and velvet finery, but in just about all of them they are deadly serious and, mostly, looking very pissed off. Mean and moody didn't exactly go with the Carnaby Street dandy look. From this period there's only the sleeve for *Technicolour Dreams/Spicks and Specks* where they're smiling – and it's not difficult to imagine that that's a reaction to smirking Roy Lynes dropped a smelly one. Roy does look noticeably older than the others, and poor baby-faced Alan looks about fourteen years old.

Similarly, looking at publicity photos from that period, their expensive clothes apart, the guys look like any other five likely lads. They don't look like stars – except perhaps Alan Lancaster, who looks like a child actor who has grown up to walk centre stage and sing the Mums' favourite. There's no edge to them, no signs of hard experience. They don't look like The Beatles or The Rolling Stones. They look as if they're about to get on their Lambrettas, or into their Mini Coopers, and go down the pub.

The one young man who does stand out in those black and white shots is John, and the difference is his stare. His eyes are heavily lidded and he looks as if he's ready to step out of the photo and start a fight. He doesn't look like a guy whose pint you'd spill and survive. You can't help feeling that all the time the photographer was focussing and setting the aperture, John didn't blink once.

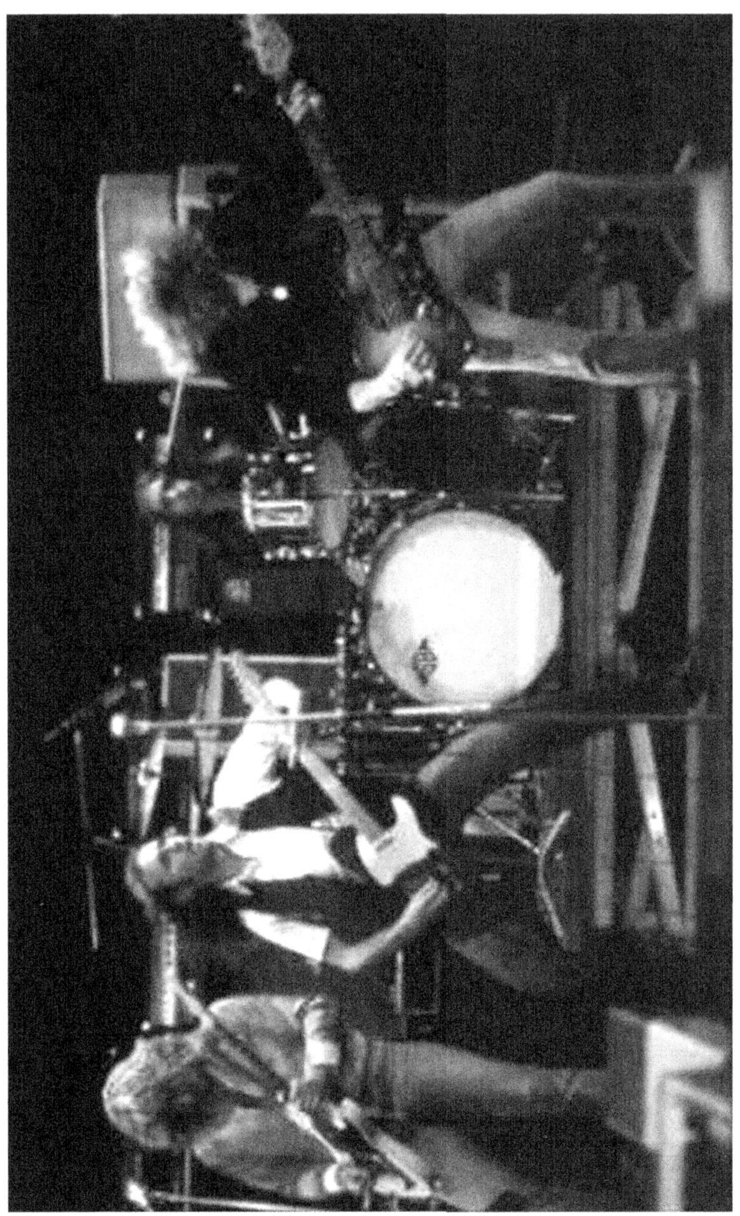

The powerhouse quartet - and the fans' favourites; (from left) Parfitt, Rossi, Coghlan and Lancaster.

5

Pat Barlow spent a lot of money with the pirate radio station Radio Caroline, in effect bribing them to play the *Pictures Of Matchstick Men.* That airplay paid off and it duly became the first of Status Quo's hit singles. It went to number seven and stayed in the charts for twelve weeks. The band had made its mark at long last.

John was 21, had appeared on Top Of The Pops – and had therefore passed the great British musical MoT test. That first TOTP performance was at the old, de-consecrated church in Dickinson Lane in Manchester, to which thousands of bands made pilgrimage. Quo very nearly didn't appear at all; they managed to get there perilously late and the producer stormed into the dressing room, swore at them and told them he was going to drop them from that night's show because of their unprofessional unpunctuality (imagine a TV producer saying that to Britney Spears ...). 'He said to us 'Just give us one good reason why I should let you perform when you're this late?' John remembers, 'To which I said 'You've got to let us go on, my Mum and Dad are expecting to see us'. It wasn't meant to be cheeky but that's rather the way it came out. It worked though and on we went.'

So he was able to show his parents some tangible evidence of his progress in life, and they in turn were about to bask in the reflected glory when they told their friends. They had every reason to be proud; the British pop scene was still very young, and though recording contracts weren't too hard to come by, hit singles most certainly were. When they pointed to their son's group's positions in the 'Hit Parade' the names of

Cliff Richard and The Beatles were in there too.

They got a lot of coverage in the music papers, all of it in the cringe-inducing style of the time. In one of the question and answer sessions, John noted that his favourite toothpaste was McLean's Spearmint Flavour, his 'Likes' were flying and 'light and bitter, and he disliked 'cold hotels'. His favourite aftershave was either Brut or Avon's Wild Honey. Not a man of expensive taste at that stage in his life then.

All the poptastic features aside, not a lot had changed. The band wasn't catapulted into the big time in any sense; though John did buy a Mini – his first car – and did find that girls knew who he was, and that he could get into London night clubs without paying.

The thing to do was to issue another single and an album, to capitalised on the success of *Matchstick Men*, and to organise a new tour while the hit single was in the charts – or at the very least, the memory of it was still fresh.

Although their hit was a psychedelic number, the band's stage act hadn't changed. They had to play *Matchstick Men* of course, but everything else they performed on stage was much heavier r 'n b. They were playing fast rhythm 'n blues like The Pretty Things or The Animals, but were wearing frilly shirts and velvet trousers.

The band's first gig headlining as Status Quo was at Ruislip on February 18. At the end of that month they undertook a short, four-date tour of Scotland, and after three more live gigs in England that was followed by a huge 28-date tour of the UK. With the established music business still trying to fit pop into its preconceived ideas of 'variety', promoters put together packages of acts. These often brought together some highly unlikely combinations of bands and solo singers, but certainly offered good value for money for the fans.

The coach that drew out of London on April 6 1968 (after the tour had opened in Lewisham in south London the night before) carried a curious assortment of musicians; some veterans with several years experience playing to live audiences, and others with just one hit to their credit.

Status Quo were halfway down the bill, with Gene Pitney headlining. He had seen his first UK hit in 1961 and was close to being at the peak of his career. He had enjoyed a string of Top Ten hits without hitting number one (and wouldn't until 1989, when he re-recorded *Something's Got A Hold Of My Heart* with fey warbler Marc Almond). He was twenty-seven years old, which must have seemed a whole generation older than the others. By 1968 his style of big power ballad was very dated, and though he was seeing a

number five position the week the tour started, it was to be his last chart place in single figures.

Also on the tour were The Mike Cotton Sound, who were backing Gene, Simon Dupree & The Big Sound, who weren't a big hit band but made a terrific sound playing live, and Amen Corner – whose first big hit, *Bend Me Shape Me* was still in the charts, and who would see a number one with *(If Paradise Is) Twice As Nice* the following spring. They were in the company of one-man band Don Partridge, who was something of a novelty act. He was a busker who had come in out of the rain, and actually did play all of the instruments himself. He had just had a number four hit with the frighteningly catchy *Rosie*. He wasn't a one hit wonder though; while they were on tour he went a place higher in the charts with *Blue Eyes*. Only then did he drop out of sight.

The acts played two shows at each venue, and of course the tour wasn't arranged logically so far as the geography was concerned. For example, after playing Coventry in the English Midlands they went to Scotland to play the Odeon theatre in Glasgow, and then drove south again for a gig in Manchester the following night. The next night they were in Wolverhampton, not too long a drive, and then they went north to Leeds. That was followed by two nights in Blackpool, and then to Derby, Cardiff in south Wales, across the Severn to Bristol (a long drive in the days before the bridge), from there back to London and then to the south coast for a show at The Winter Gardens in Bournemouth. So it went on, with a performance almost every night.

These tours were often put together at very short notice – especially if the promoter could grab a new band who had just charted; Marmalade hit the charts with *Lovin' Things* and were immediately shoe-horned into the tour. Venues were booked subject to their availability and nothing else. If this meant that the coach went from Bournemouth to Aberdeen, or from Ipswich to Truro – and then back to Ipswich via Carlisle, then that's the way it was. The musicians just had to grin and bear it – and be grateful to be on the damn tour in the first place.

At each venue Status Quo played just three numbers, always including *Matchstick Men*; Rick, Francis and Alan would each take vocals on a song.

John remembers these tours, 'You played the most amazing venues; the old Granada theatres and the Gaumonts. And they were in these obscure places, like Devizes or Trowbridge. They were absolute mayhem, but were very fiercely run. There was a guy called Ron King, the stage manager, and he'd go mad if we were late.

'One night Don Partridge was a bit drunk – he used to drink Mateus Rose, which was really exotic back then – two bottles a night, which we thought was a hell of a lot. He banged his bass drum like there was no tomorrow, and was trying to tune his guitar at the same time. And not doing too well. Someone in the audience said something and he just shouted back 'Oh fuck off'. We couldn't believe it.

'Sometimes we'd get up on stage when another act was on and start playing cards. We didn't give a toss.

The tour promoters invariably tried to get everyone in the one hotel so he could do a better deal, but that just meant that everyone was back in the same place after the show, all insisting that the bar stay open. The diversions offered by provincial Britain in the Sixties were very few and far from exciting, and there wasn't much more that the musicians could do than drink.

One evening there was a problem in a provincial night club, and they all got thrown out. John admits that it was his fault. He got into a fight. The following morning they were on the coach, waiting for Gene Pitney to deign to join them (as headliner it was his prerogative to turn up last) and it was all doom and gloom; 'We all wondered 'What's Gene going to say?' It's hard to believe, but we were terrified. He always sat at the front of the coach by right – another privilege for the headliner. When he arrived he sussed the atmosphere straight off and asked what the matter was. I stood up and owned up; it was like being back in school.

'Gene looked at me and said 'So what? That's what happens', and there was such a sigh of relief. Gene said it was okay!'

Alan Lancaster recalls one very satisfying moment at the end of the tour; 'Mike Cotton came up to us in the coach right at the end and said 'Well, we all thought you were going to be a joke band, but I've got to take my hat off to you, you can really play.' That was great, but we weren't really that good then – what we did have was energy and passion, and we made our mark by putting everything we had into it on stage.'

The pattern of heavy touring started at this point: The band played three shows in Dutch towns in August '68, and then embarked on another extensive UK tour, starting on November 2 in the Kent seaside town of Margate. On November 11 they played the USAF base at Bentwaters in Suffolk, which would have delighted John, and the tour continued right over Christmas and New Year. On New Year's Eve, what had been a momentous year for the band came to a close with a show at the Gala ballroom in Norwich.

The tour was interrupted in mid-January when the band flew to Vienna to support The Small Faces, but then it was back on the A-roads (and Britain's very few miles of motorway) of Britain. During 1969 they played around sixty live shows, as well as making TV and radio appearances and recording. The venues were old-fashioned ballrooms in the main – not ideally suited to rock 'n roll – as well as colleges and functions rooms in larger hotels. Three gigs were at RAF bases, and again John would have been in his element.

Keith Altham handled Status Quo's press relations for several years but first knew the band when he was a music journo. He remembers Quo very fondly from this period, 'I was a south London boy too – born in Balham – and they had a London sense of humour, and as guys they were great. I did several interviews with them and I really related to them.

'I loved being around them. I loved that stupid humour that they had. Parfitt particularly could make me laugh by just grinning. Rick was far more open than Francis; Francis contained himself – he didn't let you in.

'John was slightly on the periphery – like all drummers – and he was always very friendly, though you knew that he could be temperamental. I saw his temper go once, back stage at a gig, and it actually seemed so out of character. John was certainly more outgoing when he'd had a drink; a bit more extrovert, a bit more outlandish.

'Mind you it was true to say that it was the front men who were the glory boys …

'I saw the band on the tour with Gene Pitney, and there was something about them that I liked. Although they didn't have any stand-out musicians they had a core identity. They were like The Who in that respect, or The Kinks in the early days. The members made up something which was greater than any individual part.

'Rossi and Parfitt's sound was unique, and you either get that by working for a long time together, or you've born with it – like The Everly brothers were born with it being siblings.'

The band played the Marquee Club in Wardour Street in Soho several times – in the very heart of the music industry's stomping ground; 'That was great; beer on the floor, sweat running down the walls. Brilliant!' John says. They also often played at The Red Lion in Leytonstone, where they performed in a big function room on the first floor. The band used to pack it out every time. For Status Quo this was close to being a taste of the pop big time.

Their follow-up single, the depressingly-titled *Black Veils Of Melancholy* was released in April '68, and it spiralled straight into oblivion, making no mark on the charts at all. It was a charmless re-write of *Matchstick Men* (with exactly the same opening) and wasn't worthy of the band. The music business mocked them and assumed they couldn't do any better - or anything different.

The month it came out they played *Black Veils* on The David Symonds Show on the new BBC Radio One. Interestingly they also played *Gloria* again – stronger than on Brian Matthew's show eighteen months earlier, but still keeping strictly to the arrangement laid down by Van Morrison and Them.

Alan was interviewed by David Symonds – from which a nation holding its breath learned rather little – and The Status Quo ended their set with a song which showed where its strengths really lay. They played the r 'n b standard *Bloodhound*, and in contrast to *Black Veils*, set transistor radios alight the length and breadth of the kingdom.

In August '68 the first album from The Status Quo (still with the definite article, which was only dropped in late 1970) was released. It was called, unfortunately 'Picturesque Matchstickable Messages From The Status Quo', had a very naff sleeve design, and contained one track which should perhaps have been a single. *Elizabeth Dreams* was written by old rocker Marty Wilde, and was a very strong and complex post-psychedelic song with some neat wailing guitar. There was more than a hint of Pink Floyd's *Arnold Layne* or *See Emily Play* of the previous year to it. The album also contained the most honest track that the band recorded during their flower power period; their cover of Tommy Roe's 1962 hit *Sheila* was hugely unfashionable for the late Sixties – but was great rock 'n roll and terrific fun.

Ice In The Sun, released a few months later was far better than *Black Veils*, and had lyrics which actually made some sense, and was again written by Marty Wilde: The guy singing the song, poor sap, melts away like ice in the sun in the presence of the girl he adores. Again, it was beautifully produced, but it was a step in the wrong direction. Getting heavier, and going deeper into the emerging drug scene would have been a logical move – with the advantage of thirty five years worth of hindsight – but *Ice In The Sun* was very poppy, frothy and singalong cheesy. Again, it could have been penned and recorded by Herman's Hermits; not even The Hollies.

Various reviewers in the pop press thought it was simply another copycat attempt to cash in on the success of *Matchstick Men*. Nonetheless it was a very worthwhile hit; going into the charts in August 1968 and hitting number eight. Like *Matchstick Men* it was in the UK charts for a total of twelve weeks. The band was not to be a one-hit wonder; they had two top ten singles behind them. And at least the days when the group was a covers band were long gone; they were performing original material either written by themselves or others. 'The band was much better when it started to write its own stuff, and we produced some very good songs', John says; 'We had an identity. They were always very good songs for playing on the radio. That's one area where we really put our mark on the music industry.'

One recording which got away during this period was *You're Just What I Was Looking For Today*, which, surprisingly, was written by Jerry Goffin and Carole King for The Everly Brothers. Status Quo's recording of it was psychedelic and druggy, which isn't very Phil and Don (Quo recorded The Everly Brothers' The Price Of Love in 1969). *You're Just What I Was Looking For Today* starts unpromisingly with two rinky-dinky notes repeated for too long, but then broadens into a big production, with strings and big vocals. There's a touch of The Small Faces' Steve Marriott in the vocals, and Pink Floyd in the arrangement. It was very different from *Matchstick Men* and *Ice In The Sun* though, and, had it been released, it could have confirmed their droopy moustache status and confounded the they-all-sound-alike critics.

From then until the end of the decade the band had five disastrous singles, and a second album, 'Spare Parts', which also failed to impact on the charts. *Technicolour Dreams* was the first of those singles. It wasn't a bad song but was simply very old-fashioned by then, still with a touch of *Matchstick Men* guitar work. Great bass and drums though. *Make Me Stay A Bit Longer*, was followed by a re-release of *Technicolour Dreams* with a different B-side (a good cut of The Bee Gees' *Spicks And Specks* rather than the hideously embarrassing, embarrassingly hideous *Paradise Flat* – the worst song Marty Wilde ever offered the band), and then *Are You Growing Tired Of My Love* – which isn't even to be found on Quo compilations. It was the most successful of that run of singles though, in that it entered the charts in May 1969, stayed for just two weeks and touched number forty-six, left the listings, and re-appeared briefly at number fifty – and then sank. It was to be their only single that year.

The record company was getting very unhappy. John Shroeder apparently gave the band Bee Gees records to study and learn from, and had a plan to move them into a safe, Tremeloes-style middle ground. The band wanted more hits but this didn't sound right for them. Many other young bands who had seen a small number of hits, such as The Herd,

Amen Corner and Love Affair, fell apart once the initial success paled.

In March 1969 The Small Faces broke up after four years of considerable success and ten records in the top ten, including a number one with *All Or Nothing*, and an approach was made to their drummer, Kenney Jones. Born in Stepney in East London in September 1948, Kenney was the same age as Francis and Rick, and came from a background very similar to Francis's. They invited him to come and jam with them.

It was all in complete confidence, but the two Quo guitarists were seriously thinking of walking away from John, Alan and Roy. Kenney turned up at a small club in Elephant and Castle in South London, which Quo used occasionally for rehearsing.

The thought was that maybe Quo wasn't really working and it was time to leave that line-up and try something different.

The three guys, without a bass player, spent most of the day playing together. Even Pat Barlow didn't know about it; only Bob did – because he'd had to move the gear in and out. It seems that they got on well, enjoyed each other's company, and saw some future in the idea. They went their separate ways to think about it, but in the meantime Kenney got together with Ronnie Wood, Ian McLagen and ex-Small Face Ronnie Lane, with Rod Stewart on singing and strutting. It's possible that the formation of The Faces in late '69 saved Status Quo from either extinction or, at least, a seismic change in personnel – though Kenney says, 'They wanted to do something different – but it wasn't for me. They were a bit confused themselves; they wanted to do something different but on the other hand they realised that they already had something nice going on.'

The band only played thirty or so live gigs in 1970, and many of these were pubs rather than ballrooms. They were on the slide, and were also starting to support other bands rather than headlining. These included big name groups such as Mott The Hoople and T-Rex, but also the less well known, radical loonies East Of Eden. Their New Year's Eve gig for 1970, at the Dreamland ballroom in Margate might not have felt so good as the one in Norwich exactly two years before.

Finances were so tight that both Alan and Francis's wives started going out to work, which was far less common than it is now. It was also considered to be a serious stain against your manhood to be supported by a wife's income.

At this point Bob and Colin went over to Europe together and criss-crossed the continent by train, knocking on people's doors, going to see the social secretaries in universities and the owners of clubs, and simply played them a Quo record, showed them photos of the band and virtually begged for a booking.

Crucially though the band didn't leave Pye at this point, and Pye didn't sling their contract either. Pat Barlow had decided that a change of label and an injection of fresh enthusiasm was what was needed, and he opened negotiations with MCA Records. The A&R man he was dealing with was Peter Prince – who actually changed jobs during the talks, and popped up at their existing label, Pye. He had been so impressed by Pat's dedication that he renewed their existing contract, and indeed gave them a slightly better deal.

The image of the record companies in the Sixties tends to be one of old-fashioned, stuffy establishments – more like gentlemen's clubs than dynamic businesses, where everyone knew their place in the hierarchy and everybody wore a suit and tie all the time. Paul Brett, who with his band Sage was also on Pye at the time, says that the reality is very different from the cliché. He makes the point that Pye had the income from the well-established mums' and dads' stars such as Max Bygraves, Kenny Ball and Lonnie Donegan, and they used a lot of that cash to develop new acts; 'It had a structure and a meaning. They never had all their eggs in one basket; they could afford the law of averages, and see some success, and some failure.' In the mid to late Sixties Pye broke a considerable number of bands and singers; from The Searchers to Sandie Shaw, and from The Kinks to the pre-Ziggy Stardust David Bowie.

The Head of A&R at Pye was the greatly respected Cyril Stapleton, who as well as being both a record company executive and a producer for the label, was a working musician and a band leader. He understood the hopes and ambitions of the musicians on the company's roster, and appreciated their worries and problems – in a way that no purely office-based career exec ever could. Paul describes Cyril as 'a real gentleman', and praises both his breadth of musical appreciation and his support for what was then very new music.

Pye established what Paul describes as their 'left-field label' in 1970, which was Dawn. More adventurous music was released on this subsidiary - and many of its albums can now be found on internet sale sites with prices going into hundreds of pounds. Dawn made Pye a fortune soon after its launch thanks to Mungo Jerry's breezy, cheesy number one with *In The Summertime.* It's an indication that Pye saw Quo as very much a pop act that they didn't move the band over to Dawn

Pye also had every facet of its operation within the one building in central London, so that musicians met their label-mates and the guys who did have to wear suits, clean white shirts and sober ties every working day crossed the musicians' paths – even if it was only in the lift or queueing for a cup of tea. Bands didn't jet off to the Caribbean to record their albums – they went downstairs into the basement.

It's worth noting too that in the Sixties and Seventies, for a single to be a hit it had to sell a very large number of records. The current singles market has reduced so much that a number one record for The Darkness will have sold a fraction of the number sold by a Beatles number one. Nowadays a gold disc is awarded after sales of 100,000 units. In the Sixties and Seventies they were only earned after a million copies had been sold. You don't need to be a record company accountant to appreciate that the 900,000-unit gap in sales and income makes a huge difference to the business, and therefore support for its artists. Back then, if you hadn't had a top ten hit in the previous six months you would be de-selected, but Pye stuck by Status Quo through their lean years. They saw half a dozen singles turn into dismal flops, but still didn't strike them off the roster.

Everything crowded onto a stage the size of Mrs Jaworski's front room; in the stadium days they had acres of room on stage.

6

You can actually hear the first hints of what became the distinctive Status Quo style in *Ice In The Sun*. It has that breezy lightness, though there's no blues influence yet and the beat is very restrained. It was *Down The Dustpipe*, released early in 1970 and the band's first hit in eighteen months which first really defined their sound. It was still bright and cheery, and was a lovely, upbeat singalong number. The backbeat, supplied by John and Alan, was stunningly strong, and Roy Lynes played smoky-back-room-of-the-Dog & Duck piano, while Bob Young played a very accomplished harmonica line. The song also featured what was to become a favourite Quo device, a key shift two thirds of the way through the song. *Dustpipe* reached number twelve that spring. Radio One DJ Tony Blackburn hated the song though, and said that it should be 'going down the dustbin'. Tony Blackburn aside, the band, Pye and Pat Barlow were all enormously relieved. It seemed that there might be a future for The Status Quo after all.

It has been said that Bob Young – the band's roadie, harmonica player and principal co-writer of songs – first suggested that Quo played boogie. John says; 'We hadn't been having hits for a while and the bookings were drying up, so we were very much looking for a new direction. He suggested a bit of boogie mixed with a bit of blues, and we decided that it was a great idea.

'We grew our hair long and started going for more of a stubbly look. It was quite a conscious decision to turn our back on being told what we ought to play and how we ought to dress. We thought 'We're pop stars, we know best. We're going to play what we want to play'.

Bob is rather more modest about his influence on the band's re-direction. He makes the point that *Matchstick Men* completely defined the band for a couple of years and it was very difficult for them to come out from under its shadow. He says that he was 'only a part' of the band's development, but he was perhaps the best-educated so far as non-pop and rock music, such as the blues, folk and country music was concerned.

He reckons that as the guys' personal preference was for rock music with a touch of the blues mixed in, the twelve-bar style emerged organically. Certainly the Rossi and Young song-writing contributed very considerably, as Alan says, 'Francis and Bob were both keen to get away from the poppy stuff and get back to the sort of music we actually played on the road. Bob had quite an influence on the band; mostly because he told us to stop worrying about the frilly clothes!'

Sartorial advice aside, Bob's addition of the harmonica to the Quo sound certainly gave it a bluesier edge. 'It was simply the music that the band really enjoyed playing', he says, 'And they honestly didn't give a fuck if anyone else liked it or not. They weren't a blues band as such, and they weren't great blues players – but the liked blues music. Their depth and quality improved as they went on, and their sound emerged from simply not being able to do it any other way. It was something they could have fun with.'

Alan found a Bachman Turner Overdrive song called *Junior's Wailing*, which was a twelve bar shuffle. When he played it to the band Rick said 'It's not Status Quo, is it?' But it became their signature tune and they opened every show with it, and it's credited with being their first foray into becoming a boogie band.

The key to their success, Keith Altham says, is that having decided that they wanted to play music that really suited them, they then stuck to it. They played the clubs for a couple of years and simply did the work; 'They honed the sound and unified the approach – and achieved an identity of their own.

Keith says that it was undoubtedly a collective decision to identify their own sound and stick with it, but he suspects that it was Francis Rossi who was the prime mover in it all; 'He's very smart. He does sense a change of direction in the public's taste very quickly. I think he was the initiator. Francis seems to be just a good ol' boy, but watch his eyes – they're everywhere. I would never underestimate him; he's a very smart cookie.'

It's to Status Quo's credit that you can't easily cite the musical influences for the development of their post-*Dustpipe* sound. The two bands which John credits in terms of influences are Canned Heat and ZZ Top; or rather, those are the two bands which he has heard other people suggest might have been influential.

The American blues 'n boogie band Canned Heat owed far more to the purist blues, thanks in no small part to Bob Hite's phenomenal knowledge of the subject.

Canned Heat was formed in Los Angeles in 1966, and had a UK hit with lovely, moody, almost soulful *On The Road Again* two years later. Later that year they just made it into the Top Twenty over here with the breezy *Goin' Up The Country*, which included a lead flute, great bass work by Larry Taylor, and a drum line which John Coghlan would have recognised instantly - but would have wanted to play twice as fast if it had been a Quo recording.

In early 1970 they reached number two in the UK with the much heavier, upbeat anthem *Let's Work Together*, which shares all its ingredients with Status Quo songs - but is mixed into a very different recipe. *Time Was* was a delightful slow boogie, with another powerful bass line by Larry Taylor, which, if it had been speeded up by about a hundred and fifty percent, might have sounded like a Quo song.

ZZ Top - always at the very back of rock reference books - was hugely successful in the mid-Eighties but had been playing together since 1970. They were born out of an earlier blues band, Moving Sidewalks, and were almost completely unknown in Britain until their huge international breakthrough hits pulled from the 1983 'Eliminator' album (they got huge amounts of airplay, though none went high in the charts).

Their style can easily be summed up as good-time boogie, with a very commercial edge from 'Eliminator' onwards. In their earlier days they were more the genuine article; beer-swillin', hard-drivin' Texan rough-necks; with a great line in blues/rock fusion. It's rather unlikely that they were any influence on Quo.

A more likely candidate was the wonderfully-named Credence Clearwater Revival. Again, there aren't direct parallels - no-one would suggest that Quo thought 'Hey, let's copy Credence' but songs like *Down On The Corner*, *Up Around The Bend*, and the slower *Long As I Can See The Light* and *Have You Seen The Rain?* - and especially *Travellin' Band* - are out of a similar mould. But whereas Credence was John Fogerty's imaginary creation of a Cajun band drinking in the roadhouse after a hard day on the bayou

– a fantasy created entirely in California – Quo were simply drinking in the public bar of The Rose & Crown.

Until the summer of 1969 Credence's singles were covers, but they had a big hit that year with the John Fogerty-written *Proud Mary*. That was followed by equally brilliant *Bad Moon Rising*, which went to number one in the UK a couple of months later. All were John Fogerty songs, and he wrote *Rockin' All Over The World*, which he released as a solo artist in 1975. It did nothing for him so far as the charts were concerned, but Quo picked it up, made it their very own, and took it to number three two years later.

Canned Heat, ZZ Top and Credence Clearwater Revival were all American and at first glance it seems that there are no parallels or influences among British bands. If there's one though it might just be The Kinks. Formed in the north London suburb of Muswell Hill, Ray Davis and his crew are best remembered for the wistful Waterloo Sunset, and as a poor man's Who. A few of their earlier singles – *You Really Got Me, All Day And All Of The Night*, and *Till The End Of The Day* – move along like Status Quo songs, and generate the same sort of excitement.

'Quo have been called the British ZZ Top', says Colin Johnson, their manager through the Seventies and most of the Eighties, 'But that was ridiculous, if only because English rock is very different from American rock. Quo never had the depth that American rock bands have.'

Colin thinks that Quo derived most from the bands Steamhammer and Chicken Shack, and interestingly Bob Young also cites Stan Webb's Chicken Shack as an influence – particularly the post-'67 period when Christine Perfect (who married John McVie, bass player with Fleetwood Mac) was singing with the band. She had strengthened their sound and broadened the band's appeal greatly, but she left and joined the post-Peter Green Fleetwood Mac.

Bob reckons that many of the bands that Quo went on to meet in the USA, and played alongside, had a greater or lesser degree of influence on them. It was the bands that they simply enjoyed listening to, such as Blue Oyster Cult, Lynyrd Skynyrd and, yes, ZZ Top. 'They played on rock-blues packages, and those were some truly great gigs', he says, 'They were all good-time bands.'

'The twelve bar rhythm suited the way they played their guitars, and importantly, they *were* unique' says Colin. 'They created their own niche, and a couple of bands tried to emulate them but they couldn't get away with it because Quo were too far ahead of the game by then.

Radio One DJ John Peel was an early flag-waver for Quo, and they were frequent guests on his shows. He says, 'No-one else ever sounded like them, but in a way they remained fairly anonymous – which was something that Pink Floyd did as well. I always thought that any one of Floyd could walk into one of their own gigs and no-one would recognise them. It might not have been quite so easy with Quo, but they seemed to remain ordinary blokes. I came to admire the simplicity of their approach, and they were reasonably jolly blokes – and didn't seem to be suffering from the worst excesses of stardom, which I encountered a lot in the Seventies. A lot of people became demented with their own elevated status, but not them.'

'They owe a lot to Chuck Berry', says Phil May, front man with veteran British r 'n b band The Pretty Things. '*Caroline* has one of the best openings to a rock 'n roll song because of the build-up and the tension. It's a descending riff, which is weird; it's arse about face but it works.

'I suspect that Francis Rossi might really have wanted to be a free-flowing, melodic guitarist like Eric Clapton, but he thinks riffs, works round a riff format, and so Quo ended up playing to its strengths. Because of their technique they acquired a quality and a colour which no-one else had.'

Kenney Jones also reckons that Chuck Berry's music had a big influence on Quo's changing taste in music – and The Shadows; 'We were all the same age and we all liked The Shadows. We *all* learned to play listening to their records. Add in Gene Vincent and Jerry Lee Lewis, and even Booker T & The MGs and you've got it.' Kenney is an unreserved admirer of how the band developed and established their style; 'Quo had to find a way of being different from every other band that was around at the time – which they did. They developed a definite style, and they were unique.'

Alan says that under-currents were apparent to him, even then; 'The egos had started to kick in'. He adds. 'Rick and Francis started to develop quite a close relationship. I think that Rick felt he had to please Francis to stay in the band, and Francis enjoyed the attention. He was starting to play lead and Rick was playing rhythm, so there was undoubtedly a camaraderie between the two guitarists – who were also writing together.

'That relationship dominated the way the band was going to go to a certain degree. It was all very plastic, but the Rossi/Parfitt relationship rather broke up because Bob Young and Francis started writing together.'

'By the beginning of the Seventies Bob Young was co-writing a lot of the singles; some with Rick, but mostly with Francis, and *In My Chair* was a Young/Rossi composition. It was a slower song, and far more bluesy. It again had the very strong rhythm work of *Dustpipe*, but with more accomplished guitar work out front. It was released in late summer of 1970, but only went as high as number twenty-one. The B-side was *Gerdundula*, which was to become a particular favourite of Quo fans, and indeed was the first song of theirs that made John Peel sit up and take notice.

Alan says that John Coghlan was absolutely crucial to the band's shift to blues boogie; 'With a band everyone is putting their own energy in, and a chemistry develops. The drummer is very important; John was playing one of the most important instruments in that band. John had a great sound, great emotion. It's not just about when you hit a drum or a cymbal, it's how you hit it. He *drove* the band. If you take away a drummer and put in another drummer, the sound of the band changes. It might be subtle to some but though you're singing the same songs, it all changes.'

Bob Young had moved to London from his home town of Basingstoke – where he had run, and played in, a small blues club – and became Amen Corner's roadie. His path crossed with Quo's at the Hammersmith Odeon in 1968, and he met up with Francis again a fortnight later. At the end of that year Bob was working for Andy Bown's band The Herd, when Pat Barlow and co-manager Joe Bunce invited him to become their roadie. Francis had told Pat that he seemed like a good guy to have around. Bob demurred because he'd just been offered a job with Jethro Tull, which paid the generous sum of £10 a week. Pat immediately offered £15, and Bob's long association with Quo began.

At first he was merely the roadie, humping the equipment around, driving the van, and taking the blame when things went wrong. His first promotion was when tour manager John Fanning left the band's service, and Bob was promoted from driving the van to driving the band in the car. A new guy, Mal Kingsnorth came in as the lowly roadie. A pay rise commensurate with the greater responsibility took Bob's salary up to £20 a week.

His first move into song-writing was to co-write *Antique Angelique* with Alan, which became a track on the 'Spare Parts' album. However he soon found he was most comfortable writing with Francis, and the credit Rossi/Young has been on dozens of Quo hits, and the two still write together nowadays.

Keith Altham says, 'My first interview with Quo was actually with Bob Young; a piece for Record Mirror. I called him 'Status Quo's ghost. Bob was a very creative person, who in the end couldn't get all his creativity out with Quo. That was the reason that he eventually left. Sometimes he was on stage with the band, sometimes he wasn't and was just the tour manager.

'A band like that needs someone like Bob Young. He played a similar role to that of Ian Stewart and The Rolling Stones. Stu was the piano player with The Stones, who got elbowed out and became their tour manager. He was always there.

'Bob played that role for Quo. He was always there and always very grounded. The band never realised how important he really was to them. He'd been there from early on and wasn't afraid to tell them the truth.'

In the way that Stu played piano for The Stones, Bob played harmonica for Quo – so he occupied a strange position as part-time band member, road manager and co-writer of songs; 'I toured with Quo for thirteen years, and it was a real pleasure. After all these years of being in the music business I think that those years in the Seventies were really exciting. It was real music, we broke a lot of new ground and had a lot of fun. To go from driving a seventeen-hundredweight Transit van to flying in private planes, to go from sleeping rough to sleeping in five star hotels, was amazing.'

At some point, no-one seems to know quite when, John began to be known as 'Spud'. Apparently he used to wear a coat – or, according to other, a pair of trousers – which made him look like a bag of potatoes. Hence he was christened 'Spud'. Bob Young insists that it was indeed a coat, and that he was part of the successful conspiracy to steal it and then burn it.

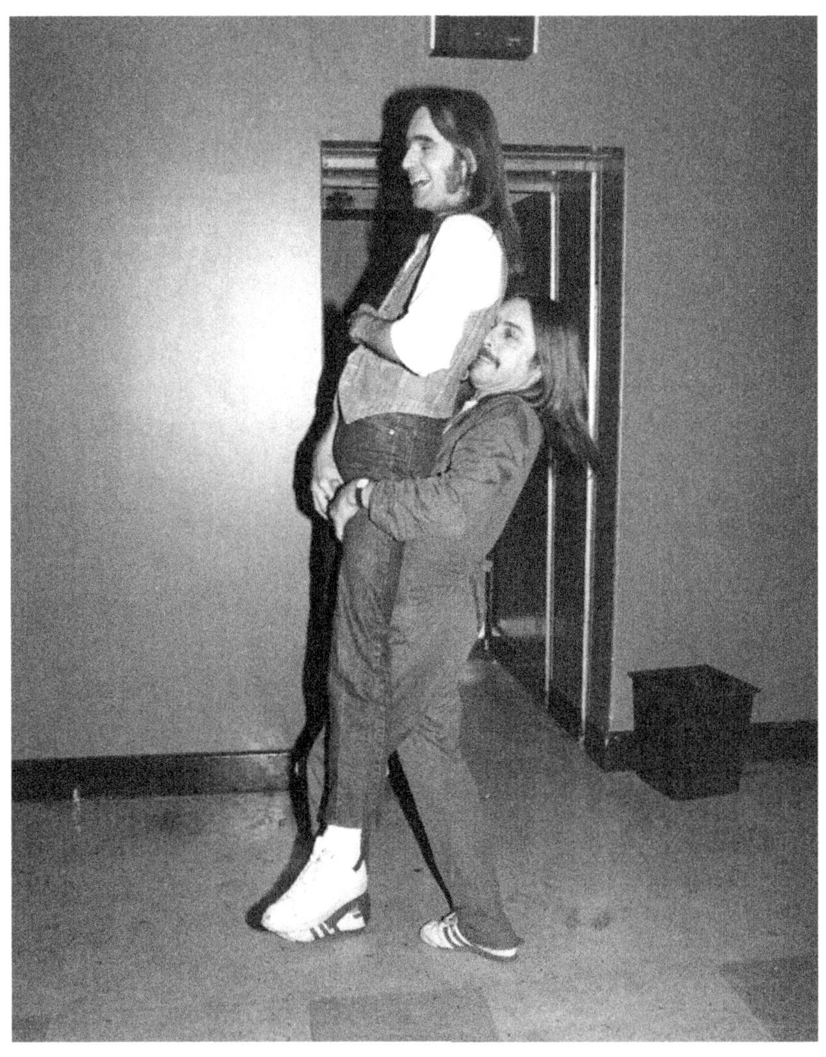

It's a funny life on the road – John gives Francis a lift to the pub.

7

1971 and '72 were leaner years again so far as record sales were concerned, with the only single, *Tune To The Music*, failing to chart. The band pulled itself out of the trough in the summer of '73 though with the brilliant *Paper Plane*. It was another Rossi and Young composition, and it was the song that set the Status Quo style forever.

Paper Plane is a thrilling song, and was also their first single for Vertigo. As ever the lyrics are largely irrelevant (an invitation to take a ride on a paper plane is a largely resistible prospect); what matters is that the song thunders along at a cracking pace. Again there's the break and re-start trick, and the key shifts. It's both – in the best sense - very simple and beautifully crafted. And there's lots more than just three chords.

It went to number eight in early '73, and was followed by the nearly as fast but not quite so special *Mean Girl*, which topped out at number twenty (lovely, bottom of the freeboard guitar playing though ...). That was followed by a run of top ten hit singles; suddenly the band couldn't go wrong. So long as it was fast and rocked it went into the upper reaches of the charts, delighted their fans everywhere and got folks dancing.

Caroline went to number five and became one of the band's most famous anthems, and was followed by the slower, bluesier *Break The Rules* which topped at number eight. *Down Down* was to become the band's first and to-date only number one single, getting there in late 1974 and staying in the charts into early '75.

It's a highly arguable point, but it's possibly the band's greatest ever single. It starts with a very long, gradually accelerating guitar duo which serves to get bums off seats and feet onto dance floors, and then – after a pause, of course, bounces into a fast, no-nonsense boogie with a couple of slow-down breaks, out of which the band accelerate at breath-taking velocity. There's no show-off guitar work; just two thunderous guitars in the front row and relentless bass and drums backing them up. What's it about? Who knows and who cares? A classic rock single.

Interestingly, *Break The Rules* and the allegedly smutty *Roll Over Lay Down* (don't you lie down first and then roll over?) were the only songs credited to all four band members. Rick Parfitt's only solo composition was the 1976 song *Rain*.

As new songs were being developed, the other band members would suggest ways that the drum line might run, and John says that he tended to go along with whatever – simply, he says, because it was 'their song'.

Roll Over Lay Down is a great song. Uncharacteristically long, if anything is Canned Heat influenced – particularly in its first thirty seconds or so - it's this. The single has a lovely, tight rhythm and some very effective off-the-bottom-of-the-frets lead guitar work. Just at the point where you are expecting the song to wrap up or fade out, its goes into a very quiet, reflective break – which comes as a real surprise. Far more characteristically though the band then accelerate out of that and back to full speed like a Lamborghini Miura pulling away in first. The band then ratchet up yet another gear as they close the song. A real treat.

There were another seven singles in the UK top twenty through the rest of the decade, including another of their great anthems – *Rockin' All Over The World*. Vertigo executives much have been hugging each other with utter delight. The guys at Pye must have been really pissed off.

On of the most distinctive elements of all these records is the hefty and dependable rhythm section created by John and Alan Lancaster. They worked very well together, and Alan played exciting and creative bass; 'Alan and I gelled very well,' John says. 'If a band hasn't got a strong rhythm section it really shows, really weakens what they're doing. If you've got a weak drummer or a weak bass player it just doesn't work'.

One of John's favourite Quo songs is *Mystery Song*, which went into the charts in 1976. Another Parfitt and Young song, with a fast bass line, it's less well known than the bigger hits, but rolls along at a whopping lick with more than a hint of *Dustpipe*. While punk rock was raging through the country's youth in the summer of 1976 the very traditional and utterly non-punk *Mystery Song* went to number eleven.

Alan (right) practises Chuck Berry's duck walk to try and get John to crack into a smile.

'*Down Down* and *Mystery Song* were fantastic. I loved them then and I love them now. Although *Rockin' All Over The World* was a hit record I've never liked my drumming on that. It's too rigid, not free-flowing enough.'

'Quo developed a very individual, unified sound' says Keith Altham. 'They used to come in for this criticism; people would say that they only played three chords, but that was much too smart-arsed and simplified. It was always much more than that. It was twelve bar blues – heads down, see you at the end, lads; and to be really good at doing something with seems simple is not easy. If it had been that easy lots of other bands would have tried it – and nobody did. They had really worked at it.

'That twelve bar blues basis is an excellent place to start from; from there you can elaborate and do other things. The reason it's good to go back to that format is that it's honest, it's simple, and it doesn't lie.'

The lyrics of Quo songs have never been big on socio-political comment or indeed carried much of a message. None of them really tell a story; they're not like what Joe Jackson, Elvis Costello or Squeeze were recording in the Seventies. By and large the lyrics just serve to add to the sound, and it wouldn't matter if they were actually drawn from the A-G section of the Montreal telephone directory.

Keith Altham says, 'Rossi was very smart in making his lyrics ambiguous. A lot of good writers do that. They mean one thing but are capable of meaning other; if you want to think it's sexually explicit, then fine. People relate to the songs on different levels, which gives the fans an empathy with those songs.'

Phil May makes the point that Quo songs always included anthemic choruses; 'After one pass the audience knew all the words to the chorus. You didn't have to listen three or four times before you could sing along. It was almost like having a little bouncing ball going along a lyric sheet.'

No-one has ever written a PhD analysing Status Quo's lyrics. Similarly, few people ever covers Quo songs – though there have been several versions of *Matchstick Men*, most notably and most curiously by Ozzy Osbourne. The songs themselves aren't that strong; it's the totality of the Quo sound that matters. And there's no point in other bands trying to improve on that.

Colin Johnson adds, 'The words to Quo songs were dreadful. The Quo song-writers were never great writers; they were never going to be in the top fifty best song-smiths of all time, but what they were trying to get across, they put across ever so well. It was the energy that mattered, and Rossi was a master on stage. He was great at getting the audience to become one with the band.'

Alan Lancaster agrees with Colin; 'What mattered was the *performance* of a song. The song wasn't the thing, it had to be fitted to the performance. You'd spend twelve hours working on a new song, getting the groove together, creating an arrangement, and then you'd try to remember how the song goes. The key was to put catchy melodies on top of heavy grooves.'

At a time when many bands were making very conscious moves away from singles and towards albums, Quo remained very much a singles band. That's not to say that they neglected long-playing records though, but their albums were, in the traditional style, a dozen or so three and a half minute-long songs. From '68 on they conscientiously and consistently produced one album every year (plus a live double album in 1977). Not for them the concept album or the rock opera though.

Similarly, the punk movement passed them straight by. While pomp rock bands like Genesis and Yes were being lambasted by punk rockers, Quo just kept their heads down and got on with it. They enjoyed many of their biggest hits while punk was raging through the pop and rock world between '76 and '78. For Quo it was irrelevant; it didn't matter.

'I hated punk', John says. 'I couldn't work out what it was all about. It was just so many people looking for attention. I am very English, and slagging the Queen off and things like that – it just wasn't on. You don't have a go at Her Majesty ...

'Also, there was a complete lack of respect for their audiences. That was strange. Couldn't understand that. Status Quo always adored their fans. Without the fans you're nothing, so spitting at your audience doesn't make a lot of sense to me.'

No Quo fans were ever likely to be converted to punk. They might come from the same street, drink in the same pubs, skive off from the same school, but working class Quo fans have always seen their beer glass as half full; to punks it was always nearly bloody empty (and there was little chance of anyone buying them another pint). Quo fans grew up to be decent citizens, concerned about their children's ability to do long division, and more likely than not to vote in elections.

8

The band's third album, Ma Kelly's 'Greasy Spoon' followed *Down The Dustpipe* in 1970 and undeniably set the band's twelve-bar boogie in solid rock. The band were pleased with it; the new direction was feeling good. Bob Young sees at the most important turning point in the band's career. All the touring was paying dividends, and they had got right into their own, distinctive sound; the twelve-bar boogie was under their skin now.

The album's sleeve was important too. Bob Young says that it was deliberately as rough and ready as they could persuade the record company to let them have it. They didn't want to be overly packaged, to be seen as slick and smart. They insisted that there wouldn't be a photo of the band on the sleeve. The band wanted their audience to know that they hadn't forgotten the times when they only had one pair of jeans and one T-shirt each. They were still reacting against the frilly shirts and satin trousers.

And the record company most certainly didn't like it. For their marketing guys it wasn't pop enough, and couldn't be pigeon-holed. They were wrong. The album was released in the autumn of 1970 and went to number twelve in the album charts. Interestingly, it didn't include a hit single among the tracks, though Quo's anthemic wake-up call *Junior's Wailing* was on there. The previous album, 'Spare Parts', which was released the year before, hadn't made any impression on the charts. Quo's music was unique, but the forms which were at its heart were very much current; that autumn the album charts included blues-rock material such as Free's 'Fire

And Water', Cream's posthumous live album, and Jimi Hendrix's (again live) 'Band Of Gypsies' – oh yes, and Elton John's 'Tumbleweed Connection'. On both sides of the Atlantic though the LP charts were utterly dominated by another UK blues-rock LP – 'Led Zeppelin III' – which was number one in the UK and the States (that was a phenomenal achievement for Led Zep, but in fact The Beatles had done it with the 'Let It Be' album a few months earlier).

Over the previous couple of years the band had built up an audience for themselves, and those numbers – fifty in this pub, a hundred in that club – had liked what they heard, and went out and bought the record.

The latest publicity shots showed them looking very different from their *Matchstick Men* days. The clothes were still fashionable but were much more restrained, the hair was a lot longer and a lot shaggier, and they had abandoned gratuitous smiling for the camera. They no longer looked like a pop band; they looked rock. They were now the sort of guys that a girl would go to great lengths to hide from her mum and dad.

One early casualty was their manager. Pat Barlow was fired by Quo just before the band became really big. They had asked Pat to represent them full time but he didn't want to lose contact with the plumbing and heating business, which had helped finance the band (along with Joe Bunce's cheque book) for so long. During a train journey to Scotland the band wrote a letter to Pat telling him that he was dismissed from their service. It was a cruel parting.

'We did the dirty on Pat', Alan Lancaster says. 'We would never have made it without him. We thought we had outgrown him. Maybe we had.'

After a short hiatus he was replaced by Colin Johnson, who had come to rock management by a curious route. In the mid-Sixties he was a machine-minder in the print industry. At a party he met and be-friended the BBC radio producer Ron Belchier. Ron invited him to sit in on a recording of his show Easybeat (always made on a Wednesday for broadcast the following Sunday). Colin adored the atmosphere, and simply became a regular at the recordings – hanging about, meeting the musicians and trying not to get in the way.

After a while people began to assume he was in the music business, and one guy he just happened to talk to suggested he'd like to try his hand at booking bands into live venues. Colin had his annual holidays coming up, so he sent his wife and children off on their own and spent his time working for Terry Oates as a booker. By the end of his holiday leave he was hooked, and he became an ex-print worker.

Not too much later he took a call from The Beatles manager Brian Epstein, who said he had heard very good reports of his abilities as an agent, and offered him a job. Convinced that someone was winding him up, Colin put the phone down on him. Oops...

The situation was recoverable though, and Colin quadrupled his salary with his move to Epstein's NEMS organisation. His responsibility was to get bookings for the NEMS stable – Gerry And The Pacemakers, Cilla Black, Billy J Kramer and so on. Soon afterwards NEMS went into partnership with The Robert Stigwood Organisation, so the roster was extended to include the likes of Cream and The Bee Gees.

Colin had a girlfriend who worked for Pye Records and she used to give him acetate's of forthcoming singles – for which she would doubtless have been fired, had her bosses known – and one of these was *Pictures Of Matchstick Men*. It made an immediate impression, and Colin checked to see if the band had a manager, and was given Pat's number. Colin called Pat and suggested a meeting, so that he could offer his services as an agent.

'Pat came into the office', Colin says, 'With his dirty overalls and his greasy hands. I was expecting a rock 'n roll manager, but this guy was a plumber!' They did a deal for Colin to arrange gigs for Quo, but a couple of days later he got a call from Arthur Howes, a rival booking agent, telling him that he already had Pat Barlow's band under contract – and would have for another two years.

By the time that contract had lapsed, in 1969, the band had seen its early run of hit singles come to an end, and Colin had left Epstein's organisation and opened his own agency in highly unfashionable Victoria, near the station. Out of the blue the band approached Colin directly, saying that the live performances were drying up, and asking him to find them gigs. Six months later they took things further, telling Colin that they felt they needed a new manager, and suggesting that he filled the post.

For a very short period Quo were represented by Nigel Thomas, who also managed The Grease Band and, for the UK, Leon Russell. That arrangement seems to have lasted for all of a fortnight, though during that time the band did secure the big Albert Hall gig with Leon.

Colin Johnson was surprised to hear from the guys, and decided that he wanted to hear them play: 'When they first got back in touch they told me they had a gig at the fashion college in Oxford Street and invited me along. I stood at the back of the hall and I've never been so excited! The pure energy that the band pushed through to the audience was amazing. It was my sort of music; I loved them.' However, Colin says that he has no idea why Quo remembered him, let alone invited him to manage them.

They were, Colin recalls, still very young and completely irreverent. They were always taking the mickey out of their new manager; 'At just our second meeting I came close to thumping Parfitt.' One thing that greatly amused the band was their manager's dogs-tooth jacket, of which he was very proud, but for them was just an eternal source of amusement.

Run by Colin Johnson and David Oddie, the company became Quarry Productions – the first half of the name being from Quo, and the second half from Rory Gallagher, whom they also handled. They were based in Dean Street in Soho, which was real Tin Pan Alley.

Colin's first move was to take Quo out of pop-orientated gigs and get them into rock clubs: 'There was no money in it. There were times when I was paying the clubs to put them on. But they went down so well at those venues that within a few gigs the promoters were saying that they wanted the band to come back and headline.' That wasn't Colin's plan though. He refused to let them headline at that point, judging that they were still developing their boogie style; 'I wanted them to do more support work and *then* come back and headline, knowing that then they'd get a really good crowd in.

'It was always a laugh. I was with them for eighteen years, and that was the most important thing; you've got to have a laugh – to take the pressure away and make it enjoyable.'

Four-fifths of the group was starting to realise that the organ sound was being swamped and was becoming redundant. As Alan says, 'When we were playing twelve bar boogie Roy would be on stage but you'd never know he was there. He had nothing to play.

'We didn't really notice. To be honest we used to forget about Roy. He was a lovely guy but a bit of a loner. He was six years older than us and it was starting to make a difference.'

Roy had met Wendy, a girl from New Zealand who was living in the UK at that time, and during a 1970 tour he sort of did for Quo what Jeremy Spencer did for Fleetwood Mac, and disappeared. Whereas Spencer went awol having popped out to buy a newspaper, Lynes simply got off the train that was taking them to a gig in Edinburgh – and from the band's point of view, dropped out of sight.

He had met the girl he wanted to marry, and decided that he couldn't stay with the band and hope to establish a stable domestic life. For the next ten years he played with all sorts of bands. He worked in and around London, and also played with cabaret bands in Spain, and worked on cruise ships.

Roy is still happily married to Wendy. He now lives in Queensland, Australia, and in 2003 he celebrated his sixtieth birthday. He occasionally plays with Quo tribute bands Quo Vardis and The Quotations. 'If it hadn't been for the guys coming down to Redhill to find me I would probably have started working in a factory or somewhere and would never have left Redhill', he says; 'I'd have done bugger all with my life.'

He says that he has had a good life, particularly since he moved to the southern hemisphere, but he also admits that Status Quo's ensuing success did get to him; 'There wasn't much happening when I left the band. We weren't getting anywhere. It wasn't another two or three years before they got going again, but hearing of their success over the years did depress me.

'I thought I was doing the right thing, but of course there were times when I thought that I should have stuck with the band. I don't think I really regret anything. I have other interests in life beside music ...'

A couple of years after leaving the band Roy began legal action against Quo and their management, alleging non-payment of artists' royalties. It does seem though that the members of the band never knew anything about the action; they insist that if they had known they would have demanded a settlement for Roy. Which may be why they were kept in the dark. The case was settled out of court, but it was allegedly ten years before he received his payment. Unbeknown to them, the four remaining members of the band picked up the legal and accountancy costs.

It can be said that Roy Lynes' departure was another turning point for the band. For the rest of their train journey north the band were very nervous about that night's show and how they would be received. Status Quo had always been a five-piece band; three guitars, keyboards and drums. Quo played the Edinburgh gig as a foursome, and found to their huge relief that it worked well. They didn't look for a replacement for Roy.

Now there was what the majority of Quo fans think of as the classic, the real, Status Quo line-up; Parfitt, Rossi, Coghlan and Lancaster.

Quo with a keyboards player and Quo without were two very different creatures. The organ creates a soft, un-rock 'n roll sound. The greatest organ playing musicians have never played rock 'n roll; from the Sixties, guys like Steve Winwood and Alan Price were firmly rooted in rhythm 'n blues, while Georgie Fame was very much a jazz musician at heart. In the Seventies, organists such as Rick Wakeman and Keith Emerson created their far more complicated, theatrical progressive rock from a highly-tutored classical base. Rock 'n roll, or even blues-rock, it certainly wasn't. Or to put the argument another way, Jerry Lee Lewis and Little Richard played piano – harsher edged and much closer to the *timbre* of a red Fender guitar – not organ.

The harmonica is very much a rhythm 'n blues instrument, of course, so three guitars and drums – plus occasionally a harmonica – suited Quo's rock-blues boogie; three guitars, drums and organ had made a different sound altogether. The band was probably at its most raw and rockiest as a stripped-down four-piece; when keyboards were gradually re-introduced towards the end of the Seventies their sound undeniably changed.

1971 was a much better year for live work than '70 had been. They played a hundred gigs, as they honed their twelve-bar boogie. In many cases they were on the bill with long-forgotten bands like If, Crunchie Frog, Grass, The Statesmen, Jerusalem, Heron, Walrus Gumboot, Easyleaf, Tricky Dicky, Angst and the dreadfully named Gnome Sweet Gnome. On the other hand, they twice played alongside Thin Lizzy, who weren't to break through for another two years, and who remained good friends with Quo. They also shared a bill with the progressive rock band Medicine Head, and – most prestigiously of all – supported the American keyboard maestro Leon Russell at The Royal Albert Hall on February 2.

As Bob Young says, 'We were playing in pubs and small clubs, and every now and again, when we could get the gigs, we'd do a Mecca ballroom. The band was still seen to be riding on the last dregs of *Matchstick Men*. We got reasonable money but it didn't go far between us. The smallest audience I remember we ever played to was three people.'

Some venues were regarded by the band as barometers of their fortunes. Along with The Wake Arms in Epping and the Kursaal ballroom in Southend-on-Sea, one was The Greyhound in Croydon, where they often appeared. If the audience was larger and more enthusiastic than last time, then that was great. If everyone was dancing, that was better still. The first time they packed the place out it felt like a real milestone.

At The Greyhound, as at some other venues, there was a tradition that the crowd invaded the stage at the end of the show. Far from having security discourage this, the band actively encouraged it, and the stage would be a single, crowded, sweaty mass of bodies – all bopping away, as the band continued to play.

In a year or two's time these venues would be replaced by the Apollo in Glasgow at the Hammersmith Odeon as indicators of the band's inexorable move upwards. Once they found they could paste up the 'Sold Out' signs there, they knew they were really in business. At the top of the scale was the Wembley Arena.

The band were busiest at the end of the year, playing almost non-stop in the UK – with the occasional foray to the continent – and this pattern became something of a Quo tradition. For many years, like many other bands – such as Lindisfarne and Fairport Convention - they played a heavy pre-Christmas British tour.

In 1972 they again played close to one hundred live gigs, including two shows in Dallenberg in Germany in July, and were back in Germany, in Cologne, in mid-December. For a dozen gigs in May they supported their chums and party pals Slade, who had finally found success late in '71 when *Coz I Luv You* went to number one. These took them to better venues, such as the St George's Hall in Bradford, the City Hall in Sheffield, the Free Trade Hall in Manchester, and most delightfully, The Orchid Ballroom in Purley.

Quo's label-mate Paul Brett supported Quo on many of the gigs where they headlined. He accompanied them on a UK tour early in the year, and describes them as being a very hard-working, professional outfit; 'They were good workmen and never failed to deliver what they promised.' He says that 'there were no egos flying about', but remembers them as being loud – and good fun; 'Even then they had a very fan-based audience. They audience were head-bangers and they really got into it. Their music was loud and simple, and very together. They really knew their audience.'

Status Quo was promoting their 'Dog Of Two Head' album, which had been released the previous December – which was well received by the fans but which didn't trouble the LP charts. Paul had split billing with Quo – which meant that his name was far more prominently displayed than most support acts – and was playing material from his own recently-released album, Schizophrenia.

Paul was playing alongside Mike Piggott, who played the fiddle accompanying Paul's 12-string acoustic guitar. They were playing what Paul describes as 'Good audience wind-up stuff; a few Irish jigs, some original material, and our version of *Strawberry Fields Forever.* We weren't lightweight though; we weren't folkie.' They were an ideal support act as they had no requirement for equipment on stage; they used Quo's PA system, and once they had finished their set there wasn't the usual thing of roadies running everywhere resetting the stage. 'The contrast between our style and theirs worked well too', Paul says, 'The audience don't want too much of the same.

'We travelled in a car not a van, we just turned up for a five minute sound-check, and as soon as we'd played we could be in the bar in five minutes later.'

Some of the venues were a really good size; Paul remembers The Shaw Theatre in London (where they played two full concerts on the same day in June) as one of the largest; 'Some of the civic halls could be a bit of a sterile environment, but they were massive. On that tour we were playing to up to a thousand people – and the halls were always full. Overall it was a very successful tour.'

These venues were a rung or two higher up than the mirrorball circuit, which wasn't just a sign that they could fill larger halls than they had the previous year, but these gigs generated considerably more revenue. The majority went to the promoters of course, but the band was at last starting to see a few more quid in their jeans pockets. Paul adds, 'You never made a lot of money touring like that, but it was consistent – and it was nice to know that your future was mapped out for the next twenty or thirty days at least.'

In late May Quo played The Great Western Festival at Bardney near Lincoln, which was one of many outdoor rock festival which blossomed fairly briefly in the late Sixties and early Seventies. It was a good airing for the band. The event was, curiously, financed by Lord Harlech and the actor Stanley Baker, and it is understood that they lost a small fortune. It rained heavily during the festival and the site became a quagmire. The line-up of bands and singers was very impressive though, and included Wishbone Ash, Helen Reddy, Roxy Music, The Strawbs, The Faces, Joe Cocker, The Average White Band, Genesis, American rock 'n roll revivalists Sha Na Na – who were particularly well received – and the cast of Monty Python's Flying Circus, who did a very rare live stage act. Quite why it was called 'Western' when Lincoln is very definitely in the east of England was a question no-one seemed to ask.

Status Quo played on the last day, Monday the 29th, between The Sutherland Brothers and Don Maclean. Those fans who were left on site were cold and wet, and Quo had the considerable disadvantage of playing in broad daylight. However they force fed their music to the bedraggled few, and they started to respond appropriately; within a song or two everyone was dancing, and the mud and the doom were falling away. In his book 'Rockin' All Over The World', Neil Jefferies tells how the band's PR man ran around the site looking for the rock journalists who were still there, and forced them to come out of the hospitality tents to see for themselves the miracle being enacted by Status Quo.

Having watched Quo perform, and been impressed by the behaviour of the crowd, the Bishop of Lincoln said, 'These people have a lot to teach us, at least in the way they live so simply'. Heaven only knows what planet he was on. The Lincolnshire Chief Constable, George Terry, saw things rather differently; 'The misuse of drugs on the site was so great it must be amounting to a threat to society. You only had to see the degradation amongst the people that we had to arrest; young and otherwise decent people on an LSD trip and stinking of cannabis.' A little known fact about The Great Western Festival is that the then-young record company Virgin sponsored the toilet paper.

Quo's New Year's Eve gig for '72 was close to home, at The Greyhound Hotel in Croydon, and though it wasn't a prestigious venue it's not difficult to imagine that the band felt that although record success was eluding them, at least they were gigging more, working regularly and were definitely thought of as a very good live rock 'n roll band.

Within weeks everything had changed. Just as *Paper Plane* was heading into the top ten in the middle of January, the band was packing their suitcases to fly to Australia. It was terrible timing, being exactly on the other side of the world when your biggest hit for five years is breaking, but the signatures were on a contract to tour Australia with Slade and Lindisfarne and there was nothing they could do about it.

They returned at the end of February and again started criss-crossing the UK, but now they were headlining in the largest British venues (in the day before huge stadia, of course) – where only a few months before they had been the support act. Quo played twenty-five gigs through to the end of April, and on April 1 played the BBC's Paris Theatre in London. Throughout they were supported by a band called Byzantium, which included guitarist Shane Fontayne, who went on to work with Mick Ronson, The Mamas And The Papas and Bruce Springsteen's Lone Justice band.

From there the band went to the USA for the first time, and played about ten gigs during May, in Los Angeles, Las Vegas and El Paso. Broad-minded LA makes sense, but what the natives made of Quo in Vegas and El Paso is anyone's guess.

After several more gigs back home, three shows in Switzerland in August and one in Sweden, it was back to Australia and New Zealand at the end of that month. The band had been hugely popular there when touring with Slade and Lindisfarne, and now they returned as headliners. That tour, says Bob Young, was, 'Ground-breaking, body-breaking and just about everything else-breaking.'

Again they managed to be halfway round the world when they had a real hit. When *Caroline* went to number five in September they were in

Beauty and the beasts. Quo meet Joan Collins backstage at Wembley. John thinks he's odds-on to pull. The others disagree.

New Zealand, but fortunately they were scheduled to return to the UK in the middle of that month and could capitalise on the highest chart entry they had seen to date.

Back home the band returned to the large British venues, and was supported by the greatly respected British blues band Savoy Brown, led by Kim Simmonds – famous for his Flying-V guitar - who founded the band in the mid-Sixties. It was then in its second incarnation, and augmented by musicians from Chicken Shack and Blodwyn Pig. A year or so previously the original Savoy Brown had headlined on a lengthy tour of the USA, with Rod Stewart and The Grease Band as their support act. Savoy Brown supported Quo on more than a score of occasions in '73. Another support band was The Sensational Alex Harvey Band, Glaswegian rockers and professional drinkers, who had a big hit with their re-working of Tom Jones' *Delilah* in 1975.

In August '73 Quo made another festival appearance, this time at The National Jazz and Blues festival. It had changed its venue just about every year, but by '71 it had found its permanent home and was better known as The Reading Festival. The event began in '61 for high-brow jazz and blues fans, who very much looked down on rock 'n roll, but it was soon swamped by pop and rock.

The '73 bill was terrifically broad, ranging from Aerosmith to Tim Hardin, from George Melly to Richard and Linda Thompson, and from Georgie Fame to Commander Cody And His Lost Planet Airmen. Rory Gallagher received rave reviews for his performance; The Faces less so. The bands could be described as the very top of league division two, and a couple of teams from the first division (together with the older-style jazz and folk acts, for the traditionalists), and like The Great Western it was an excellent outing for Quo.

A live album was released from a recording made at Reading, and it included Andy Bown's *Long-Legged Linda* as well as Quo's *Don't Waste My Time.*

At the end of '73 Quo played in Finland, France – at the Olympia, a terrific venue – and in Holland, Belgium and Germany. Most of these were one-off raiding trips to the continent, so the mileage tally the band was racking up was becoming enormous. The pattern was the same as '74 opened, with four gigs in Scandinavia before the band returned to the USA in February. There they were supported by the Liverpudlian group Badfinger, who had been signed to The Beatles' label Apple at the end of the Sixties with three top ten hits. Badfinger collapsed in a legal and financial morass and two of its members committed suicide.

Back from the States Quo played one UK gig before setting off for a long tour of Germany – via four gigs in France. Germany was to become a real stronghold of Quo music, and remains so to this day. They spent the summer touring Britain, with three consecutive nights at the huge Empire Pool at Wembley. The venues were now as big as they came.

The touring schedule was getting frantic; through the rest of '74 Quo played in Holland, the Isle of Man, twice in both the States (supporting Rory Gallagher) and Canada, Norway, Sweden, Finland, Denmark, back to Sweden, another short tour of Germany, Switzerland, back to Germany again, and then a further tour of Australia. Quo had just returned from the Antipodes when they saw their first number one. *Down Down* soared up the charts through December '74 and brushed aside the truly dire festive hit *Lonely This Christmas* by Mud to become number one in the middle of January (after just a week they were knocked off the top spot by *Ms Grace* by the 1950s Philadelphia close harmony group The Tymes, who had were seeing their first chart success since 1962).

Quo had moved into its heyday. They were back in the charts in a big way and were now major contenders. They had their own sound and their own look, and while they might be on the move almost endlessly, they were having a damn good time. In his book, 'No More Mister Nice Guy', Keith Altham says, '(Quo) were always generous, good hearted and good humoured, and it was humour that took them through some of their most difficult times. Francis and Rick were the most amusing combination I have encountered off-stage or on. High-octane fun and games.'

Kenney Jones says that sharing a bill with Quo was always great fun; 'It was like being in one giant band back then; we all knew each other really well. The love of the music, that we had in common, was what bonded us – but we used to drink the same drinks, enjoy the same parties, like the same girls and listen to the same music – well, similar – and it was nice to be with each other. We were young and we were great mates.'

The gold discs were starting to stack up, and the band members could put up rows of them on the walls of their new houses.

Already though the band was being dismissed as un-hip by some critics – and, the worst tag of all, simply not cool. At early progressive rock gigs Francis would tell the audience, 'You're really going to hate us. Tough luck.' Those who were becoming Quo fans however saw them as a refreshingly honest change from the likes of glam rock and they saw as 'pretentious crap' from arty bands who wanted to be considered serious artists, and who wanted their audiences to sit quietly and savour every carefully-wrought note. No matter how boring. On the other hand, if Quo didn't get absolutely everyone up out of their seats and dancing then they didn't consider that they had done a good night's work.

The music press were often less than generous to the band; or downright rude, to be more precise. Writers whose egos were bigger than the musicians they were writing about wanted to be associated with exclusivity for the elite few, not good times for the many. John Peel says, 'I think I liked them because they were so extraordinarily uncool. I did a gig with them in Nottingham – for which I don't think any of us got paid – and there was hardly anyone there, and Quo came on and shouted 'You're not going to like us!' and I rather admired them for that. I thought it was the right attitude and I started to pay them more attention. I identified with them not being cool.

'I initially subscribed to the belief that an audience had to sit cross-legged on the floor, and I strongly disapproved of anything other than a deeply spiritual response to music. With Status Quo a spiritual response was rather out of the question ...

'I always play *Down Down* and *Caroline* at gigs nowadays. I played *Down Down* at a Tribal Gathering once - which was a very dance-orientated event in a field outside Luton – and half the people left the tent immediately and the other half thoroughly enjoyed it. I can always detect a frisson of pleasure when I play a Quo track.'

DJ and television presenter Chris Tarrant has long been a Quo fan; 'They are uniquely British', he says, 'There's none of the flash nonsense that comes with some of the American rock bands like Kiss or Guns 'n Roses. They are also unpretentious, and they are actually musically very, very good. They are a really tight band and all that stuff about them only ever playing the same three chords is actually complete nonsense. They couldn't have survived for as long as they've done or sold as many records as they have done, without being genuinely talented.'

Like John and Chris, Quo fans couldn't care less about the concept of cool; maybe they even preferred being a persecuted minority. The band hated what they saw as the unprovoked snootiness of the rock press, but just learned to live with it.

On the other hand, it meant that the band weren't being ignored. They were rapidly on their way to being a permanent fixture on the rock 'n roll scene. It's when people stop talking about you that it's time to worry, as they'd found out in 1969 and '70.

John admits that the success did change them. 'We all became a bit more flash. More than a bit. In fact, we were downright arrogant at times. We assumed that we'd get in places for free. We'd just walk straight in. I don't think I ever said 'Don't you know who I am?' but that was the feeling behind it. It was just accepted that you'd get recognised in a club or wherever and walk straight in. I enjoyed it enormously.'

It was all very casual though; very laid back in a late Sixties, early Seventies sort of way. 'Rick Parfitt used to ring me up and say he was coming into London. I'd get the train in and he'd pick me up in his Singer Gazelle, and we'd go 'up town'. We used to go to Soho – to The Marquee, and to The Ship in Wardour Street. All the bands used to hang out there; it was a brilliant scene.

'Sometimes we'd go to The Shaz, which was a drinking club, and then he'd drive home again. Another favourite was The Speakeasy, and some nights, if I'd run out of money, I'd walk all the way home. It's amazing. You simply wouldn't do that now.' Well, Kylie wouldn't.

John was still living at home, in that his parents' house was his address. They were touring so much, living in hotels, that he saw no need to acquire a house or a flat. At the age of 24, 25, with half a dozen hit singles behind him he was still living mostly in his parents' three-bed semi in south London. Kylie wouldn't do that, either.

After the Mini there had been a Ford Zephyr, which was probably the poshest car in their street. Bright red. They were huge cars with lots of chrome trim, and tail fins which boasted the American influence in the styling. There were three-seater bench seats, front and back, with a column-operated gear stick to get the power out of the two and a half litre engine - more than twice the size of that in a Hillman Husky.

'A lot of it was great fun. Playing my drums was fun. Drinking with the band was fun. Being with the women that playing in a band seemed to attract was fun. We were on our first Australian tour and they showed us the Sydney Opera House, and I just thought how incredibly lucky I was to be being paid to be there.

'We did manage to do some of the tourist things when we were on tour. We went sand-boarding in Australia, went deep sea fishing off New Zealand, went up the big tower in Seattle – arriving in LA for the first time and driving into Hollywood; it was all thrilling. People made such a fuss of us. Nothing seemed to be too much trouble.'

Colin Johnson describes John as being quite introvert though, and says that he was often happier with the road crew than with the other members of the band – though one reason for that arose from John's love of large vehicles. Given half a chance John would desert the band's limo and volunteer to drive the truck; 'We used to travel in a red Bentley S3, and we took it in turns to drive. John wouldn't drive the Bentley, but he'd sit in the back and he'd be forever tapping out a rhythm with his fingers. He never stopped'.

Colin describes John as being quieter than the others, and not much of a conversationalist. Perhaps that was a relative state though, as John Entwhistle of The Who said, 'They describe me as 'the quiet one', but I'm not especially quiet – it's that the others are incredibly noisy'. John was never tolerant of people though – or rather, of new people. He was not so bad with the people around him who he knew well and was comfortable with, but he couldn't handle new people. And he hated the record company functions, the record company people and all the glad-handing that you're expected to do; 'Someone like Rick Parfitt was always a good ambassador for the group – good at communicating with people and having a laugh with them, make them feel at ease – but John just wouldn't.'

9

For John, the real reason to be in a band was the fun of being on stage, playing live for hundred or thousands of adoring, bouncing fans; 'Playing, I love. That's what I do, that's what I've always done', John says.

Those fans had a great affection for John and knew how important his style of drumming was to the Quo sound. 'I made my mark in the business by the way I played – or so I'm told – but I always found it very easy to do. It was just making it swing. I put my own identity on it as far as I could, but it's the way you attack the song.'

'I always used to do a drum solo when we were playing live. That came about by accident. There wasn't too much of an outlet playing a shuffle for most of the songs, so when we ended with *Bye Bye Johnny* I'd extend it a bit. It got longer and longer every night until the guys said 'Oh fuck it, why don't you just do a drum solo?'

Living and working in the studio wasn't so good: He admits that he always found the discipline of recording difficult; 'I didn't like doing the same thing again and again. Someone would say 'Let's do it again' through my cans –often over and over, again and again, and I'd be wondering what on earth was wrong with what I'd just played.'

Alan Lancaster understands that frustration, 'We were a better live band than a recording band. It needed energy to perform the sort of music we were playing and that didn't come across as well on record. Recording was secondary in a way because it was only a snapshot of what the band did.'

Quo have used many recording studios over the years. The first was Pye Records' own, near Marble Arch. Then the band recorded in the IBC studios near the BBC in Portland Place – which brought its own problems; 'That was next door to the Russian Embassy and from time to time we'd get Morse Code or Russian voices coming out of the amps. We should have told GCHQ. It might have been useful.'

Curious studio adventures recurred when they were cutting an album at a studio they used often, near Hilversum in Holland. The studio was set in some woodland, and while they were recording, lightning struck a tree and bounced onto the studio. It cut all the electrics in the middle of a take – leading to suggestions about the critical faculties of the gods.

The best bit of recording, according to John, was always getting an advance copy of the single or album. The thrill never paled: 'When everything had been laid on and we heard it back though, I'd think 'Wow, that's good!' The best bit though was getting the first copy of the record, back at home, and playing it – playing it to your friends or your family. That was great. Then you'd hear it on the radio, which was also wonderful. I was always very proud of our records. And I loved the fact that my mum and dad used to hear them and take so much pleasure from it all.'

Their fourth album, the curiously and illogically named 'Dog Of Two Head' had been released in late '71 This didn't include any hit singles, because there hadn't been any recently, but what was to become both a single and another firm favourite in years to come, *Mean Girl*, was on there. Alan Lancaster says that they were especially proud if it.

'Piledriver' was released the following year, and the cover photo showed the three guitarists on stage, blue denim jeans straining against sweaty thighs, heads down hair swinging, faces obscured, and three guitar fretboards running in parallel up to the top right. The majority of the tracks were co-written by Francis, and The Doors' *Roadhouse Blues* was the last track on the second side.

Colin Johnson made two other important moves at this stage; he aligned the band with Rod Stewart's Gaff Management to gain some clout, and negotiated a move to the Vertigo record label. Vertigo was a subsidiary of the huge Dutch-owned Phonogram conglomerate – and its records were unmistakable; all the written information was on one side of the record, while the label on the other side was a stark pop art swirl which, if stared at unblinkingly at either 33 or 45 rpm, would make you feel very poorly indeed.

Colin had discovered that the band's deal with Pye gave them a royalty of 1.5% of 85% of the wholesale price of their records for British sales, and half of that for foreign sales. This was not a lot of money. Colin tried to negotiate it upwards, as you might expect, but Pye's boss, Louis Benjamin, simply said no and wouldn't negotiate further. The bid was for 4% UK and 2% worldwide – which was still fairly modest, and is absolutely tiny by later standards, and Benjamin described it as 'ridiculous'.

Pye then made a curious mistake. For a PR campaign to promote Status Quo they unwittingly used photos of Paul Brett's Sage. Considering that Quo had been with them since 1966 it was a strange mistake to make, and it was even stranger that no-one in Pye noticed it. Colin Johnson didn't just complain – he sued them, and won. So that didn't help relations between the band and their record company.

Colin also says that Pye didn't understand how the band had changed, and were still trying to promote Quo as a pop band. Maybe they could have lived with that, but the percent return had to change.

Moving labels was a problem though. Colin wined and dined executives from the majors, and piled them into limousines so that they could see the band in action. They were all hugely impressed by Quo as a live band, and could see what a dedicated fan base they had created for themselves. The verdicts were the same though – no-one thought that such live ability and excitement could be re-created on record.

The exception was Brian Shepherd, who was Head of A&R at Phonogram; Colin took him to a Status Quo gig at Weston-super-Mare – where the band were supporting Rod Stewart and The Faces – and once he had heard the band play and had seen the audience's reaction he said 'Yes' there and then. Colin cut a deal for them to be on the nausea-inducing Vertigo label – and to receive 7% of the wholesale price of every record. So in late '72 the band left Pye.

'Piledriver' was their first album for Vertigo and the band took the opportunity to do away with a producer and handle all the production themselves. With many bands a lack of a third party opinion and a fresh and independent pair of ears could be an utter disaster, but for Quo it worked, and their self-produced work is probably their best and their most honest.

The next album, 'Hello!', was released in September '73 and it took no time at all to go to the very top of the album charts. To this day it's considered by many Quo fans to be their best ever LP. As well as *Roll Over Lay Down* it included *Caroline*, and a Rossi/Parfitt song *4500 Times*, which was to become a huge favourite with their fans at live gigs.

The '74 album, simply entitled 'Quo' went to number two, and included the single *Break The Rules*. The following year the band were back at the top with 'On The Level' – which had a curious, claustrophobic cover, with Rick and John shown as very small figures in a room set, with Francis crouched and normally-sized centre stage, but the diminutive-in-real-life Alan was shown giant-size. Very strange. 'On The Level' was full of potential Top 10 hits yet 'Down Down' was its only single release, and Quo's only number one on the UK singles chart in January 1975.

Early in '76 they were back at the top of the album charts with the 'Blue For You' LP, the cover of which showed the band in a sea of blue denim, with John - at his most hirsute – sitting cross-legged, and other three standing behind him.

Because Quo hadn't gone the purely album-orientated route they were still at their very best as a live band. Their role in the rock world was to get people up on their feet, bouncing like good 'uns and generally having a great time. It's not what, say, Pink Floyd or Genesis did for a living. The West Midlands band Slade were out of a similar mould though, and having spent several fairly fruitless years trying to find their niche, they began to break through at the beginning of the Seventies. They recognised like-minded souls in Quo, and they toured together often and became particular chums.

For Slade, the 1972 British tour with Quo was the newer band's first big tour, and they were just enjoying the first of what was to be a long run of hits through the Seventies and early Eighties. The two bands had a similar fan base; mostly guys, who just wanted to have a beer and get their heads down and boogie.

'They were fantastic to have around', Slade's drummer Don Powell says, 'We were like brothers; we hit it off from day one. We always had a great time together – we used to take the piss out of each other all the time.

'We were like Quo in that we went for a long time before we had any success on record, so we had that in common; we went through the same mill, backing other people and playing the clubs. We understood each others' language. Plus we went in for the same sort of things. We liked a pint ... though at that time Francis didn't drink. It was all booze then, very little drugs.

Don describes John as being very quiet on those tours; 'The two of us got on very well together and I felt I had a real affinity with him. People used to say I was quiet – but I wasn't as quiet as Spud.'

Don also remembers with great affection the two bands touring Australia along with Lindisfarne in the early Seventies. John says of Slade, 'They were good friends; great fun. Noddy was always a laugh. When we toured Australia together we were just dangerous; we drank like it was going out of fashion. Both bands were pissed all the time.'

Keith Altham explains, 'Quo and Slade always did get on well together. They identified with each other because they had both struggled. Both bands went through three or four flop singles; they hadn't just suddenly arrived as overnight sensations. They'd worked really hard, sweated at it, got through the heartache and above all stuck together; if you've got something and you're prepared to work for a few years – and you stick together you could really achieve something. Of course, it's easier said than done. You have to go through fire. When you're working hard and not getting the reaction that's what breaks bands up.'

As Quo went on stage at these gigs they often found that the audience was shouting its appreciation so loud that the sound was being picked up by the microphones and was feeding back through the monitors. 'You just had to put your fingers in your ears,' John says; 'It was always absolutely incredible. And some of those gigs would be incredibly hot, and you'd be soaked in sweat by the end of the first number. When you came off stage you had to get the roadies to drag your trousers off.

'There was never any point in getting a seat at a Quo gig. I took a friend to one show and he complained that I hadn't got him an allocated seat. I told him he didn't need one; no-one sat down for long at one of our shows. The audience were up on their feet from the moment we walked on.'

In 1974 Quo had embarked on a UK tour with legendary British r 'n b band The Pretty Things. At one point three of The Prettys, aided by the chemicals for which they were famous, borrowed John's beloved Range Rover and decided 'to find how good it really was off-road'. They headed for the woods, stoned out of their brains, and almost totalled the car.

There again, John had his own problems with vehicles on occasion. As the band was setting up for a gig in Germany they found that their truck needed moving. Ever happy to get behind the wheel of something really big, John volunteered for the job – which should have been the responsibility of a mere roadie – but something went wrong as he was manoeuvring. The result was a runaway truck rolling down a hill, and five wrecked cars.

'They were great guys to tour with', Phil May says. 'We had a lot of fun. It was all very raucous. All very aggressive, but then rock 'n roll is. It was very much a rock 'n roll tour.

'Quo were laddish, like The Faces with Rod Stewart – men behaving badly. The very best British rock 'n roll comes from amateurs with attitude. Original amateurs. For example, we were doing a sound check in Atlanta once, and there was a band called Cactus there. Everything they did was very complicated. One of the guys said to me 'You know with The Who, how long do they rehearse that guy Pete smashing his guitar? Do they have a choreographer who travels with them? Who works that out?' I thought he was pulling my chain for a moment, but that's why a lot of Americans simply didn't get the best British bands, like Quo.

'At one gig John told us they were going to be playing three new numbers, and asked us to go out front and tell them what they thought of them. Later on he said 'What did you think of them then?' and we said, 'Er, yes, they're fine' because for the life of us we couldn't work out which were the new numbers and which were the old ones.'

'Quo music was just in yer face. There was nothing to dissect, nothing to think about,' Colin Johnson says: 'A lot of people thought their music wasn't cool – it's not Pink Floyd and it's not Fleetwood Mac. Quo were just a heads-down, let's get on with it rock 'n roll band.

'I've seen a lot of bands on the road and not seen anyone who had as much fun on the road, and had such a healthy attitude towards what they were doing. Rod and The Faces were the only other ones. The majority were so miserable; Black Sabbath and Roxy Music we knew, they were always sitting around moping. There's no other band that I'd have preferred to manage for that length of time. Most of the time it was pure joy.

'A real camaraderie had built up between the guys after all the years of hard work they'd put in together. You'd get something like the first time you filled The Roundhouse in Dagenham, fifteen hundred people crammed in and water running down the walls. After the show you'd count the money and we'd be amazed by what we'd come out with. Hey, we actually made money here tonight!'

John decided at one point that what he needed on stage with him was a huge Arthur Rank-style gong, and that was another headache for Bob Young.

'I wanted a gong because people like Pink Floyd had one. Everyone else seemed to have a gong in the drum kit so I wanted one as well. It was like when John Bonham got a timpani drum; I had to have one too. Everybody got one. Things like that were always a fad. After a while you'd realise it was just getting in the way, and then it'd sort of disappear …

John was supplied with his kit by Premier (and cymbals by Paiste), and

Premier thought he might also like a gong, so they simply delivered one to a Quo gig in Switzerland. It was massive – 'I think they were taking the piss' - about three yards across, and it needed four or five roadies to lift it into position.

That afternoon, at the sound check, once it had been miked up, John gave the gong a trial thump. It was louder than three guitars combined, it drowned them out completely, and deafened everyone in the hall. John compromised and decided on a smaller version. He only ever hit it a couple of times in every gig – and then only during his drum solo, and he had to half-dislocate his spine to turn on his stool and do so. It was Bob's responsibility to arrange for it to be shipped around and set up. 'That gong drove me mad. But then drummers are different creatures from the rest of us', Bob sighs, 'I mean … they hit things for a living.'

A feature of Quo tours throughout the Seventies was Blackie's Bar. Two brothers, surnamed Blackie, worked for the band setting up the PA system, and in whichever hotel they were staying, the crew and the band set up Blackie's Bar.

A room was booked and kept empty, and then it would be specially fitted out; crew members would appropriate pot plants from reception, the nicest chairs they could find in the lounge bar, and so on. The spare room was turned into Quo's private drinking venue, but it was a members' club with proper membership cards, and rules. It was a ritual, and a huge amount of effort went into it. Every member was allowed one guest, who tended to be female.

It was Bob Young's job to make sure it was the most appropriate room to be Blackie's Bar for that night, and he had his underlings bring back all the alcohol from dressing rooms or wherever else it might be found. A record deck and sound system would be set up and someone would be the designated DJ for the night.

The Blackies would work as barmen, and would also create cocktails – in the loosest sense – usually just flinging together whatever came to hand first; 'They were good fun on the road – but lethal'.

If you forgot your membership card you weren't allowed in, no matter who you were. If you misbehaved you were fined, with all proceeds going into the drink-buying pot. If you misbehaved repeatedly you could be banned for a period, which was terrible social ostracism. John remembers Rick Parfitt being ejected from Blackie's Bar because he was wearing lipstick. Two of Quo's security guards stood at the door and enforced the rules, and kept out those who had been banished.

It was a sanctuary, Bob says, and far less trouble than going out to a nightclub. If in doubt, create your own. John was ejected from Blackie's Bar for being 'out of order' on more than one occasion, and had to be carried out, and then be kept out, by security; 'I hated getting thrown out, and I'd do everything I could to find another entrance, or climb back in through the window. I'd say 'I'm in the band. You've got to let me in!' and they wouldn't. The alternative was drinking in the hotel bar on my own … '

By this time getting Quo on the road was quite an undertaking, and the number of people needed to do so had increased considerably. Their tour manager was John Fanning, who treated the band as if they were school kids and he was the class prefect, or some sort of traffic warden marshalling unruly parkers: 'He was a good tour manager. He got the job done, but he'd tell us that we had to be up at nine o'clock the next morning, and we'd tell him that it was far too early and say that eleven o'clock would do. He'd say 'No, it has to be nine', and one of us would say 'Bollocks to that!', and he'd immediately fine us five quid for insubordination. We'd swear at him, so he would up the fine to ten pounds. We'd tell him to fuck off, and he'd say 'Right, that's fifteen pounds!' Honestly, he used to fine us!

'It was like getting the cane at school. He was from Liverpool and we used to take the piss out of him. We'd ask him if he ever knew The Beatles, and he'd go 'Mmmmm, I knew John Lennon'. So we'd all shout 'Lying bastard!' Maybe he had known John Lennon but no-one believed him.

Another important person in the Quo personnel was Mal Kingsnorth, who died unexpectedly in the spring of 2004. His responsibility was 'the back line' ensuring that all the amps and speakers were in place on stage, all facing in the right direction and all plugged in and ready to run. John remembers him as 'a lovely guy, he never did drugs but he was a great guy to have a beer with'.

John's personal roadie when they were on tour was Hotdog, the drum roadie. By this time each band member had their own roadie to ensure that their equipment got to the venue safely and was set up exactly where it was needed, and was in tip-top conditions. Guitarists have 'guitar roadies' who line up their instruments on racks, keep them tuned, and undertake any running repairs. Drummers have drum roadies to do ensure that the kit is set up to within a millimetre of where they like it, and the skins are tuned. This allows the drummer longer in the bar.

On some tours they would have their own master of ceremonies, whose sole job was to introduce the band on stage. This was Jackie Lynton, and every night he made a meal of it. Jackie was an old-school rock 'n roll singer (and indeed, still is), who had joined the inner circle of Good Friends of Quo; 'He was the funniest man in the world. He'd come out with some great jokes – none of which could ever be repeated'. John would often sit in on drums for Jackie's own band; 'There were so many places that bands could play, back in the Sixties and Seventies', John says, 'And if Jack was playing somewhere we'd all just turn up. He was often on at The Marquee or The King's Head in Fulham, and it was great pub rock 'n roll – so we'd all go along and it'd be party time.'

Status Quo was now a very big deal indeed, and increasingly Quo was becoming Rick Parfitt's band; not in the way that Jethro Tull was Ian Anderson plus a few other fellas he drafted in when he needed them – or Dire Straits was to be Mark Knopfler plus the best musicians he could find, but Rick's became the dominant voice and opinion within the band. To some degree a move like that is inevitable; rock music and democracy don't go well together, and someone needs to stand up and shout the odds. With Quo it was always going to be Rick that emerged ahead of the others, partly because he co-wrote the majority of the songs, partly because of the strength of his personality, but also because he was, and is, a very bright man, and a good communicator. He always seemed to know exactly where he wanted to go, though history has shown that perhaps he hasn't always been right.

The problem with the alpha male is that he's never happy with, pardon me, the status quo; he gets restless and wants to move on. That has always been exactly what Quo fans didn't want, and don't want. They're not looking for 'The Dark Side Of The Moon' or the next 'Sergeant Pepper's Lonely Hearts Club Band'. They want more or the same, only faster and louder. In time Rick started to move towards a country music influence and away from blues-boogie. He was also, surprisingly, happy to trust others with the band's albums – which was illogical and unproductive.

In the late Seventies keyboards player Andy Bown joined the band full-time. He had already played on half a dozen or so Quo singles, and the decision was made to add him to the line-up. The first album where he played on every track was the 1977 recording 'Rockin' All Over The World', the single from which has his piano intro on it.

Andy and John over-lapped as band members for four years. Having previously been in The Herd with Peter Frampton in the mid-Sixties (and had three Top Twenty hits), Andy at first considered it a come-down to be playing piano with 'a three chord outfit'. They were a fairly easy band to join though, he says, and not particularly tight-kit – though there were constant rows between the existing members, and he came to adopt a peace-keeping role. It was all pretty tense.'

He says that Status Quo were not like any other band he had ever played with for the simple reason that 'none of them listened to what the others were playing. The sound, the full-on-ness came from everybody trying to play louder than everyone else.' The sound of the rhythm guitar in Quo's music, Andy says, is four times louder than it ought to be. But that's what makes it work, makes them different.

It is, he admits, fundamentally a guitar-based band – and his keyboard playing only really serves to add a little to the overall volume; 'The guitars have always been mixed louder than the drums, which is weird.'

10

In the mid Sixties there was a brief appearance among teenage motorcyclists of a movement which wasn't the old-style Rockers of the late Fifties and early Sixties, or the more modern chopper-riding, Easy Rider-inspired bikers. They were 'Greasers' or as they preferred, 'Grebos'. They wore denim jackets with the sleeves cut off, usually over black leather jackets, heavily decorated with studs and chains. There'd be some German World War Two insignia on there too, just to upset their parents and other adults; chrome-plated iron crosses and the like. They rode mildly modified British bikes, called 'cowboy bikes'. They didn't really have a lasting impact in the great tapestry of British youth cultures – and weren't, to be honest, the brightest stitch – but they were easily parodied by cartoonists.

One thing they did bequeath to the rest of us was a curious sort of dance, which had first been seen in rocker circles years before. It was some sort of atavistic, primeval display – and was originally just a guy thing (for males to dance almost exclusively together wasn't that rare; it was what Mods did, outside of TV studios, all the time).

Two guys faced each other in the gladiatorial arena that was the dance floor, with hands on hips or thumbs stuck into belt loops, and feet wide apart. Then they bowed from the waist to each other, to one side and then to the other, until they were leaning over almost a full ninety degrees. This one manoeuvre they repeated again and again, faster and faster.

The danger was that they'd smash their skulls together, but maybe this was where the skill came in to it. Especially when they feinted to one side or bowed twice to one side inside of just the once. Very long hair, swinging manically from side to side, made all this far more effective, for both the dancers and onlookers. After a while the dancers would be oblivious to the outside world and would disappear in a fine mist of sweat and dandruff.

What was needed for this dance was a very heavy beat, and early Heavy Metal was great – it's no coincidence that the phrase first appears in the lyrics of Steppenwolf's *Born To Be Wild* - but even better was the fast boogies of Status Quo. Greasers adored Quo music and everyone copied their frantic dancing. Quo are one of the very, very few bands that has its own dance form, and nowadays there isn't a wedding reception anywhere at which some sad dad doesn't embarrass his family, and strain the trousers of his Burton suit, by dancing like this to a Quo record. Frankly, it looks better when teenage girls with long *Timotei* hair do it.

At the same time the band developed a new on-stage uniform. Or rather, they did what everyone else did and simply wore their normal, everyday street clothes on stage. Except that what they were wearing at that moment rather became frozen in time, and became as much a uniform as the preposterous satin frills.

The Quo 'look' is, from the waist down, blue denim jeans worn with what were then called sneakers. These were soft, flat-soled, high-topped, lace-up shoes with canvas walls, which owed something to a sport which may or may not have been baseball. They were comfortable on and smelly off. They were proto-trainers.

From the waist up the form was to wear a T-shirt or a blue denim or white collared shirt with the sleeves rolled up; often under a waistcoat which had obviously been originally designed to make a very different fashion statement. Sometimes this would be less formal and be, too, made of blue denim. For 'best' they would, and still do, wear suit jackets with blue jeans – oblivious to the belief that middle aged men and blue denim jeans are not natural allies.

It was only what many other people wore; not 'smart casual' but 'just popping down the pub, can't bothered to change'. Somehow Quo – Rossi and Parfitt in particular – turned it into their uniform.

At the time of their 'Blue For You' album a deal was struck with jeans manufacturer Levi Strauss, and the clothing company's posters of Quo wearing their products seemed to go up everywhere – they were certainly in well over 6,000 jeans-orientated clothing shops, which was exactly where

Quo fans gathered. It amounted to an early form of sponsorship, and it was very clever, in a smart-alec marketing sort of way. On the poster Francis looks villainous, and Alan is sporting a walrus moustache and a studded wristband. None of them, of course, is smiling.

The record company tied this in with hoarding advertising at football matches, which was an interestingly innovative idea (Pink Floyd's people wouldn't have thought of it ...). There's some debate to this day as to who paid whom between Vertigo and Levi's, but the band members are certain that they saw nothing out of it personally – except those of them who were bright enough to turn up for the photo shoot wearing Wrangler jeans, which at least ensured that they got free replacements.

As to the appeal to their fans, Alan Lancaster says, 'We were the punters' band. It was as if four guys out of the audience had got up on stage and started to play. We were doing on stage what the air-guitarists did in front of their bedroom mirrors. We were the band of the people.'

'It was like a gig in your front room when Quo played', Colin says, 'You thought the band were your mates. Francis did this thing where he'd identify one person jumping up and down, ten or twelve rows back, and he'd point to him – then he'd point to *him*, over there. You'd get fans who really wanted to be the person that Francis pointed to; they'd move forward. It was camaraderie, all that 'Alright? How y'doing mate? Y'alright then?' It just grew and grew.'

'They were always a blokes' band – a football supporters' band', says Keith Altham. 'The blokes could just wear jeans and T-shirts, and turn up looking exactly like the guys they were going to watch on stage. Quo knew that. It wasn't luck. They decided that it was important that they looked like their audience. Then it started to have a kind of feedback effect; the audience look like the band, the band look like the audience, and then the audience really *want* to come looking like the band.'

To a very large degree it has been the fans that defined Quo. Phil May says, 'At a Quo gig the audience was always so *locked* in – getting what they wanted. And everyone at a Quo gig would be in blue denim! The girls that were there looked like the blokes; they didn't get dressed up to go to a Quo gig, they wore blue denim and a T-shirt too.

Andy Bown says, 'Every band thinks they have the best fans in the world. The difference with Quo is that our fans *are* the best in the world.'

'It was like being a member of a club, being a Quo fan', Alan Lancaster says, 'Fans would come up to us and tell us that they'd changed their lives!'

Chris Tarrant says that he's a typical Status Quo fan, and what he feels about the band would be echoed by hundreds of thousands of other Quo fans; 'I seem to have been a Status Quo fan forever. I'm not so sure that I was that keen when they were into their rather worryingly pretty, psychedelic stage. I do remember thinking that tunes like *Pictures of Matchstick Men* were utter, utter twaddle. And looking back I think I was probably right. However, once they got into *Down Down* and *Caroline*, as a long-haired constantly jean-wearing headbanger myself, they seemed to be absolutely my idea of a rock n roll band.

'Long before I'd ever met any of them I just felt that they were kindred spirits. Guys who liked a beer or three, essentially good lads and when I finally got to meet them, that is exactly what they were. I must have seen them all over Europe dozens and dozens of times.

Chris agrees that they are 'very blokey', and adds, 'A Quo concert really is a great lads night out.'

Unlike many bands, Quo never stood apart or aloof from their audiences, in Bob Young's opinion; 'The audience could relate to the band, and the band could relate to the audience.' The fact that the band wore, simply, jeans, T-shirts and trainers was very important, he says.

John adds, 'We had the best, most loyal fans any band could ever want. There were English fans who would take their annual holidays when we were touring and would follow us from gig to gig. If we saw them we'd sometimes give them a lift to the next town or wherever. True fans.'

As well as devoted fans, Quo were lucky in having a very dedicated manager. Keith Altham says, 'Colin Johnson really cared about the band. Cared passionately. I went to one gig with them, up north, and the record company had laid on a really big spread for the press for after the gig. Colin and I went to check on the room just before the end of the show, and there was this guy stuffing food into his mouth. Colin, in his laid-back, understated manner said, 'Nice food then?' And the guy said 'Yeah, it's good' as he shoved another vol-au-vent into his face. Colin said, 'What do you think of the band then?' And the guy said, 'Can't stand them. Every number sounds the fuckin' same'. Well, those were the last words he spoke. The next minute he was ploughing up the buffet table with his nose. I grabbed hold of Colin. He was saying 'Let me go Keith, I can handle *him*!' I said 'I know you can handle him, Colin – *I'm frightened you're going to kill him!*' He only calmed down when all the others started arriving.

11

As well as touring and recording Quo spent a lot of time in television studios, which John says he enjoyed greatly. The waiting around didn't bother them too much as there was usually other bands to chat to and drink with if they were performing on a music show, and almost invariably girls to chase too.

Quo performed on a huge number of television shows, and the recognition factor went off the scale accordingly. John says, 'I always enjoyed doing television. I think we all did. Playing Top Of The Pops was always a thrill. It's such an institution and you know that so many people will see you. It was such fun, and it meant that you'd really made it.'

On many occasions the band was required to mime to their songs. The record was played in the studio, and over transmission, and the solo singer or group had to pretend that they were performing it. It made life easier for the production team and minimal changes were needed between acts. It was utterly illogical in musical terms, but for years it was how British pop TV worked.

There would be a large fold-back speaker behind the drum kit, and John would try as hard as he could to appear to be really playing; 'I did actually hit the drums, but not very loudly.' A lot of drummers didn't bother keeping up the pretence, just as a lot of guitarists lost the will to strum real chords and pluck real notes. The Faces, miming to *Maggie May*, dispensed with the charade and played football on stage instead.

These were the far-off, and now unimaginable days before the prerecorded music video. On occasion a show such as Top Of The Pops would save money by re-playing a tape of the previous week's performance (so long as the single being performed was still heading up the charts), but this wasn't popular with the band. A trip to the TOTP studio was an event.

The other attraction of TOTP for John, as for many musicians, was the 'house' dance troupe Pan's People. These girls were the focus of the sexual fantasies of the majority of the nation's adolescent males, but the musicians regarded them as quarry to be chased and bagged. John did his share of the chasing and bagging; and possibly more than his share. His particular 'friend' in Pan's People, as he describes her, was Ruth. Her dark, exotic looks particularly appealed. 'I remember driving her home one night in London. She was pissed and I had to drive – in her black Morris Minor 1000, which wasn't very rock 'n roll as cars go. We got to the roundabout at Marble Arch and she couldn't remember where she lived and we ended up going round four or five times.'

John claims that there was never as much sexual activity as rock 'n roll mythology would have us believe, but at the same time he says cryptically 'there was always something going on'. Then again, he adds that there were many occasions when the band couldn't wait to go to bed and catch up on their sleep. But having said that, he then bemoans the fact that most of their earliest fans were guys, and the large female following didn't really appear for a year or two. After that point it seems there might have been a quantitative rather than a qualitative problem; 'Every town had its gang of girls, who would always turn up at our gigs. Probably turned up at everyone's gigs. One night they all arrived at a single show – the girls from Liverpool, Birmingham, Manchester, from everywhere – there were twenty or thirty women backstage for the five of us and they were rowing between themselves. We went 'Oh fuck!' and hid.

'The worst ones were known as The Manchester Heavies. They used to get upset if they didn't get shagged. They used to get so *angry.* They'd be going 'We'd best see some action soon. The Move are playing down the road – we'll go and see them!' We used to compare notes whenever we could. That was when you found out that there was half a dozen other bands shagging the one you liked.

'There were times when you'd be on stage and you'd like the look of a girl at the front of the audience. You'd have a quick word with a roadie and make sure she got backstage afterwards. The big problem was that you'd find they weren't actually that good looking; the stage lights had done them a few favours. The lights that were there to make us look good worked on them too.

Before Quo had broken really big, when the band rehearsed at the Elephant and Castle, they had their own crew of female admirers – who called themselves The Elephant Mob, and used to hang around the rehearsal rooms and see how they could do. Bob thinks of them as the very first fans of the boogified Quo, and they worked hard at being their first groupies too. Without great success, apparently.

In both America and Germany the girls could be almost frighteningly persistent. They would turn up at the different hotels, one after another, and what they did was simply get in cars and follow the tour bus. They networked and shared information about where the band was going to be next.

That wasn't always wise. Quo were on tour in the States with Bob Seger and The Silver Bullet Band or Blue Oyster Cult. Two girls had followed Quo for several days from their hometown of Chicago, and when they finally got backstage just before a show, and made their way into the band's dressing room they were expecting something quite positive from their heroes. But that wasn't what they got. John was in one of his moods, and didn't want to know. 'Fuck off,' he roared at them. Colin Johnson explained to the drummer exactly how dedicated these girls were. 'I don't give a fuck. Tell them to fuck off.' One of the girls started to take objection to the language, and told John that she wasn't going to be spoken to like that. To which John shouted 'Just get out off my fucking dressing room, alright?'

So she took a swing at him. He picked up a can of Coke and threw it at her, hitting her. Her friend picked up another and caught John a great shot right on the eyebrow. Then it got a lot worse. When they finally managed to get John on stage there was still blood trickling down his face.

'We seemed to do alright with air hostesses', John says. 'I don't know if I was attracted to them or they were attracted to me. We had a party with a British Airways Jumbo crew in a hotel room once, and everyone was seriously pissed. I thought 'this is going to be fun', but I know for a fact that no-one scored at all that night.

'Me and the lads used to climb out on hotel balconies and look in through the windows – trying to find an orgy.'

Keith Altham remembers things slightly differently; 'John was always a ladies' man. Always had an eye for the girls. He wasn't sort of 'under the counter' about it.'

'John always liked to have a young lady around,' Colin Johnson says, adding archly, 'No matter what she looked like.'

Bob Young says that John was slightly more selective; 'John certainly had his share, all shapes and sizes, but he definitely liked them to have big tits. If she had big tits she was okay by John.'

For a while John was involved with Sharon Arden – better known now by her married name as Sharon Osborne. John pre-dated Ozzie by a long time, but, it is said, he was so scared of her father – the greatly feared rock manager Don Arden – that he eventually, quietly, wandered away. If you displeased Sharon's dad there was a strong likelihood that your kneecaps would be shot off. Coincidentally, at the same time Gillie West, who became John's second wife, was working at NEMS which represented Black Sabbath, and was Ozzie Osbourne's regular darts partner.

12

Status Quo was far from being the only band that has undertaken exhaustive touring – then, before or since – but reading the old schedules does show just how potentially exhausting the itineraries were. Even now that the band had re-conquered the charts, the gigs were still booked according to when the venues were available, rather than in any logical geographical way. There were fewer international air routes and less frequent flights, so flying took longer that it would do today, and the flights rarely took the band exactly where they needed to be.

In 1975 the band undertook a tour of France and Germany, before whizzing back to the UK to play the great Kursaal Ballroom in Southend-on-Sea and then Trentham Gardens in Stoke-on-Trent the following night, before leaving for Spain.

On most of these continental trips the group travelled by cross channel ferry, again, slower than the modern vessels, rather than flying. For most of the summer and autumn they were touring first the UK, then Sweden, France and Germany. They were supported either by The Pretty Things or by the heavy rock band called Snafu (armed forces slang; 'Situation Normal, All Fucked Up'), whose guitarist, vocalist and harmonica player, Mickey Moody, was to remain a friend of the band's, and who played with John in the Eighties.

September saw Quo in Japan, and in October they returned to Australia, playing a dozen gigs in seventeen days. Through December they played France and Holland, and got back to the UK in time for Christmas. Their New Year's Eve gig for 1975 was again on home ground, at The Great

British Music Festival at the Olympia exhibition centre in west London – along with Snafu, The Baker-Gurvitz Army (with ex-Cream drummer Ginger Baker), The Moody Blues, and Welsh rockers Man.

At the end of October '76 the band took the Glasgow Apollo for three consecutive nights and played to packed houses, but there was another reason for the trio of gigs. Quo were planning a live album, but not one stitched together from several dozen performances, recorded in as many countries. This was to be from one venue, at just about one moment in time.

The previous year they had released a three-track EP (extended player, 7-inches in diameter – the same size as a single), which went to number nine. Now they wanted a real crack at capturing their live performances on vinyl.

They had hired The Rolling Stones' mobile studio, and Andy Bown played keyboards on stage with Quo for the first time. They had no problem selling the tickets for what had been one of their biggest 'barometer' venues; all the tickets for all three nights were snapped by Quo fans within hours of going on sale.

Entitled 'Live!', the resulting double album was released early the following year and went to number three in the album charts. The record kicked off with *Junior's Wailing*, just as the set did, and roared through four sides of black vinyl to end with *Roadhouse Blues.*

The band had insisted that there should be no over-dubbing, bravely, and that what they played would be what the fans would hear. One adjustment they did make was to turn up the crowd microphones so that on the record, better still on the CD, you can actually hear the Apollo's balcony creaking (the band's sound crew on the mixing desk, who were a lot nearer to it, claimed it moved a full nine inches). For Quo fans those were the gigs to have been at. The album's sleeve notes were written by John Peel, which was a coup in itself.

The now almost inevitable success of Quo singles continued through the second half of the Seventies and on into the Eighties. The even heavier than usual *Rain*, written by Rick alone, went to number seven in early '76. It was characteristically Quo, though with a slightly surprising ooh-aah vocal back line, and John couldn't have put up a heavier, chunkier, heftier drum beat if you'd put a gun to his head. That was followed by the even-faster-still *Mystery Song*, which just failed to make it into the top ten that July, and at the end of the year *Wild Side Of Life* (which had an understandable story running through its lyrics) stopped at number nine – while one of the worst songs of the decade, *Under The Moon Of Love* by Showaddywaddy hogged the number one spot.

Wild Side Of Life was a surprising choice for a Quo. For a start it wasn't written by the band, but by Airlie A Carter and William Warren in the late Forties. It had been recorded by several country artists, but the best-known cut was by Hank Williams. It had also been a very small hit (it topped out in the UK at number thirty-three) for the Liverpudlian Tommy Quickly And The Remo Four (who was one of Brian Epstein's least successful acts) late in 1964. There's often been a hint of country in Quo music, if you look closely enough, and the band speeded this one up and made it very distinctively their own. An interesting departure.

1976 was a splendid year for head-down-and-boogie Status Quo fans, who had lots of reasons to dance, and lots of records to dance to.

The same year they tried their luck in the States for the fourth time. At a huge Bill Graham-run concert in San Francisco they were bottom of the bill – despite all the time and effort they had invested in the USA - opening for the American former child actor and friend of George Harrison, Gary Wright, who was enjoying a hit with *Dream Weaver.* He was followed by Fleetwood Mac (who had just recruited Stevie Nicks and Lindsey Buckingham, and who would top the album charts on both sides of the Atlantic the following year with 'Rumours'), and the bill was topped off by Peter Frampton, who was riding on the back of his huge 'Frampton Comes Alive' album.

Rockin' All Over The World saw '77 out, and was followed early the following year by *Again And Again* (credited to Rick, Andy Bown and Jackie Lynton) – which, surprisingly, only made it to number thirteen. Though listening to it afresh it's easy to find that it isn't as strong a song as you remember it to be. For that single, and the album it came from, the band brought in a third-party producer, rather than over-seeing everything themselves. The guy they chose was Pip Williams, an ex-session guitarist. That choice, indeed, the very decision to go back to using a producer, has been a source of heated debate among Quo fans ever since. The consensus is that it marked the end of Quo at their most raw and rocky.

The recording session for the 'Rockin' All Over The World' album had to be postponed for a while when John was taken very ill. He was diagnosed with acute appendicitis and taken to hospital, where the offending organ was removed.

As John Fogerty had written everything that Credence had ever recorded, he probably wasn't short of a bob or two, but doubtless the unexpected extra royalties generated by Quo have come in handy over the years.

There was also one uncharacteristic flop in this period; *Accident Prone,* which only touched number thirty-eight in the British charts, and has been expunged from subsequent compilation albums. At the same time Quo's twelfth album, 'If You Can't Stand The Heat', was in the LP charts (it topped at number three). It included *Again And Again*, and the old Andy Bown song *Long Legged Linda.*

Quo didn't touch the charts in 1979 until late on in the autumn, when *Whatever You Want* – with its surprising, contrasting, riff-heavy opening and typically relentless, thundering beat - went to number four. The song was co-written by Rick and Andy Bown. It was also the song, which more than any other, Status Quo's critics pointed at derisively; proof that they were uncultured simpletons turning out simplistic songs pandering to a lowest common denominator. As if the Quo fans cared what the poncey, high-falutin' rock critics thought.

The album of the same name (again produced by Pip Williams) went to number three, again, as did the greatest hits compilation '12 Gold Bars', which was released in the spring of 1980. In the same year the band released 'Just Supposin'', not their strongest album, which went to number four.

The single *Whatever You Want* was followed into the charts shortly afterwards by *Living On An Island* (by Rick Parfitt and Bob Young), which stopped at number sixteen. Opening with a strumming acoustic guitar, this sweet ballad was uncharacteristic Quo, and wasn't welcomed by many of their fans. It didn't play to the band's strengths, and the line '*Waiting for my friends to come and we'll get high; gonna touch the sky*', seemed very unQuo-ish, and harked back to the half-forgotten nightmare of *Matchstick Men.*

In 1980 they were back to basics, to the reassurance of their fans, with the unsubtle *What You're Proposing* – which is utterly deafening, even played quietly. At number two it was their biggest hit since *Down Down*, and was kept off the top spot by, startlingly, Barbra Streisand with her unlikely hit *Woman In Love*, which was eventually replaced by Blondie's far more rock 'n roll *The Tide Is High.*

A double A-side single entered the charts in December of that year, with *Lies* – with its hint of country in its lyrics - on one side, and *Don't Drive My Car* on the other. This latter cut was a great rocker, but wasn't the strongest song in the world, and simply didn't sound like Quo. The single wasn't memorable Status Quo, but it made number eleven. That was followed by a number nine for the very characteristically Quo *Something 'Bout You Baby I Like.*

The last Quo single that John played on was *Rock 'N Roll*, released late

John, almost smiling, with the 'send your entries to this address' caption on Tiswas. Chris Tarrant is on the left and a hysterical Andy Bown on the right, next to Rick Parfitt. Note Sally James' boobs on the bottom left.

in 1981. Unpromisingly the record starts with someone whistling over guitar chords – and it's a well known fact that whistling on a record has always been a disaster, apart from *Jealous Guy* of course (being the exception that proves the rule). Then the violins start. It was slow, autobiographical, and would have been bluesy without the strings, and did play up Quo's undeniable naff side. However it was Status Quo's twenty-fourth hit single in thirteen years, and those records had spent a very impressive total of 229 weeks in the charts over that period.

And then there were the live shows: The tour schedules for those years, indeed for the whole of the end of the Seventies, show that Quo was still gigging constantly. TV appearances would be fitted in whenever they could and the only real breaks were for recording sessions and the occasional, increasingly expensive and exotic, holiday.

The pattern was the same each year; about thirty gigs in the major cities of the UK (and Bridlington), plus tours of Germany, Scandinavia, the Low Countries, Austria and France – and further afield, Japan, Australia, New Zealand, and occasionally the USA. In '77 they played more than twenty shows in France across the end of January and into February, with a gig almost every night. Then it was twenty shows in Germany, three gigs on consecutive nights in Ireland, and back to a full-length British tour – which ended with six nights in London; three at Hammersmith Odeon and three at the Odeon in Lewisham.

The following year they played even more gigs on the mainland of Europe, so much so that they hardly played a thing in Britain (the '78 UK tour didn't happen until '79). Australasia was getting huge for Quo, and that year they played nearly thirty big shows there, including several stadium appearances. The first night they played in Australia that year, on what was the 'Rockin' All Over The World tour', appropriately, was recorded by boot-leggers and the unofficial recording, called 'First Night Stand', was widely distributed.

In July 1979 Quo played a rare rock festival in Dublin in the Republic of Ireland, compered by John Peel. The line-up also included the Brummie heavy metal band Judas Priest, and local lad Christy Moore, late of Planxty.

Bob Young describes the band's itinerary as 'dart board touring', with gigs everywhere and in no logical order. He recalls the band having to break off a European tour and dash back to the UK for a single gig or a Top Of The Pops appearance, and then turn straight around and head back to the ferry terminal. He says that it was satisfying though, as they saw the

A young girl from the audience looks on in horror as John poses as an Arabian Sheikh on the Tiswas set.

venues getting bigger and better – going back to a town and playing in the civic centre or the football stadium rather than the small club they were in the previous year; 'You did see progress. You knew you were breaking into new markets. It was very satisfying.'

They did have a day off – sort of – in November 1979, when The Sun newspaper organised a rock 'n roll five-a-side football competition at Wembley. They dribbled, tackled and took corner shots with the likes of Manfred Mann's Earth Band, and The Electric Light Orchestra. Strange.

Another distraction was Tiswas. In 1974 Central Television launched the Saturday morning show Tiswas, hosted by – among others - Chris Tarrant (who also produced the show) and Sally James, and featuring the then little-known Lenny Henry, and Bob Carolgees and the infamous Spit The Dog. Ostensively it was a children's programme, and in retrospect it is credited with having revolutionised British television – but it also had a huge audience of grown-ups and not-so-grown-ups, who adored the improvisation and the chaos.

Chris explains, 'I suppose just because nothing had ever been seen that was remotely like it. It was supposedly for children and yet the average age of the audience rapidly became something over 17 or 18. It was seemingly watched by every student in Britain and an awful lot of mums and dads as well. It was a kind of anti-kids show.'

On the other hand, large numbers of men watched every week just to catch a glimpse of Sally James, who, with her low tops and thigh boots, was a greatly admired, though slightly bemused, sex symbol.

Pop and rock music featured on the show every week, and many musicians were fans of the programme. These included Status Quo, and in particular Rick and John, who would frequently arrive at the studio for the live recording. At this point they seemed to lose what inhibitions they had and join in with the madness.

Chris Tarrant remembers, 'Quo were certainly regular guests on Tiswas, mainly because we liked them a lot and if you're the Producer of a show, why the hell can't you have a few chums on rather than people that you genuinely loath? They always gave good value; there was nothing stiff or starchy about them, they'd always somehow drag themselves into the studio, whatever state they were in the night before, answer questions that were asked and join in all the antics ... custard pies, gunge, the lot.

'I do remember the famous celebrity cage that we had one week. We had a regular feature called The Cage which normally featured members of the public - grown ups who really should have known better rather than to

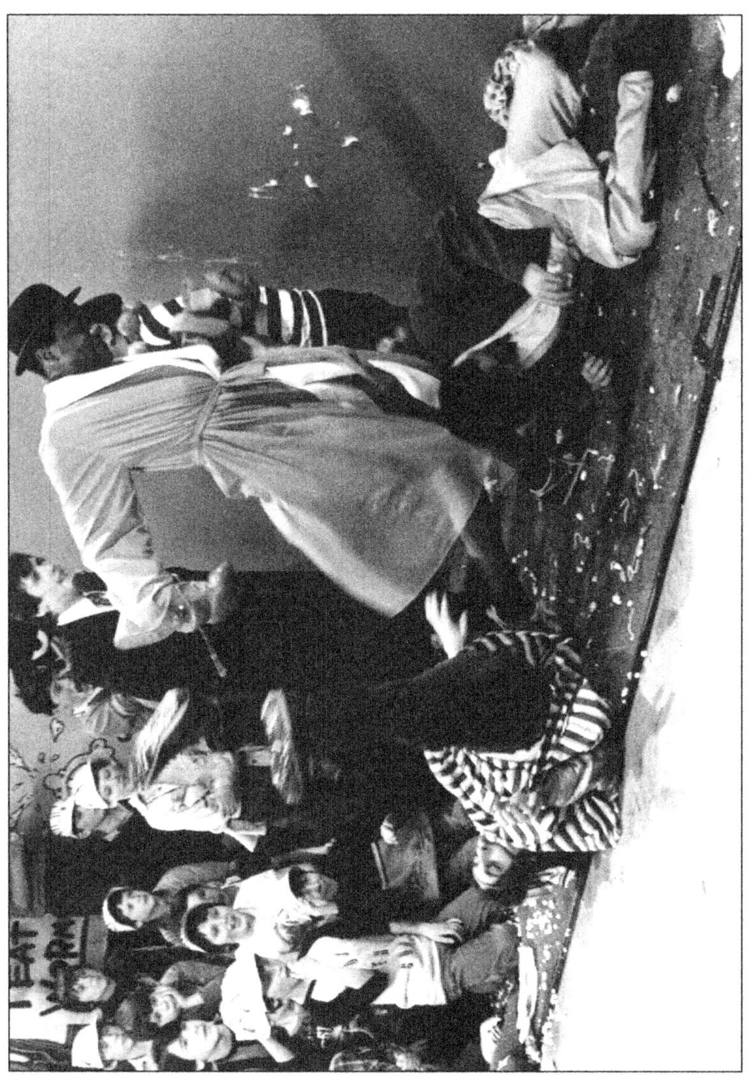

The young audience wonders about the things that grown-ups get up to; John and Bob Carolgees on the floor, with Lenny Henry in boxing gloves and bowler hat.

be in there in the first place, VAT men, tax inspectors, school teachers etc, and they were always drowned in gunge and God knows what else.

'One week, as a PR exercise, I decided to have a Celebrity Cage. We had Quo of course, a couple of the guys from Motorhead, including the magnificent Lemmy, John Peel from Radio One, Cozy Powell from Rainbow, a couple of journalists from music papers and an extraordinary American girl rock band called Goldie and the Gingerbreads. I was in the middle of a sketch with Lenny Henry when I suddenly got the unmistakable whiff of marijuana in my nostrils …

'Here was I, the producer of what was ostensibly a kids' programme with somebody smoking dope live on air in among all the children. I grabbed a bucket, pelted the offending celebrities with gallon after gallon of ice cold water and happily the smell and the joint disappeared. I've never revealed who it was on that occasion smoking the joint ... but I know in my heart of hearts it was Parfitt.'

What tended to happen after Tiswas had been transmitted was usually even less suitable for a children's audience, especially as the action took place in the studio bar – and then in the pub, and then in another pub. Chris will only say, 'I would always go for a good drink with them afterwards and it was always a splendid night out.'

Back to business, and the band received the Silver Clef award from the Nordoff-Robbins charity, which uses music therapy to treat children with learning difficulties. Pioneered by Paul Nordoff and Clive Robbins in the Fifties and Sixties, music therapy had been found to be enormously beneficial to ill or disabled children, and the charity had long been supported by the rock world. Quo received the award for 'Outstanding services to British music', which is awarded annually as a reciprocal gesture to the industry which has given so much to help the work for severely disabled children'.

It gained them considerable publicity, but it was also indicative of something more subtle. They were now on the inside, they were part of the British rock scene – part of the rock 'n roll establishment indeed.

The tour itineraries show that between '76 to '79 Quo were allowed their New Year's Eves off, which was nice.

13

In 1972 John married Carol Rodd, a Walthamstow girl. The band frequently played The Wake Arms in Epping at the beginning of its move to boogie; 'It was a great venue; a little pub, it probably only held a hundred people, but we used to play there regularly. I met Carol there. She was a blonde, and worked as a secretary. We went out for a while and I suppose I fell in love with her.' John's memories of the period aren't detailed.

They had a full-scale wedding in Carol's home town, and the other members of the band turned up, together with most of the road crew. What the Rodd family made of this leery, hairy invasion is anyone's guess. John has no memory of the wedding (or even the time of year it took place, let alone the date...), except that it took place 'in a very nice church'.

The newly-weds set up home together in Roding Valley in Essex, in a small semi-detached house. Carol's father was a master builder and he worked long hours getting the house up to the standard he thought the newly-weds deserved.

The marriage was probably never going to last though. 'I was in one of the hardest-working bands around, and I was simply never home. That's what destroyed the marriage', John admits; 'There was no-one else involved on either side'. They were together for two years, during which time their daughter, Charlotte, was born.

Friends describe Carol as being possessive and very jealous. It is said that she wouldn't let John go to the pub, even in the company of her own

John looking very rock 'n roll, at his first wedding in 1972, with his bride Carol and her mum Lilian.

brother, in case John started chatting up other women. She could be said to have had a point.

Colin Johnson – whose then wife was friends with Carol - says that one of the most important differences was that Carol wasn't from a music business background, and didn't either understand it or want to; 'Carol was a nice girl, but she didn't like the music scene and didn't encourage John. She wasn't supportive of him. I think that, like with my wife, it was a case of always having to be at her parents for Sunday lunch, running round there twice during the week – not letting them get on with their lives.'

Bob Young recalls them as fighting all the time, like cat and dog; 'The first time we went to the Isle of Man there was a hell of a battle going on between them on the bus. We were just going from the airport to the hotel and there was a real old barney going on between them.'

Gillie reckons, 'She couldn't cope with his job, and she couldn't cope with her jealousy. And for John she was 'too Essex'; they *had* to live near her mum and dad, where the family was. There was pressure on him to be something he wasn't and he couldn't live like that.'

'I imagine it would have been quite hard, with that kind of lifestyle', Charlotte says. She has never spoken to either Carol or John in any detail about the break-up of the marriage, but she shrugs; 'Sometimes these things just don't work out.'

After the divorce Carol married another drummer – Lee Hayes - a friend of John's, by whom she later had a son. Lee was very actively Charlotte's step-father, though she always kept contact with John. She always retained the Coghlan surname too.

'Lee was always saying what a great drummer Dad was. Lee's a really good drummer, and still plays out and around now with The Paul Harper Band, but he was a great fan of Dad's', Charlotte says; 'Lee and Dad always admired each other, so there was never any hostility between them.'

She doesn't recall that having a rock star for a dad was any big thing. She says that friends simply found it 'interesting', but even today people still ask her if she will get his autograph for them; 'I didn't go on about it. He was just my Dad, and that's what he did.'

Status Quo featured at number twenty in a February 2004 TV programme which listed the fifty bands and singers who had sold most singles in the UK since the charts began. The following day Charlotte's boss was the first person to say to her 'I saw your dad on tele last night!' When pressed she will admit that she was far from unhappy with that; in fact she was really proud When she was young though she was always embarrassed when fans came up to them and asked for his autograph.

Charlotte and Carol went to see Quo playing at Wembley once, when she was very young. They got lost driving there so they missed a lot of the concert, but Charlotte remembers that they did arrive in time for her to see her dad under the spotlight, doing his drum solo; 'We were at the side of the stage, and the solo was really impressive - but it did seem to go on for an eternity.'

Her father can be hard to talk to at times, she says – but after a few drinks he'll do the world's funniest Dudley Moore impression. They talk more, and more deeply, now than they ever have; 'I know how to deal with his quiet moments now; I'll just go off and have a girlie chat with Gillie. He likes his own time, he likes to be on his own every now and then. He loves the country life nowadays; he adores Ellie the dog. He's in his element when he's talking about planes and army vehicles. He loves to show me his flight videos, though sometimes he forgets that he's shown me them before. If I see an unusual plane I'll call him and tell him and he loves it; he'll get really excited about it. And he loves taking me out in his army truck.'

She knows that he has a reputation for having a temper, but argues that he has mellowed with age; 'I'm still learning things about him, still getting to know him. I love spending time with him. I think he's proud of me; he loves introducing me to friends. And he's always been terrific with my boyfriends.'

John says he is glad that Charlotte has never wanted to get involved in the music business; 'It must be nice for a musician to have a son or daughter who has hit records, but when you've seen what all the trappings entail you think that she's probably better off out of all that.'

Charlotte is a fan of early Quo music, but doesn't care for how it changed through the Eighties. She says that the overall style changed irrevocably, and cites *In The Army Now* as the nadir for her ('a terrible song!'). She has a Status Quo platinum record on her wall at home – a gift from her grandmother at the point where she moved into a nursing home - but will reluctantly admit that she doesn't own any Quo records or CDs.

John first met Gillian West at a Quo gig in Hammersmith Odeon in 1974 – the year Charlotte was born - in the back stage bar at the Hammersmith Odeon. Gillie says that their eyes met across the crowded room, in the time-honoured fashion. He was with his wife, but Gillie didn't know that so the fact didn't cramp her style. 'It was instant sizzle', she recalls, just a touch misty-eyed, 'There was a bit of chat and he invited me to meet him in the dressing room. So I did, and I gave him a blow-job.'

Gillie's father, Bill West, was a stage director for Rank – one of the big national entertainment groups – and her mum was an ex-Tiller Girl. Born in Windsor and brought up in west London, Gillie gained a scholarship to the girls-only boarding school Westonbirt, near Tetbury – not far from where they live now.

After a period in a secretarial college – which her dad insisted on – she started working in the music business, though the first jobs she had were more Vera Lynn than rock 'n roll. It was an environment she adored, and was, she says, all she had ever wanted to do. When she wasn't working, she was having fun, and her preferred company was rock and pop musicians.

She says that she fancied the drummer with Status Quo long before she ever met him. She had a box file in her office, with a photo of John stuck to the lid. 'I always fancied long-haired drummers. I liked guys with long hair, and John had the longest, the best long hair.'

Gillie was still taken by her photo of him – with his blue jeans tucked into long suede boots, fashionably, and just a leather waistcoat over his otherwise bare chest; 'That was when he was really muscley'. Gillie still has

John (centre, with a drink) receiving a gold disc from a Phonogram executive. Alan Lancaster is behind the mike stand and Colin Johnson is on the right of the picture.

the box file, with the Sellotape fading and now with a couple of back stage passes stuck it. John is sitting at the front of the drum riser, leaning forwards slightly so that his hair reaches almost to his waist. What you notice though, and what doubtless caught Gillie's attention, is a very engaging little boy smirk. He's glancing off to his left rather than looking at the camera, and looks the very definition of merry mischief.

'These days if I open a newspaper and see a photo of Justin Timberlake or whoever the little girls are supposed to be going for, I just go 'aaaargh', Gillie says: 'Show me a photo of Jon Bon Jovi or Robert Plant though – or even The Darkness – and I'm away!' Gillie says she simply always had 'a thing' for drummers; 'I went out with a lot of drummers; I can't remember any of their names – but I've got a list somewhere ...

'Whenever I wanted someone I got them. I used to see someone at a gig or on TV, and I'd say 'I'm going to have him', and I did. I never didn't get anyone I said I was going to get.'

After their very brief meeting at the Hammersmith Odeon, John phoned her and suggested that meet up at The Marquee. That was a disaster: 'He was in one of his Mad Turk moods, didn't buy me a drink, got all stroppy and went home. So I thought 'Fuck you mate; what a wanker'. I wrote him off and I thought that was the end of that.'

Two years on, she had moved on to MAM, who represented Hot Chocolate, The Kinks, Black Sabbath, Neil Young, Barclay James Harvest, and Deep Purple. Her boss received an invitation to the opening of The Kinks' new studio, Konk, in Highgate. Scribbled on the edge of the invite was 'And bring Gillie – the one with the big tits'. Well, it was the Seventies...

Gillie had been living for some time with, uncharacteristically, a guitarist, by the name of Roy (at Roy's parents' house in Kensal Rise). So she and he went to the Konk party – where she was re-united with John. They spent the entire evening together, and Gillie learned that John was no longer with Carol. Gillie decided that what she wanted was him, and possibly for rather longer than it took to give him a blow-job.

The next day, Gillie opened up to Roy's mum, telling her that what she really wanted wasn't her son but this long-haired moody drummer. Roy's mum listened carefully before announcing that she never thought that he son was going to amount to much, and that from the sound of it Gillie would be better off with John!

As if by magic, and certainly as an auger of what life was going to be like, John sent round a chauffeur-driven limousine. Gillie got in and was whisked away.

John had recently bought a farmhouse on the Isle of Man, but hadn't actually moved in. Just five days after they had met up again at Konk, over dinner at Musto's Bistro in Primrose Hill, John invited Gillie to live with him, and she unhesitatingly moving into the flat he was renting in Wimbledon. A few months later he suggested she join him on the Isle Of Man. Gillie claims that she said, in her educated, distinctly refined voice, 'Yes, I'd love to. Where is it?'

She adds, 'If you'd told me at the time that we'd still be together nearly thirty years later I'd have laughed at you. Don't be ridiculous! I wasn't the sort of girl who was looking for the man of her dreams; I wasn't going to get married. I was thinking 'This is a fun shag; let's see what happens tomorrow.' I didn't want marriage and I didn't want to have children. I wanted to have fun.'

She wasn't even, particularly, a fan of the band. Her music was heavier, by choice.

Quo, like very many rock bands, had a very ambivalent attitude towards

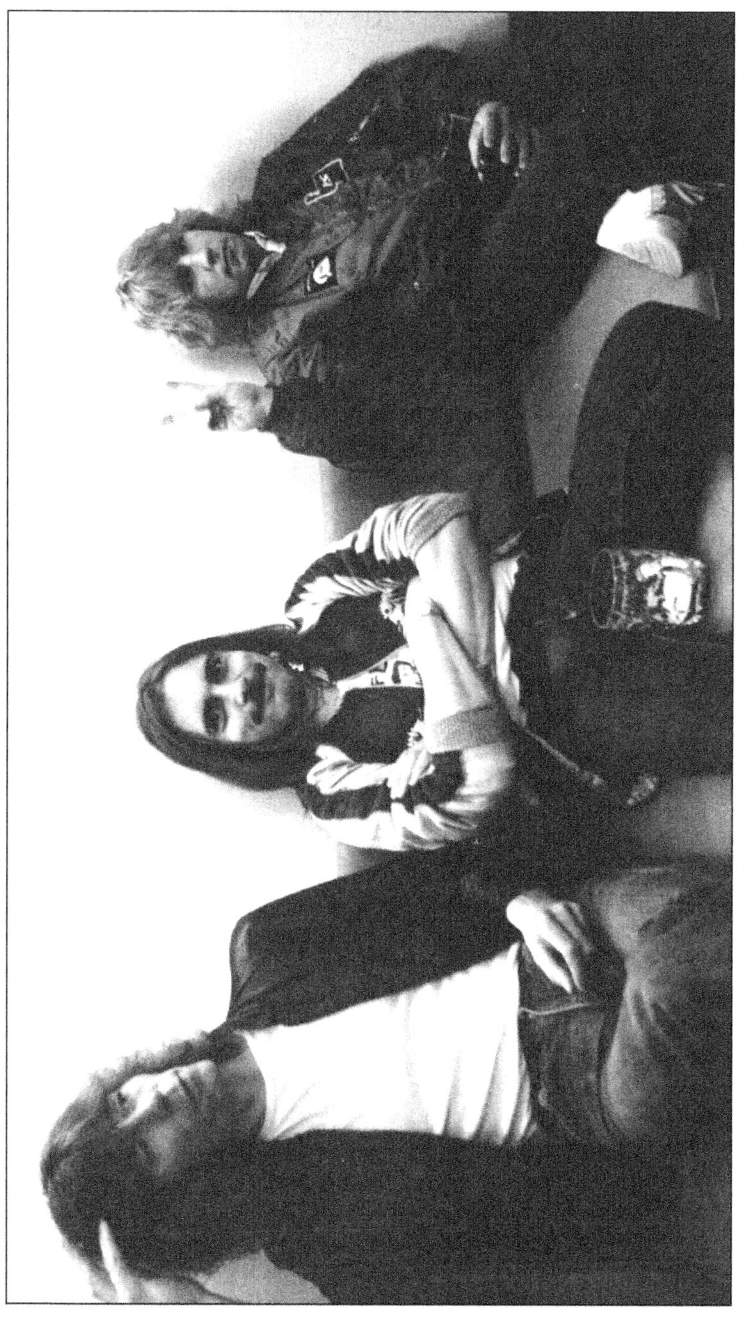

A rare Seventies shot of John smiling (centre, with a drink), with Andy Bown on the left and a cheery Rick Parfitt on the right.

women. 'Wives can be murder for a rock band; they get in the way, they mess up the rhythm,' Colin Johnson says, 'Usually because they don't want you to be away. They can make things very difficult.

'They're always seen to be interfering, and we *tried* to ban them from going on the road with the band. It lasted for a while, but they'd just turn up ... and then you'd get caught out. Wives were a funny commodity. Always a threat ...'

Gillie says that she always got on well with the other members of the band; says that Francis could be 'a bit quiet – and weird – always fine with me but never close', but says that both Alan and Rick were 'lovely'.

'Gillie had been around the business for ever', Colin says, 'She'd been hanging around rock 'n roll musicians, and was always Mrs Showbiz. She was always wonderfully turned-out and very flamboyant.

'I must admit I thought 'What's her agenda?', but they were a very well-suited couple. Gillie is a one-off. She has always given John great support, and has the utmost faith in him.'

Bob describes Gillie as 'always good fun, always bubbly – and very tolerant.'

Having made a commitment to a rock star, Gillie was completely relaxed about what inevitably went with that; 'I was never bothered if he had a quick bonk while he was on tour. I'm likely to have a quick bonk while I'm away as well, and that doesn't mean a thing to me. Sex and love are completely separate things as far as I'm concerned. Sex is a bit of fun, and it's a sport and great. Lust and love are different. I'm not a feminist at all. I believe that women are equal, okay, but if a man is happy to pay for me to be me, and have a nice time, and he's happy with my company, what more do I want? I haven't got a career-minded bone in my body.

'If John fell in love with someone else it would be a shame, but I've always been confident enough to think that he will always come back to me. If he didn't then it would mean he'd have found something better. It's never bothered me; I think like a man where sex is concerned.

'I want him to be happy, and out of sight *is* out of mind. I don't *want* him to fall in love with someone else ...'

14

In the Seventies the Labour government's Chancellor Of The Exchequer, Denis Healey, declared that he was going to tax the rich 'until the pips squeak', and he introduced a terrifying top rate of personal taxation at 97%.

The previous decade and a half had seen a cultural explosion in the creative arts in Britain, and the wealth this created – especially in terms of foreign earnings and, in particular American dollars brought into Britain – was enormous, and was gratefully welcomed by the government. It resulted in embarrassments like The Beatles' OBEs, and a Trade Minister giving Led Zeppelin a special award for their export achievements. It also gave the country a huge boost in terms of its international prestige; one which we are still, perhaps mischievously, trading off.

The Chancellor's punitive tax rates were initiated as a result of Labour dogma, which was outdated even then. It meant that the successful were to be allowed no more than the most modest rewards for their talents – no matter how brief their creative lives might be. The effect of this was to drive many of the cleverest and most creative people into exile abroad. Many of the brightest and best of the rock and pop musicians, who had brought in such huge sums in foreign earnings, were now scattered across the globe.

'We had a meeting with the accountants, and they told us straight; they said 'You've got to get out'. It was an amazing situation.' John says.

Led Zeppelin wasted no time in leaving the UK in order to hang on to their new-found wealth, moving out in 1975 when the highest rate of tax was a mere 87%. Earlier in the decade The Rolling Stones moved to France to escape impossible taxation demands, and, interestingly, they all moved to the same small area. At one time, indeed, they were all living in Keith Richard's home in Nellcote – and he charged everyone for bed and breakfast. They recorded locally and very much remained a single unit.

For Status Quo it was very different. Francis Rossi decamped to Dublin, Rick Parfitt went to Jersey and Alan Lancaster, who had already gone to Australia, simply stayed there. Maybe the fact that the four band members left for four different territories tells us something, but John denies that it caused problems; 'It was only a problem with Alan, simply because he was so far away. We did actually, famously, do a Top Of The Pops without him. We used a dummy that had been made for some promotional thing. We put a wig on it, with his jeans and his leather jacket, and strapped a bass guitar to it. We were playing *Rockin' All Over The World*, and Colin Johnson was up in the lighting rig pulling the strings on this mannequin like it was a puppet. It was very cruel. Alan's granny saw it and phoned his mum and said 'I've just seen Alan on the TV and he doesn't look at all well'.

'We were told that we could only spend so many days in England, sixty a year I think it was, and I wondered how they'd ever know. Whenever I flew into Heathrow there was always Special Branch officers there checking identities for immigration or looking out for villains, and all us tax exiles assumed that they'd clock us in and out too, and report our movements to the Inland Revenue. Someone said 'Oh they can't do that!' but no-one wanted to be a test case!'

John moved over to the Isle of Man on his own, intending to simply start a new life from scratch. He says he went at Trevor Baines's suggestion; 'He said 'Why don't you come and live over here?' So when the accountants ordered us out of the country I decided it was a good idea. I thought that having friends on the island would give me a head start. The idea of going somewhere where I'd know no-one was a bit scary'. The ready availability of British beer might have been a small factor too, but it was the obvious place to go.

Trevor had became a great fan of the band, as well as a friend of John's, and went to their gigs all over Europe, often with his girlfriend of the time, Caroline Nettlefold – now Lady Caroline Windsor - to whom Rick Parfitt would dedicate *Caroline*, telling the audience 'That's the girl at the back with the big knockers'. (In the 2004 Sunday Times Rich List, Trevor was noted as the richest IoM resident, with a personal wealth of £126,000,000.

John (on the left, with a drink) receiving the Silver Clef award from comedian Tommy Cooper - and almost smiling. Rick in smart jacket and Colin Johnson on the far edge of the shot.

This made him better off than David Bowie or Ringo Starr, but slightly less blessed than Phil Collins ...).

Without doing too much research or giving the matter a great deal of thought John bought a substantial house on the island's north-west coast, by the coast road to Jurby. Set in four acres on top of the cliffs, it had its own access to the beach down a flight of steps. Instead of a rented apartment he now had a sizeable house – and all the expense and responsibilities that went with it. It meant that for the first time in his adult life a real base; a home. It was to quickly become a much-loved haven for him.

He wasn't there for long before Gillie joined him – a matter of a few weeks - though it was to prove to be less of a haven for her. She'd never heard of the Isle of Man. It's said that when she heard the word 'isle' and the phrase 'tax exile' she assumed their destination was a sun-drenched island in the Med.

With a few clothes and her box file, Gillie got on a plane and flew to a part of Britain she had never heard of. A city girl through and through, she was about to get a considerable shock when she set eyes on the house she had agreed to move into. Harvey Nicks wasn't just round the corner, there wasn't an underground station within walking distance, and the only creatures that ate out were sheep. Come to that, there weren't even street lights – or other people.

'John turned up with this terrific girl', Trevor says, 'I think she had a T-shirt and a couple of pairs of knickers to her name.'

'The first house was on the edge of a cliff, and though it was the most beautiful setting, the house itself was completely shitty', Gillie says. 'It was a very old farmhouse; obviously no-one had done anything to it for years and it was falling apart completely'. It perhaps wasn't what Gillie was expecting, and certainly wasn't the sort of home that she would have nudged John towards if she'd been involved in the process a little earlier. In fact, she says now, not only would she not have bought the farmhouse, she wouldn't have picked the Isle of Man.

His description had been of a romantic dream; the reality had the potential to be a nightmare. John had been attracted to the isolation, the miles of beaches and the mountains not far away. It was a wild landscape, quite unlike anything he was used to, and miles away from any facilities. Scotland was in one direction and Ireland in the other, and the mountain of Snaefell was to their back. John found that the pace of life on the island was the perfect antidote to the rigours of touring. As he says, 'Just about everywhere you know when it's Monday morning because of the increase

Gillie at the gates of the farmhouse; their first home on the Isle of Man.

of traffic on the roads. Over there you didn't. Every day was a Sunday.'

'It was nothingness, but for John it was the right place at the right time. At that point in his life it just appealed to him', Gillie says.

The two of them had one crucial, deciding factor on their side – and that was cash. They didn't stop to think about whether or not the farmhouse was a good investment, whether or not it was worth pouring a fortune into – they just opened the wallet; just started writing cheques. As Gillie says, 'John saw that if he opened his cheque book he could do anything, and in those days he didn't think about what things cost. He just said 'Right, I want it, it can be done.' We got architects, builders, everyone – and just started taking the house apart and then putting it back together. We had lots of walls ripped out, put in lots of bathrooms, and built a huge kitchen – which I loved. It was the mid-Seventies so the décor was all William Morris; there were Sanderson prints everywhere – it was just a mass of Art Nouveau swirls and flowers.

It was all hugely impractical. The house was at the opposite end of the island from the airport, and two-thirds the length of the island from the ferry terminal – and the infamous Manx mists often made travel difficult – if not actually impossible. John was away for long periods of course, and Gillie couldn't drive. She did learn though. John bought her a Mini.

John says, 'I found the island very strange at first, but after a while I came to love it. I found it a bit like Ireland; very slow, no-one rushes, everyone just ticks over slowly. It was a seriously social scene back then.

Lots of parties, lots of drinking, everyone having fun. The only down side was that you'd start off with a nice sunny day, and the next thing you knew the rains would come in and there'd be a howling gale. Crossing on the ferry could be a bit hit and miss; I'd be feeling queasy on the ferry from Liverpool, thinking 'Why on earth am I doing this?'

'Actually, we usually flew over there rather than used the ferry. It was always such a nice feeling when we landed at the airport. Even the policeman, just standing there, watching people coming and going, we'd know him and he'd ask if we were alright. It was like going on holiday, every time; like arriving at your favourite place for your hols. It was a very nice place, and around Christmas time everyone had their drinks parties ...'

They were at the farmhouse for just eighteen months, but as they were setting off on holiday in 1981 they spotted a much larger house for sale: Walton House at Ballasala, in the south-western corner of the Ireland, near to the airport. John had suffered a medical crisis at the farmhouse when his appendix nearly burst, and they realised – *he* realised – just how isolated and impractical that house really was. The other factor, Gillie says, is that drinking and driving was becoming a problem. It was always less so in the Isle of Man than on the mainland, especially if you were a celebrity, but any late night and sozzled journey home meant navigating tiny, tortuous lanes across mountains and over narrow bridges in dark glens.

Walton House was a big place, and needed a lot of work. An elderly couple had lived there until their deaths, so the house was in poor repair. Gillie phoned the estate agent immediately, and arranged to see it on their return. They sold the farmhouse to Margaret McAlpine of the wealthy building family, bought Walton House, and proceeded to pour a fortune into it.

'It was brilliant being so near the airport. We were about a mile away. If we were flying out they'd ring me up if the plane was late or anything, and I'd tell them which seat I wanted,' John says.

The band always had 'the office' to organise them; 'the office' made all the bookings, sorted all the arrangements – from fees to cars – and phoned the four band members with the simplest instructions possible; 'They'd just call up and say 'Be at such-and-such a place at ten o'clock on the fifteenth', and we would. That was all there was to it.

'They'd send a plane for me. If I was doing Top Of The Pops there'd be a private plane to fly me to London from the Isle of Man, and there'd be a car there to take me to the studio.

'If we were flying in from abroad we'd land at Gatwick, and the office would charter a helicopter to fly us to Heathrow so that I could fly home from there. We were doing a gig in Italy once and I invited everyone back to my place, so Colin Johnson said he would arrange a direct flight by private jet. Then he phoned the Manx airport authorities and insisted that they kept the airport open.

'We all got hideously pissed on the plane, and when we landed and they opened the door we all rolled out – like Dudley Moore falling out of the car at the beginning of Arthur. All the bottles rolled down the steps, going clink-clink-clink. There was a policeman there, and he said 'Oh we thought it'd be you, John. Can you fuck off home so that we can go for a drink? By the time we'd got to the cars, all the airport lights had gone off and they'd all gone to the pub.'

'It was a totally decadent life', Gillie adds. 'We didn't live a normal life. It was fantasy time. We had a housekeeper who had a standing instruction to wake us up with a pot of tea at midday.'

At this point, unsurprisingly, John was at his wealthiest. Everything he did – recording, playing live, television appearances – was bringing in cash. It all went to 'the office' though and was processed and whatever before being credited to John's quarter-share account. What he didn't get, of course, was song-writing royalties, but there was still a very large amount of money washing around.

Keith Altham says, 'They all found themselves with big houses with swimming pools (and in Rossi's case aquariums between all the rooms!), and flash cars. The money didn't actually change Quo as much as I've seen it change some other bands, but it altered their perspective. For one thing, in that situation you start to get suspicious of the people around you; you want them to justify their existence.'

Andy Bown says, 'They were making an awful lot of money – though who was actually pocketing it in the end is a different story. They were working class boys who didn't really know anything about money; didn't understand it. It was all a bit strange for them.'

Bob Young agrees that the change in their fortunes was dramatic, but he says that it didn't fundamentally change anyone in the band, and it wasn't inherently corrupting in any way. There was an awful lot of money washing about – 'More than we ever knew about' – and there were 'dodgey deals' going on somewhere or other. As Bob says though, they were too busy working to even think about business, and anyway, didn't they have people to take care of all that sort of thing?

Certainly John was in a position to buy anything that he wanted. The cash came in; he and Gillie spent it. The office told him that adequate funds were being put aside for his 'pension', but beyond that he didn't give the future a thought. He never made his own investments or asked for an independent audit of the wealth being generated. In all the time he was with Quo, he and Alan agree that they never saw a statement of either monies in or monies out.

'We were young', Gillie says, 'And it sounds stupid now but we were simply enjoying it. It simply didn't occur to us that it was ever going to stop.'

'I don't know how rich I was', John says. 'I couldn't tell you how much I ever had.' Having said that, an examination of John and Gillie's spending only puts them on a level with, say, a successful company director. They were spending a lot of money by most people's standards, but not by premier league rock 'n roll standards. They were extravagant but weren't in, say, Elton John's league when it came to spending cash. Not by a long way.

When it came to the restoration of the new house though, money simply wasn't a factor. 'We spent a massive amount of money', Gillie says, 'Over £100,000 in total, and a lot of it went on things you didn't actually see, like designers' and architects' fees.'

The house had everything a Seventies rock star could desire, including a full-fitted bar, and a music room complete with juke boxes and pinball machines.

Walton House is a Victorian villa, very much a 'gentleman's residence'. It's large but not overly grand or formal. It's pretty well in the middle of the village, a hundred yards from the pub, and the longest side of the property stretches down a lane that leads off the centre of the village. Along this side there is a large white-painted stone arch that opens into the garage and stable yard, and gives access to the back of the house.

It was set in four acres; mostly rolling lawns. Inside there were large, beautifully-proportioned rooms. Like the farmhouse, it turned out, it needed absolutely everything doing to it. 'We got it as a wreck and started ripping it apart', Gillie says, 'Again, John had an open cheque book – which everyone knew. I think we got ripped off left, right and centre.'

But then ... Gillie didn't just want the ankle-deep, shag-pile bedroom carpet pink, she wanted it the *right pink*. And when it was fitted and wasn't right, she had it taken up, taken out and dyed. When it was re re-fitted yet again and still wasn't what she wanted – out it came once more. The bedroom carpet was dyed three times to get the right shade of pink. Doubtless the final, exact colour reflected beautifully off the mirrored walls.

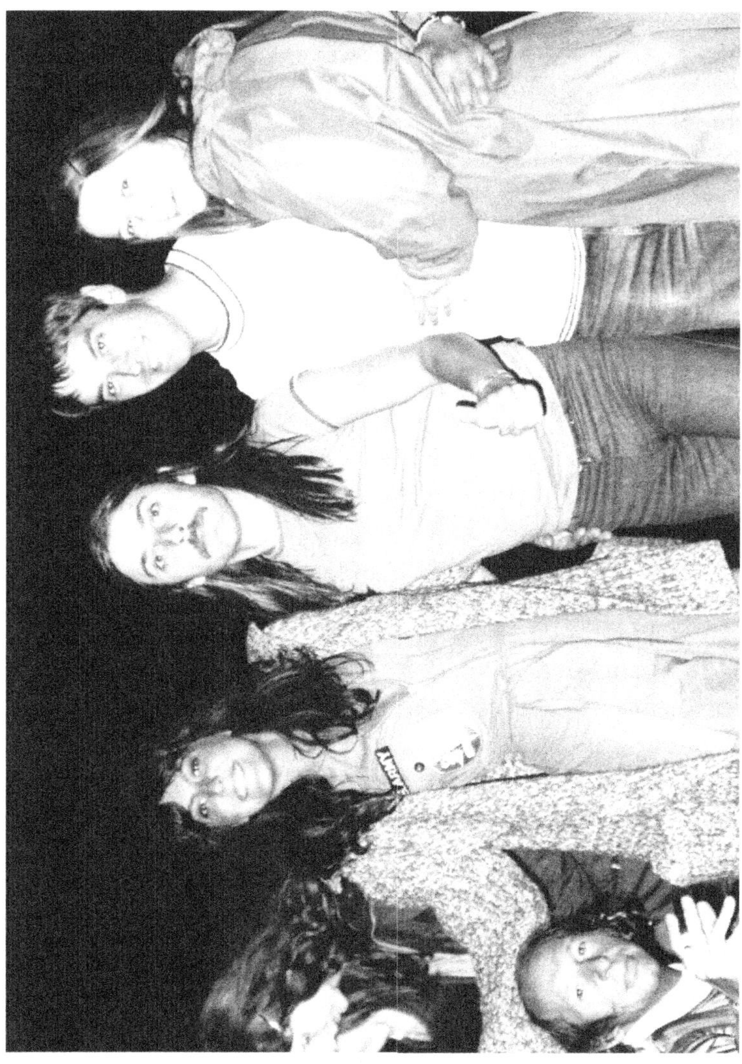

A late-night party on a Manx beach, with John, centre, Gillie to his right, and Trevor Baines in the bottom left corner.

The bathroom came, piece by piece, in boxes from Harrods. The bathroom wouldn't have been out of place at Gracelands. The sunken bath alone cost £4,000 – at 1970s prices. In some places you could have bought a decent house for that.

The bar – 'John's Bar' – was the centrepiece of the drawing room. It was handmade out of Manx stone and oak, and was at its best when John was pulling pints for showbiz and island friends. The comedian Frank Carson often took his turn as bartender, Gillie recalls. It's one feature of Walton House that everyone seems to remember.

'That house was wonderfully over the top. Absolutely right for us at that time', Gillie says, 'You could describe the style as 'William Morris-chintzy meets over-the-top Seventies rock star'.'

'Not my cup of tea', says Colin Johnson of the house, 'I don't know what era it was meant to be ...'

Years later, when the actor John Inman rented the house he complained that the flowery Sanderson décor gave him hay fever.

While John was never happier than when he was at home on the island, and 'at home' to as many guests as possible, Gillie's heart was back in London: 'I loved the house but I got back to London as often as I could. That was home. I wouldn't stay on the island for longer than I had to. It wasn't a girlie place. It was a boys' place – pubs and fishing and sheep and motorbikes. Also, there was almost no sunshine; if it had been Bermuda I would have loved it.'

Manx society has always been a closed, rather claustrophobic one. The island is ruled by a small clique of the rich and powerful, who dominate the island's government, and whose influence trickles down into just about every aspect of life. It was, and still is, a very conservative place – but, in apparent contradiction, it's not without its Rabelaisian, Bacchanalian shadows. It's also a society which looks kindly on outsiders' money, but not on outsiders themselves.

Asked if they really fitted in there, Gillie says that the real answer is both yes and no; 'Our best mates were well-established islanders, and they were all young and beautiful like we were at the time – eccentric men and young girls with short skirts and endless legs. Life was all about having fun, and because our friends were the centre of everything, we became the centre of everything too.

Their broader circle of friends on the island included the local landowners, the parliamentarians, the lords and ladies and the Governor. Curious company for a long-haired working class guy from South London – but then John wasn't the only rock star in tax exile on the island. His compatriots included members of the Scottish heavy metal band Nazareth, poppy popularists The Bee Gees, the saccharine Smokie (who had dominated the radio waves in early 1977 with *Living Next Door To Alice* – which reminded everyone why punk was a damn good thing), Paul Thompson of Roxy Music, and, later on in their stay, keyboards player Rick Wakeman.

Another famous rock drummer was one of the very first musicians to discover the fiscal advantages of the Isle of Man though. Ginger Baker, who had enjoyed enormous success with Cream in the late Sixties doesn't seem to be a likely financial wizard, but Trevor Baines says, 'I think that Ginger Baker invented off-shore banking. I used to see him in Victoria Street, carrying a suitcase, ominously heavy. He was our first.'

'If you were a celebrity you became part of the clique', Gillie says, 'If you were asked to open fêtes and your photos were in the paper, you were definitely in. So long as you were part of 'the set' you were fine.'

'Everyone on the island knew John Coghlan', Trevor Baines says, 'People were always trying to get hold of him for some reason or other, but he wouldn't turn up for anything if he didn't want to.'

Although John was at his most relaxed on the island he could still be impossibly difficult when he wanted to. 'He would tell people to fuck off if he wasn't in the mood. Mind you, on the other hand, he could light up a room when he wanted to.'

The pastimes of the set seem to have been drinking, partying and sexual adventurism. Gillie says, 'I don't remember what I did on normal days – because there weren't any normal days. It was party after party. We slept a lot, ran around in John's military vehicles, and then went to a few parties. Then we went on holiday. There was no normal life.'

Trevor says, 'We partied every night, and I mean every single night. There were maybe ten or twelve hard-core fun people; no boring people. It was brilliant; no-one ever had any clothes on.' He does insist though that drugs played no part in the fast set's life; lots of sex and drink, but no drugs of any kind.

Their other, non-rock 'n roll friends on the island included the racing magnate Robert Sangster, Peter Lilley – heir to the Lilley & Skinner shoe shops, singer Iris Williams and her husband-manager Clive, Quentin Summerville, Warwick and Belinda Charlton, and Sir Dudley Cunliffe-Owen – who ran the big hotel and ballroom in Douglas, The Palace.

Sir Dudley was great friends with John, whom he re-christened 'Bongo-Bongo'. On one occasion John turned up at The Palace without the regulation jacket and tie, as ever, and a flustered *maitre d'* phoned Sir Dudley at home to enquire if it was alright to allow him in, in breach of the dress code. 'If it's Bongo-Bongo then of course he must come in', drawled the baronet, 'But while he's there do tell him that if he keeps on taking my waitresses home I'm going to charge him corkage.'

Every 'turn' who starred in a summer show on the island, be they musicians, comedians, ventriloquists or whatever, were invited to the huge parties John and Gillie threw on the lawns at Walton House. These could be really big names like Des O'Connor or Dick Emery: Trevor remembers John playing drums with Kenny Ball's Jazz Band in the disco beneath his new home; 'I expected him to be all rock 'n roll and wacky, but he didn't take over; he decided that he was 'just a member of the band', and Kenny had to ask him to do a solo. John said 'If it's okay with you?' It was actually magical.'

There was a certain point, Trevor Baines says, when 'Gillie discovered posh frocks'. She 'got a bit carried away with the party frocks', he adds.

There was something of an upset in their 'set' when Peter Lilley's wife, Sue, moved in with Robert Sangster – after a lively romance – they went on to marry. John and Gillie had been letting them use Walton House in the afternoons as their affair unfolded.

There was absolutely nowhere on the island for Gillie to shop – she remembers 'an ancient Marks & Sparks' being as good as it got, so on the frequent occasions when her wardrobe needed topping up she would fly to London or Paris. Or both, in turn. 'It was just as Maggie Thatcher was emerging, and everyone was looking like ladies who lunch. I wore the huge shoulder pads, and, in fact, dressed much older than I was. We all went to Ascot and all those things; with the girls in silk designer frocks and the guys in top hats and tails. The style was very much early Princess Di. She dressed older when she was young and then became 'rock chick. I had started off as the rock chick, then I became lady who lunched, and I dress far more 'rock chick' now than I did then.'

Gillie usually stayed at home when Quo was touring, but did accompany John to 'the good places, the fun places'; the destinations which offered great shopping or sun bathing; 'I did Paris, Geneva and Nice – but I didn't do Essen or Dortmund'.

The rich islanders adored their dressing-up events, when they could show off their finery, arrive in splendour in their Roll-Royces, Bentleys and Range Rovers, drink far too much – and, often, leave with someone whom they hadn't arrived with.

Rather the worse for wear; John, Alan, Rick and Francis come off stage after a gig in Wales in 1976.

'The Manx Derby was the big fixture', Gillie remembers. 'Christmas was always huge, a great time to show off'. There were also endless charity balls. Everyone vied to make the most money for the charity in question, and competed with an awesome ferocity to arrive with 'the best' guest. Either hosting the most successful auction or bringing a tame Royal was a great coup. Achieving both was pure heaven. Curiously, John was usually happy to turn out in a dinner jacket or whatever for these functions, though. He might throw a strop at some point in the evening – but nothing serious. He loved it all really.

One moment that stands out in John's memory of those years is buying a Rolls-Royce. He was never into sports cars and the like, preferring instead big 4x4s and military vehicles – of which he has had many. On one trip to England however he bought himself a Silver Shadow, on a whim; 'It was a fantastic car, and as I drove to the ferry terminal I was thinking 'Look at me! I've got a Rolls-Royce!' It was a fantastic feeling.

'As I was driving off the ferry on the Isle of Man though I started to have my doubts. I began to wonder if people would resent me having such a nice car. Would they think 'Oh look at him, flash bastard'? Still, I kept it for a few years. I wish I had it now.'

One Friday night Manx Radip phoned to ask John if they could borrow his Rolls. Billy Connolly was arriving at Ronaldsway and the radio station wanted to send something better than a mini cab. John, who had met Billy before, said he'd be delighted to go and collect The Big Yin himself. Billy was stepping off a plane when John arrived, and he swept him back to Walton House.

John showed him round, made a fuss of him, took him to his bar and gave him a drink. Or two. Then gave Billy a tour of his military vehicles. Then they had a couple more drinks. Then John took him out for a ride round the village in his tank – which Connolly apparently adored. Then they returned to John's Bar for a few more drinks.

In the meantime Manx Radio was phoning everybody, desperately trying to find their star guest. Eventually a ray of sobriety shone through the party, when Billy looked at his watch and announced; 'I'm supposed to be doing a fucking live fucking gig on Manx fucking Radio … in five minutes time.' The two fell over each other in the race to get back to the Rolls, and apparently John got him there with seconds to spare.

John's other transport on the island was one of a string of Range Rovers (one of which had the witty Manx registration A69 MAN), and various rare and exotic military machines; 'I just bought military stuff that was

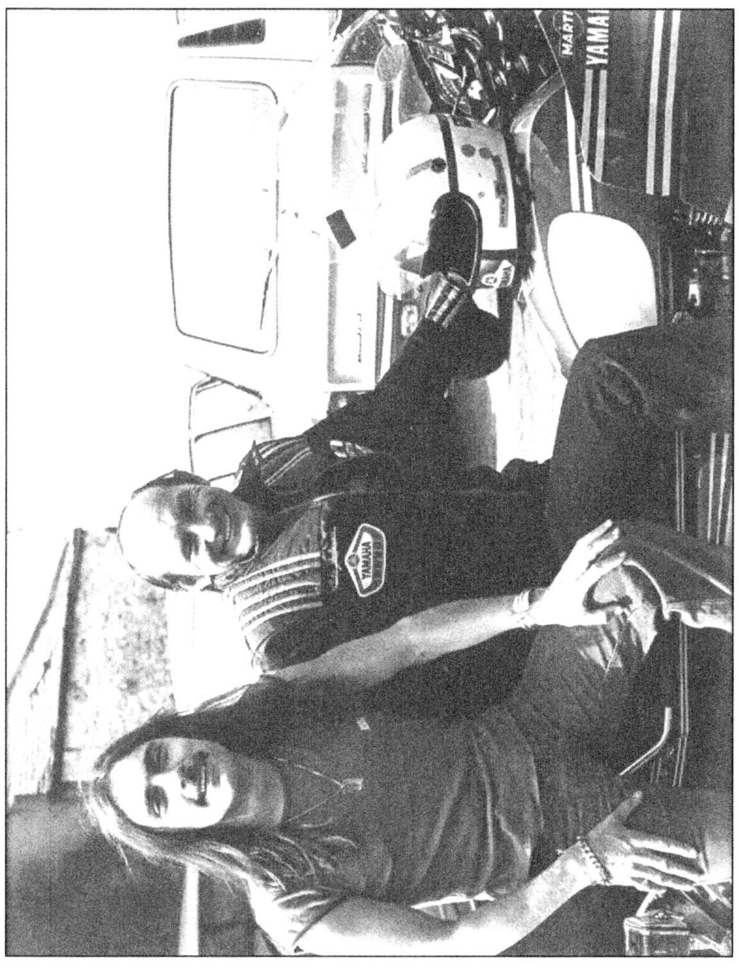

John, relaxed and happy, with one of many famous friends - motor racing champion Mike Hailwood.

unusual. I wanted to have vehicles that no-one else had. I had a Volvo Sugga, a Dodge Mowag, a Bofors tractor and a Humber Snipe command car – that was used on a couple of TV programmes; it was in Yanks.' One of John's military trucks was so huge that he had to take the Manx equivalent of the Heavy Good Vehicle License test to be able to drive it on the roads.

'I did own an MGB once but it was a complete mess. Gillie loved it – she drove everywhere with the top down - but I hated it. I'd have sooner been driving a Kenworth truck.'

John fell in love with Range Rovers as soon as the model was first introduced. A friend of Rick Parfitt's, Hugh Bryan, owned a dealership in Thames Ditton in Surrey. He invited Rick to a drinks reception in the showroom and he brought John along. John had a couple of drinks and a handful of sausages on sticks – and bought a Range Rover. It was worked over by a specialist company, who added tinted windows, a sun roof, and a host of other luxurious touches. Range Rovers were rarities on the roads of Britain, and customised ones were rarer still. Needless to say, John adored it.

Shortly afterwards he was introduced to the All-Wheel Drive Club, who raced 4x4s in muddy fields and up and down hills. Rick and Francis both also bought Range Rovers, and the three of them went off-road racing. Their discipline was 'competitive safaris', where the cars raced an off-road course, being sent off from the start line at one minute intervals.

The next step was to buy a specially lightened Range Rover, just for racing – and to keep the dents and the mud off the road car – but that was soon followed by a full-on racer, acquired from well-known 4x4 ace Alvin Smith. It was bright yellow, and had no back. Behind the rear wheels there was nothing, so that the car could exit from holes at the greatest possible angle. The next move was to modify the car very dramatically; John lightened his Range Rover by simply taking the bodywork off and throwing it away. There was a full roll-cage around the driver, for protection, and the petrol tank was relocated to the middle of the car to even up the weight distribution. You then had a long-haired rock star in a skeletal machine – looking like the Toecutter from the movie Mad Max as he roared across the English countryside.

The man who is now President of the All-Wheel Drive Club, Richard Beddall, says that as a racer John wasn't that much cop; 'He was absolutely bloody useless, but he had great fun doing it. And he was a great laugh to have around. You didn't race to win; you raced to have fun.

'He would be the first to admit that he's got no mechanical aptitude whatsoever, and he'd tear round, thrash about, and the thing would break and he'd stand there hoping that someone would come along and mend it. He didn't worry about winning things ...'

For a while John also sponsored a radical Ford Escort race car which was campaigned by a driver called Ray Vall in the 'hot rod' stock car class. He was a drinking mate of John's, and mentioned that he was looking for sponsorship. John tried to get the band to sponsor the car, but was met with indifference, so he simply did it himself. Instead of having the name of a construction company or a car dealers on the side, the car – which was very successful – raced with 'John Coghlan of Status Quo' sign-written along its length. It was a very rock 'n roll thing to do.

As well as being in the All-Wheel Drive Club, Richard Beddall was also into military vehicles, and he invited John to see his collection at his home in Buckinghamshire.

When John was very young, his dad had shown him a wartime snapshot of himself and his comrades sitting in huge trucks in France, waiting to be driven into battle. John had never forgotten the image, and in particular the lorry. It was, he learned, a Bedford QL, and Richard had several of these. As soon as he saw them John was taken back to Sainsbury Road and his childhood – and he'd found a new love.

He and Richard started going to military events together, and John found even greater satisfaction in learning how to drive military vehicles and get the best out of them. Then, of course, he started buying himself a collection.

'It's a very English thing to do, in a way', John says, 'As soon as you get the nice weather in summer, all these vehicles suddenly appear out of garages; old sports cars, traction engines, vintage tractors, military vehicles, whatever. The rest of the year you'd have no idea they were there. It was great fun, and the parties at the military vehicle runs were always great.'

Some of the Walton House collection of military vehicles were sourced from and by Richard, including his Humber staff car, the armoured car, and the huge Volvo Sugga staff car – which Richard says John absolutely adored.

John loved the 4x4 and military vehicle scenes, and the people those pastimes attracted. With them, Richard says, he was very outgoing and extremely generous; 'He gave the most fabulous parties for the off-road and military vehicle folk; they really were splendiferous events. He would invite an awful lot of people whom he only vaguely knew'. These parties became famous for their extravagance. On one occasion he took over an entire hotel in Sloane Street and invited everyone he knew whom shared his passions.'

This was his antidote to rock 'n roll. He wasn't just another enthusiast; of course he was popular because he was a very high-profile rock 'n roll star, but the worst sorts of sycophancy were deflected by the shared passion for a subject which was completely divorced from the madness of the music industry. It was also a scene where people enjoyed a drink or two, but shied away from drugs, which was perfect.

The way he is remembered by the 4x4 and military vehicle people is very different from the memories held by some in the music business; the former think of him as outgoing, gregarious and welcoming; the latter see him as moody, difficult and unpredictable. But then Richard Beddall contrasts the people John knew through the All-Wheel Drive Club and the Military Vehicle Trust with friends of John's he met on the Isle of Man. The former, he says, were a genuine cross-section, and included people with real depth and genuine enthusiasms, while his impression of the Manx residents – particularly those who had gone there for tax reasons, some of them fellow musicians – were that they were unimpressive and very shallow.

John's parents were occasional guests on the island, but they didn't feel at home there. The showbiz lifestyle and the high life on the island were utterly alien to them. Doubtless they were delighted for John and Gillie, but they weren't comfortable with the trappings of rock 'n roll excess.

When she was very small Charlotte would sometimes arrive home from school to find that John had sent a limousine to collect her from their fairly ordinary Essex home. The chauffeur would put her luggage carefully in the boot and open a rear door for her; she would snuggle in the back; a tiny figure on a large bench seat – with the driver several feet ahead of her.

The car would take her to the airport, where there would be a first class ticket waiting for her, and a kind, fully-briefed stewardess. John would meet her at the airport on the Isle of Man, in the Rolls, or a Range Rover – or an armoured personnel carrier – and whisk her back to Walton House.

Charlotte remembers all this as very exciting, but she didn't regard her dad's life on the island as being another world in any sense, simply because, she says, he was always very down to earth and matter of fact. For her at least he never played the rock star role. 'It was really nice out there. The house was lovely. Very old, with huge doors,' she says, 'I was very young but I remember the spiral staircase, the juke box and Dad's bar in the sitting room.

She also remembers that there were donkeys in the field next to the house, and a tennis court that she and her dad could play on. 'I slept in a lovely big room, with french doors that lead out to a conservatory. Gillie and I used to sunbathe in there.

'There was an area where Dad had all his army trucks and bits and pieces. We used to go out in Dad's tank, round the island. We'd end up at a restaurant on the cliff-tops and have a cream tea. That was a bit special ...'

On other occasions John would meet up with his daughter in London. One of his Range Rovers really impressed her – because it was the first car she had ever been in that had heated seats; 'We used to go to Epping Forest, or when I was a bit older we'd meet up in town. I used to like watching TV in his hotel rooms, though I think I always fell asleep.'

Charlotte has nothing but the happiest memories of her childhood times with her dad. She spent just one Christmas at Walton House, and that, she says, was magical.

Gillie recalls that when Charlotte came over for holidays she would insist that her mother was at the house at the same time, to deal with it all; 'John would go to the pub, I'd have a blue fit, and eventually Charlotte would go home.'

Gillie's mother was bemused by their lifestyle; 'She loved coming over but she knew we were living in a complete fantasy world. She would never have dreamed of telling us what we ought to be doing. She would never have interfered. She let us make her own mistakes.' Years later, just prior to her death, she confided in her daughter that all along she had been terrified that all the money was being spent; nothing was being put aside for a rainy day. But then of course her generation would have that perspective.

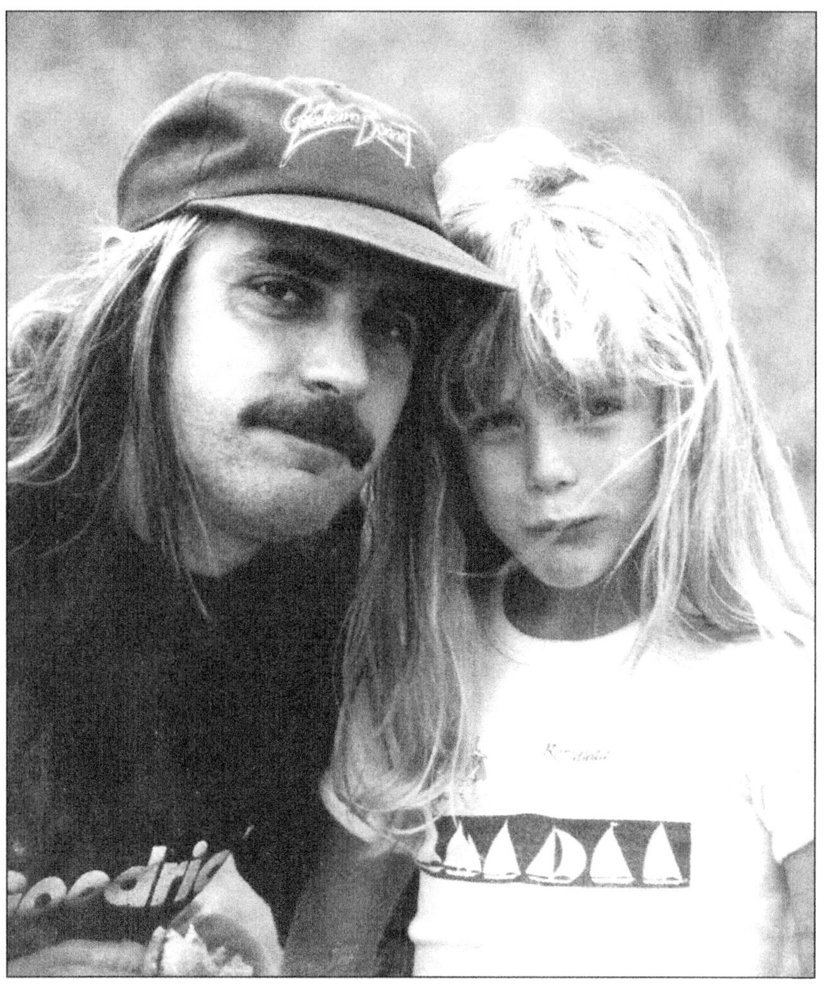

Father and daughter; John and Charlotte on the Isle of Man, 1976.

15

For all musicians, the downside of playing live is the requirement to be constantly on the move; always travelling to the next gig. Colin Johnson makes the point that Status Quo needed to tour to introduce their new records to the public. Word of mouth got them some record sales, but it was important to show the fans what they were doing; 'In the early days everyone thought they were a pop band, and we had to work very hard to get the pop image out of the way and show the world that they were now a rhythm and blues band.

'We always had to put Quo in front of audiences. Bands like Pink Floyd only toured every four years or whatever, but still sold records. But then you listened to Pink Floyd's sort of music – or Dire Straits - on your own, but with Quo you listened to it with your mates. Mind you, the biggest-selling album Quo ever had sold three million around the world; Dire Straits' biggest album sold twenty-four million. Dire Straits didn't have to tour. Quo did.

'Once we stopped 'the campaign' the sales stopped. Touring kept the whole thing going. Quo had a punishing schedule but it couldn't have been done any other way.'

Bob Young describes it as a very tough schedule, with frequent gigs over a period of several weeks, and then just a couple of days off before it all started again. The band was away from home a lot, and for John that was a pressure in its own right. He says, 'I know John found it hard. He used to get wound up quite easily, and that was more frustration than anything.'

Most musicians take near-endless touring in their stride, and a few thrive on it. John was in neither of those camps: 'We seemed to be on tour endlessly. And at first it was good. I always enjoyed Germany because the audiences were just so appreciative; they were fantastic. We did all the main European countries – frequently, we played the USA and Canada, Scandinavia, Japan, Australia and New Zealand. We were really big in Australia; I think they saw us as a bloke's band more than anyone – get your head down and go for it. Americans were always trying hard to be cool. Mind you, our first gigs in the States were a residence at The Whisky-A-Go-Go early on, which was really prestigious.'

Music publicist Keith Altham had been interviewing Doors frontman Jim Morrison one afternoon when Quo were playing The Whisky, and invited him to come down to the club to hear his compatriots' set. Morrison had a drink, gave Quo five minutes, and told Keith 'Tell them to turn down, give up and go home', and left. Keith didn't bother passing on the thoughts, but agrees that they were playing far too loud for the venue; 'Bands of that period seemed to play very loud if they were lacking in confidence. It was as if they were thinking 'We don't care that we're not going down too well; we're going to deafen you all'. They played well but there was an element of that. Mind you, Jim was so chemically assisted that he wasn't the best possible critic ...

Bob Young recalls one drunken night after a show at the Whisky; he and John ended up at John Mayall's home in Laurel Canyon. John had brought along a waitress from the club, and though they were all very drunk John seemed much further gone than anyone else, 'He was well pissed, and then he really got out of order'. They had a limo and a driver waiting patiently outside, so Bob took out to the car, pushed him inside and told the chauffeur not to stop until he'd got back to the hotel – and to leave his passenger there.

Los Angeles was a culture shock for the band. It was very different from south London: 'A woman came up to us when were playing there; she had a black car with a black interior, and always wore black. She introduced herself and said 'I'm your local cocaine dealer. Everything you want, I have.' I thought she was really scary. She gave me a lift back to my hotel – driving down Sunset Strip at sixty miles an hour – and I realised that she was spaced out of her head. A very dangerous woman.

'It was all so different for us English boys though. One night I walked back from the Whisky to our hotel, and the next day I told one of the American roadies about this in passing. He said 'You walked? You walked down Sunset at two in the morning? You must be crazy!' He could hardly believe it but I couldn't see the problem. He said, 'Don't do that again. You'll get yourself killed!', and I said 'Nah, I'll be alright'.

'We had a love-hate relationship with America. Because we were enormous in Europe we felt that we didn't really need to try to hard in the States. It was funny over there; popularity can be very patchy. In some places we'd be top of the bill and in other towns we'd be half way down the bill.

'It was definitely an eye-opener; they had so many rules when you were playing – like the stage crew weren't allowed to walk on stage else there'd be a strike.

'They were very well disposed towards English bands though, and we eventually started to relax over there. I think that one option for the band would have been to re-locate, to set up in the States and try and really establish ourselves there. I think we could have done it.'

Bob Young agrees that that might have been a strategy; he points out that when John Mayall realised that the market for his music lay largely in the States he simply moved there. On the other hand lots of British bands have been prepared to shuttle backwards and forwards, especially as air travel became quicker and flights became more frequent – and Bob cites Queen as a good example.

His thinking is that American management was needed though, just to represent them in the States; 'You need someone on the ground; someone who knows the territory. Working with American producers would have been good too. It was hard to understand why Quo didn't break the States. When you're touring with the likes of ZZ Top and Skynyrd and getting fantastic reactions wherever you play, it's doesn't make sense. It was hard, having toured successfully over there but not managing to sell records.'

The Quo camp had been confident that *Down Down* would break them into the American market in 1974, but it simply didn't happen – good though the single was. They were contracted to the prestigious and well-connected Capitol label in the USA, but still they couldn't seem to sell records over there in big numbers. When the contract expired in '78 Capitol didn't renew it, and they weren't represented at all in America for a couple of years.

Keith Altham sums it all up; 'It was sad for Quo really. The Americans didn't understand either their humour or their reserve.'

Colin Johnson says that Quo actually got kicked off a ZZ Top tour of the States, in the bearded-ones' home state of Texas to be precise, because they were going down too well – to the embarrassment of the headliners: 'Overall though, for the States, the lyrics weren't enough to think about. The kids in Britain simply liked the sound, but the American like to have something that they can think about, and *'Won't you ride my paper plane?'* wasn't enough. They like to dissect songs; Quo deliberately gave you nothing to think about, it was head down and wallop-wallop-wallop for three minutes.

'The Americans like a guitar hero and they like a really out-front raucous vocalist. So, the songs weren't up to it, for American tastes, there wasn't a front man, and Rossi wasn't a guitar hero – but then I don't think he ever wanted to be. That's not what Quo were about.'

'When we first went to France everyone said the band wouldn't mean a carrot over there', Colin says; 'But they adored Quo. We played these little places like Poitier and Lyons; the kids had no idea who Quo were, and when the band came on they'd all be sitting on the floor, cross-legged. They were expecting something like Pink Floyd or Tangerine Dream, and Quo would come on and get them up on their feet and boogying. We earned ten gold records in France.'

Bob credits Quo's success in Europe, Australia and Japan to the fact that they toured so frequently, but also because they got the radio plays in those territories.

'It was only ever Germany that really gave us problems', John says. It was the beer. The beer was too strong and we always seemed to end up insulting people. We were always getting a bollocking'.

The band worked as hard as they could to make touring fun, but they were never really hotel-smashing rock 'n roll loons. However, when they toured Australia with Slade and Lindisfarne the airline thought it wise to have guards on the planes, but although the massed musicians could and would get as drunk possible as quickly as possible the misdemeanours didn't extend much further than unravelling toilet rolls down the plane's aisle and bouncing bread rolls off the heads of Japanese businessmen. All harmless enough.

John insists that he has always found touring incredibly tiring; 'I found that if I wasn't playing I was sleeping. It's very difficult for any band. When you're touring you're around each other twenty-four hours of the day. You get on each other's nerves. We had lots of arguments – about songs, changing the set – someone would want to change the set and someone else wouldn't – or about money, or just a drink, or a woman. You'd argue over anything. We were in each other's pockets so much that having a good row was a sort of release. There's not much you can do

Rockin' all over the dock of the bay in '78 - Rick and Francis (back) watch Alan and John Boogie. Platform-soled shoes make short drummers look taller.

about it. The next day you'd be fine about it as a rule. You had to be.

John doesn't remember the band ever coming to serious blows, but does say that as time went on they used to shout at each other an awful lot. He puts it down to tiredness and a simple lack of sleep. For him at least there was just far too much travelling. Often they were simply falling out with each other for no particular reason, but then people who work together in normal situations have rows - in the curious and artificial situation where you're together every waking minute, and everyone else around you is behoven to you to a getter or lesser degree, it's surprising that touring musicians don't actually end up murdering each other.

Andy Bown says, 'There was a lot of touring, and it was very, very hard work. During the *Rockin' All Over The World* year there was a tour which was two months in Germany and a month in Spain, and a lot of work either side. That was totally flat out and completely away from home. It was really, really hard work – and pretty much non-stop.' His solution was to get out of the hotel at all costs, and usually by the fire escape; 'You have to get away from it all for a bit, and I've done that on dozens of occasions. It was the only way to preserve my health.'

'On the other hand it was fascinating to play in front of different audiences,' John admits; 'To see how Germans or Swedes or the Japanese responded to your music. Actually, the Japanese were the strangest. They were very polite and would just sit there. They'd leap about during a song, but as we finished they'd clap very politely. Then they'd sit down again. As soon as we went into the next song they'd be up on their feet again – and so it went on. And of course they had no idea what we were on about.

'The amazing thing about Japan was that often hundreds of fans would follow us around. We used the bullet train to get between cities – which was absolutely great – and it'd be packed out with Quo fans, also going to the next gig.'

By the late Seventies the strains of the incessant touring were taking their toll on John. Along with his colleagues' drug taking it's the one factor that he credits with bringing him to crisis point. The fatigue, he says, just built up relentlessly and never seemed to go away. He admits too that his reaction to this wasn't hugely helpful: 'Depending on how I felt I could be difficult. I could be miserable if I was in the wrong sort of mood. I seemed to be tired such a lot and that wasn't good.

'Gillie used to tell me that she could tell what mood I was in by the length of my drum solo. If I did a long one, I was happy, but if it was short – stand by!'

Very few photographs taken of Status Quo in the Seventies show John smiling. He preferred to keep people at arm's length. He admits that 'I would only talk to people I really wanted to talk to', and otherwise the shutters would go down and he wouldn't mix at all. He could certainly look very intimidating. He doubtless knew that and made the most of it.

'After a gig I needed at least half an hour to calm down and dry off. I used to hate it when people came straight into the dressing room as you'd walked off stage. You did get people coming to see the band straight after a gig and they're going to ask you exactly the same questions that you were asked last night and the night before. I thought 'I don't want to say that again', so I didn't.

John adds, 'People often took pictures of us when I had no reason to smile' – which is perhaps rather telling. It's supposed to be an automatic showbiz reaction that you smile for the camera – smile and wave, smile and wave – but John was having none it; 'I thought I was going for mean and moody. I hate that thing where the curtains go back and there's six people standing there beaming like idiots. That's pop cabaret. Have you ever seen Van Morrison smile?'

Colin Johnson recalls the band being in Rome, and there was a queue of kids trying to get the band members' autographs. John said, 'Colin, tell them to fuck off. *There's too many of them.*' Too many of what, Colin asked. 'Too many bloody Italians. They're everywhere!' John replied. Colin says, 'I tried to explain to him that we were in Italy, that's why, but he stormed off. He would get very impatient. He stormed off a lot.'

He did actually punch Bob on one occasion, in a club in Frankfurt in the company of Queen. John got wound up about something, and starting shouted and swearing. Hugely embarrassed, Bob escorted him outside and told him to cool off. John's reaction was to throw a punch. Bob, to his credit, didn't thump him in return, but firmly insisted that it was time for the drummer to go back to the hotel and get into bed.

Gillie Coghlan thinks that the band weren't as close by this time; they were no longer best mates; 'They didn't spend their free time together - but then why would they? They lived together for nine months of the year, why would they, say, go on holiday with each other? Apart perhaps from Rick and Francis, they weren't mates any more.'

'They were never really sociable with each other. None of us were. They didn't take holidays together.' Colin says.

Along with his long-time nicknames of 'Spud' and 'The Mad Turk', John started to be known as 'Grumpy'. Andy Bown is forthright in his opinion that John simply 'lost the plot'. He says that John simply wanted to get through the day, get through the gig, get through the tour – and go home; 'But the one instrument you just can't play badly in a rock band is the drums. You can carry anyone else, but you can't carry a bad drummer. It stands out like a sore thumb.'

16

When Robert Louis Stephenson wrote *Dr Jekyl And Mr Hyde* he didn't try to define what the catalytic potion was which turned the civilised, clubbable Dr Jekyl into the crazed Mr Hyde. The simplest explanation is that it might have been alcohol.

There's almost a tradition of rock 'n roll drummers having tempers which operate on a hair-trigger, and shifting from reasonable, affable men to demanding, obnoxious monsters once the alcohol has started flowing through their veins. Keith Moon of The Who was one, but even he couldn't hold a candle to Led Zeppelin's drummer John Bonham. After a few vodkas Bonzo metamorphosed into a demon, known to fellow band members and the crew as The Beast; someone who was almost invariably verbally and physically violent, and had no regard at all for the sensibilities or safety of others.

It's unlikely that John was ever in Bonzo's league, but with a few drinks inside him the eyelids would close slightly and a fearsome temper would not be far from the surface. His normal speaking voice is a soft tenor, but his pissed-up voice is harsh, accusatory and aggressive. And rock 'n roll drummers are very fit and very strong. John Coghlan's Mr Hyde is not someone you would be advised to mess with.

John admits, 'I could get very nasty, very horrible when I'd had too much to drink. I would say something, upset someone, and I would always regret it the next day.

'John always had a dark side to him,' Bob Young says, 'And when he'd drunk too much the dark side would kick in. We called him all sorts of names – Chief Blackcloud was a good one. He'd take things the wrong way and could get very stroppy with people. He was always getting himself into trouble.'

'I used to wake up in the morning with a hangover, and my mind would click into 'What did I do last night? What did I say?' And I'd remember something awful. Or Bob Young would say to me 'You were totally out of order last night'. It was always a horrible moment. I'd get that terrible sinking feeling. Bob would say there'd been a complaint from the management, or tell me what I'd broken or who I'd insulted, and I used to wonder why I did it. Why did I do it? I just did.

'I spent a lot of my mornings apologising for what I'd said the night before. I'd go and knock on their hotel room door or whatever and apologise, and they would always say that it's alright, don't worry – but they got fed up with it after a while.'

Bob says that if John didn't remember, he had to remind him. It was his job to either keep the peace or restore order after everything had been upset; 'It was my responsibility – just as it was my responsibility to get the band around the world, make sure they got on stage every night, and move on to the next gig the next day.

'An apology now and again doesn't go amiss. An apology doesn't necessarily make it all right, but it shows you do care. I didn't want the band as a whole getting a bad reputation.'

'I had my moments of being fine', John claims, then adds, 'But more moments of being not fine. There was always those moments when I thought 'I don't want to be here'. I would even look out of a hotel window and think 'I wish I was over there, not here'. You think the person across the road is having a better time than you …

'There's always a reason though, isn't there? I got homesick a lot. I missed my wife, missed my daughter, missed England, missed the Isle of Man. I'd look at the date sheet and see that we still had thirty cities to play before I could go home and I'd really wonder why I was doing it. I daydreamed about being able to go home, have a good night's sleep in my own bed, and be back on the tour in time for the next gig. But you can't do that if you're half way round the world'.

Colin Johnson says that John would often lock himself in his hotel room and play music really loudly; 'And of course he got a lot more aggressive after a pint or two. He'd get even more short-tempered. Something would just spark him off, put him in a really black mood.

'We were in Germany and he was in a mood, and he was playing Led Zeppelin really loudly in his bathroom. The volume was ridiculous. A guest complained and the manager went up to his room and politely asked him to turn the music down. Eventually the police arrived and took the stereo off him.'

Bob Young: 'The rest of the band could always tell when he was going into a mood. It was always 'Fucking hell, we don't want John kicking off again tonight'. He could very easily get pissed off and kick his kit over, and then piss everybody else off. But to a large degree it was just accepted – we all had our bad points, but everyone else had to live with them. I used to keep an eye on him, try and keep him calm. He could be good fun; I enjoyed his company – but you always had it in the back of your mind that something could happen and he could turn.'

'John wasn't a complete bastard', Andy Bown says, 'I have a soft spot of for Spud; I had some pleasant times with him. The rest of the band were quite surprised by that. They didn't think that was any longer possible. They thought they'd left the nice Spud behind at Butlin's in Minehead years before. I saw a very gentle side to him, but yes, he could be very difficult on the road at times.

Andy Bown says that it got the point where John regarded just about everyone as 'the enemy'. He would say something and the other guys would blank him, then he'd get annoyed and say something like 'I suppose I'm only the fucking drummer'. But, says Andy, it wasn't the case that it was John versus the rest of the band; 'There were constant divisions in the band, but you get that on the road. Someone isn't talking to someone else, someone has sided with someone else. But the next day everything's fine.'

'You'd hear , Francis saying 'Watch it, Coghlan's on the warpath', and you'd know there was going to be a row of something. He's got those dark eyes anyway, and large eye-lids, when they lowered even further you knew there'd be trouble', says Colin Johnson.

'John was always a straight forward bloke', Keith Altham says, 'What you saw was what you get – a bit like Bill Wyman in The Stones. There was no 'side' to John. He wouldn't run round and stab you in the back ... if he didn't like something he'd come straight at you, head-on. He would absolutely roast people. You'd sometimes think 'Is this for real? Does he mean this or is he just joking?' No, he'd bloody well mean it! It was a way of letting off steam, I suppose.'

'It just got so tiring', John says. 'We went to Australia and it took us twenty-five hours to get there, and after a few hours sleep there were seven interviews to do. I used to get serious jet lag, and I'd be battling to keep awake – knowing that the worst thing you can do is go to sleep too soon.

'The record company always had stuff lined up for us and we had no say in it. One journalist at a press conference asked us 'Do you play better music when you hair's longer?' Well, what a stupid fucking question! What do you say to that? I was never any good at the quick John Lennon quips.'

John had no patience for all that sort of thing; the glad-handing with record company executives, being nice to rock journalists, posing for the cameras – none of that was for him. On one occasion, during a record company meeting, he decided that he had had enough and was going to go to his room. There were twenty people sat round the table in an admittedly small room, and John climbed up on the table, walked along its length, and left. 'It was quite spectacular', says Andy Bown.

'When you're on tour you do forget what town or city you're in', John explains. 'The gig feels like the gig you played yesterday. The set you're playing is the same as the one you played last night, and the same as the night before. The lighting plot's the same. And you could be anywhere.

'I got very run down. I think we all did to a greater or lesser degree, but on the other hand, when we were actually at the gig and the band was announced, from that second we'd whizz back up again. We felt fine instantly. We'd start with *Caroline* and everything was fine again.'

The touring itinerary wasn't what it had been though; amazingly Quo played no live gigs in 1980. Those that had been lined up had been cancelled when Francis developed a severe spinal problem. John told the rock press at the time that he was really bored by the inactivity; so the assumption has to be that he hated touring, but was bored when he didn't.

There were frequent rumours that Status Quo were on the verge of calling it a day and splitting up for good. Although he still wrote songs for the band, Bob Young had left their employment and no longer toured with the band in his unique role of tour manager, harmonica player and even-handed peace-keeping force.

Through the first half of '81 the band did play extensively throughout Europe - including a brief, eight-gig visit to Italy (which was never big for them) and two gigs in Portugal, which were to be Quo's only visit to the country – but that tour had ended in the summer and there were no more gigs until the end of the year. John's last live gig with Quo seems to have been at the Gaumont Theatre in Southampton on June 3 1981.

The other big problem for John was the hugely increased levels of drug taking going on around him. For years there'd been odd bits of dope

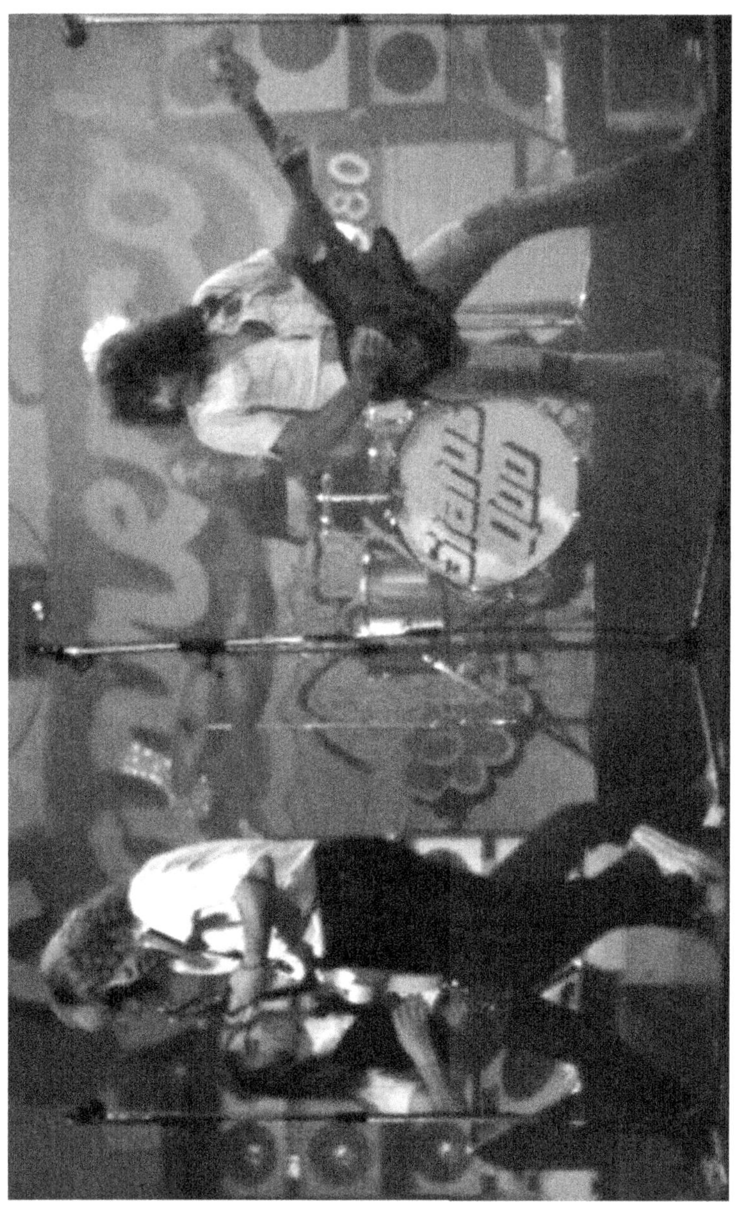

around, but now there was cocaine too. Lots of it. The other band members, the crew, the management – everyone seemed to be snorting coke as if medals might be handed out. Everyone, that is, apart from John.

'I've never been into drugs, and although I used to drink far too much I don't think I was ever going to be rock 'n roll casualty. The drink is bad but the drugs are far worse.

'I like beer. I like a pint of bitter. I drink wine on occasion but I don't drink spirits apart from a very occasional glass of brandy late at night. From a medical point of view I don't know how destructive my beer intake was - but it's a hell of a lot less now than it used to be.

'I like a couple of drinks before I play, but I've never tried to play when I've been seriously drunk. I can't play pissed. I wouldn't because I'd be too scared of fucking it up.

'I had an occasional joint, but I hated putting smoke in my lungs. That was the bit I hated about cannabis; why would you want to put smoke into your body? I once had a joint after I'd had quite a lot to drink and the two really didn't mix well. The room started to spin and I couldn't get off. Even that was too nasty for me, too frightening.

'I don't have a real problem with cannabis, but overall I'm fairly anti-drugs. Especially cocaine. I've had a few lines of coke but I think it's bad news. There was always a lot of it around – especially at recording sessions, which is a problem because you're not working it off. We felt we had to keep awake and get the job done. It was nice briefly, but I thought 'I don't want to get stuck on this. It isn't going to do me any good'. Francis was big on cocaine – he even had that problem with his nose falling off or whatever it was – but it was totally destructive, totally unnecessary.

'Cocaine changes people. It's very tough trying to work with someone in those circumstances. Instead of having a friend you've got an enemy.

'Drugs crept up on the band. Initially more on recording sessions than at live gigs. It was the one subject on which, after all these years, we totally disagreed. We were like chalk and cheese on this one subject; they were all out of it and I was straight. It meant that I was no longer part of the gang. I felt I had to drink a bit to catch up.

Bob Young rather agrees and says that John was excluded because he wasn't part of the dope-smoking crowd. He was simply not interested in taking drugs.

'It sounds old-fashioned, but it did worry me that it was illegal. I actually did worry about them being busted', John muses. 'And I wanted to say to them 'will your mum and dad be impressed if you're all over the papers for drug possession?' I can't believe that we never got caught. Francis and Rick used drugs in private places like recording studios, but also in very public places like TV studios. There really were musicians who took their own drugs abroad, through immigration and everything, and it made me think 'Is it really worth it?' It makes me sound seriously straight, but that was what I honestly thought.'

17

By the early Eighties John had a wonderful life on the Isle of Man, but when it came to the band, everything seemed to be wrong. He had got to a point in his life where, he says, 'I thought 'I don't want to do this anymore', and I just couldn't help myself.'

Alan Lancaster reckons that the rot set in for Quo during 1978, and he equates the drug-taking with the band stopping producing their own records. From the 'Piledriver' album released in January 1973, the first post-Pye recording (they were now with Vertigo), the band had acted as their own producers.

There were other tensions too. Colin Johnson agrees with others who say that songwriting fragmented the band. There wasn't a clearly defined song-writing source, as Jagger and Richard were for The Stones, Lennon and McCartney were for The Beatles, and Pete Townshend alone was for The Who. Colin says, 'Once a band becomes successful everyone wants to write the songs. And jealousy comes into it. Francis Rossi was writing with Bob Young, Francis was writing with his old friend Bernie Frost (which is when it got really poppy), Alan Lancaster was writing a bit with Rick Parfitt and a bit with Bob Young and a bit with Mickey Green (who used to be in The Pirates). It became all so fragmented, and they lost the plot. There were so many influences they didn't know where they were going any more. It didn't gel.'

Phil May adds that it's often difficult for band members who aren't part of the song-writing process; 'You can't take away the fact that two blokes have written almost all the songs. A lot of bands have problems with that. That's often where the problems start, and it can be an ego thing as well as a money thing. The writers have a lot more power.'

The only person who wasn't trying to contribute to Quo's song-writing canon was John. But then, while Mick Jagger, Keith Richards, Ron Wood and even Bill Wyman are song-writers, how many songs has Charlie penned in his forty years on The Stones' drum riser?

Those who write the songs get more of the glory – they're seen as far more creative than 'mere' musicians – and they can get a lot more money, and for a lot longer. The case which really brought this home to the industry, Colin says, was the other members of Spandau Ballet trying to sue Gary Kemp; 'Gary's a multi-millionaire and the others haven't got a pot to piss in. So they tried to sue him, saying they wanted part of the royalties. The judge said that it was nothing to do with them; Gary had done the work so he had earned the money.

'On many, many occasions Francis Rossi would go back to his hotel room when he'd come off stage, get his guitar out and start writing. That's what he did. Two years down the line, when it came to pay-out time Rossi got the lion's share, so the jealousies set in again.'

'There was money floating around all over the place. Parfitt would go off and buy a boat, and then buy his two Ferraris and his Porsche and a Rolls-Royce – so he wouldn't be writing. Francis Rossi always continued writing though; he always had his feet on the ground.'

Colin also says that the drug taking was at 'ridiculous' levels by this point: 'On and off the road it was coke for breakfast, coke for lunch and coke for dinner. The drugs – and the money – made everything go haywire.'

It was November 1981, and the band were at the Queen studio in Montreux in Switzerland, to record the album that became 'Never Too Late', and they had been working for the best part of a week.

It had become almost routine for the band. It was something which they had done often enough over the years; the only real difference, apart from the equipment getting ever more sophisticated, was that they were recording in more exotic locations. Everything was about to change though.

John says, 'I was in the studio that one night and could hear all these strange sounds in my headset. I didn't know what was happening, and by all accounts I kicked the drum kit over – but I've no memory of that. The next thing I knew, I was on a plane flying back to London.'

From Montreux he phoned Gillie, who was at home at Walton House;

From left, Bob Young, John, Colin Johnson, Alan, Rick and Francis – with more gold records than they know what to do with.

her mother was there too. He told her he had left the band: He didn't say that he had been fired. Gillie had been due to fly to Switzerland but John told her to stay put, and that he was coming home. Gillie remembers simply bursting into tears; 'My mother was horrified. I thought 'Oh, he'll calm down tomorrow', but he didn't. Then I was horrified. Immediately I could see it all falling apart. I could see it being the end of life as we knew it. Which it was.'

Colin Johnson says, 'John just wasn't into it from the moment he arrived at Montreux. He was being an unbearable bastard. He'd had a bit of a row, and there was some upset about some of the songs that were to be put on the album; they weren't all happy with the songs.

'Our sound engineer, Dave Richards, had a new piece of equipment. It was incredibly expensive and he'd had to put it behind the door because it wouldn't fit anywhere else. He told everyone and asked them to look out for it, and three minutes later John comes in and Wallop!, the door hits the new kit. His reaction was to tell everyone what a fucking silly place it was to put it. Dave had asked John to be careful, but John was just shouting and screaming.

'In the studio he apparently couldn't get a drum sound through his headphones and he threw a tantrum. It was unbelievable. He kicked the kit over and everything – but then he did that quite a bit. Sometimes we made a laugh out of it, but this time we told him he ought to go.'

John, says Colin, was sent back to his hotel room, and then given his passport and told to go home. The tour manager, Ian Jones – who was known as The Axeman because he was never backward when it came to sacking roadies, sound engineers and the like - went to see John and told him that the band had decided that they were going to use a drum machine in future: 'What a feeble thing to say. A band like Quo don't use a drum machine. I felt 'If that's how you feel, fuck it'. I phoned Gillie and she was in tears, and I just flew home to the Isle of Man.'

John says simply that twenty years of hard work had caught up with him; 'Someone should have taken control, stopped the session. We should have got together the next morning – or taken a couple of days off - but they didn't want to do that. Alan Lancaster said 'Let's leave it for now. You'll be alright in the morning. Let's leave it for now' – but that never happened. What I found out later was that Pete Kircher was already on a plane; he was on his way over to finish the session.' Francis Rossi had been working with Pete Kircher on other work, and Pete was an obvious first choice for him.

Colin says that John was out of the band from that point, 'That was it.' He wasn't told to go and cool off. He was told to go.'

How insulting that the founder drummer in a hugely famous, hugely successful rock band shouldn't even get the chance to sit down with the rest of the band, and was summarily fired not by his colleagues, and not even by their management, but by the tour manager – whose responsibilities didn't normally stretch beyond booking hotels and making sure that the roadies got the right gear into the right venues. It must have felt like being sentenced to death by a traffic warden. And the notion that Status Quo was going to get their backbeat from a drum machine in future was an excuse from the far side of Planet Weird.

Alan Lancaster remembers it slightly less definitively. He describes the scene in the studio as just another of the sort of rows that the band used to have occasionally; the sort of rows that are almost inevitable when folk spend far too long in each other's company – and under increasingly heavy pressure.

Alan holds something of a conspiracy theory, but the biggest villain, in his opinion, was cocaine. He says that John wasn't told he was out of the band, but that he was told to leave the session – and that the whole thing ought to have blown over.

Andy Bown denies the notion of a conspiracy though and says that in no way was John's departure from the band inevitable. Despite it all, despite the moods and the anger, he says that no-one was desperate to get rid of John.

There was a school of thought that explained John's actions by suggesting that he was suffering a nervous breakdown, and Andy Bown agrees; 'I think he was depressed. Clinically depressed. He needed to see someone.' Alan agrees; 'I don't think that John really knew what was going on at the time.'

Rick Parfitt has said in interviews that he now agrees with that theory. He recalls John locking himself in a hotel bedroom some time before, and they could hear him through the locked door, sobbing his heart out. That was the first indication that something was wrong, and Rick now sees it as the beginning of the end for John's relationship with Quo. Rick also agrees, again with hindsight, that the drug clique in the band actively excluded John – 'If you smoke a joint you go somewhere else, and laugh at things you wouldn't normally find funny. If you don't smoke you don't feel part of the crowd; you don't feel as if you're in the circle'. It rather sounds like children in a school playground who won't let one classmate be part of their gang.

Even nowadays it can be enormously difficult for a man to admit to anyone else that he is suffering from any kind of nervous problem. It's simply not a manly ailment; men get back pain, smoker's cough and fractured limbs; real men don't have nervous breakdowns. Twenty-five years ago that feeling was even more strongly felt, and symptoms would go undiagnosed (with the sufferer probably convinced he was actually losing his mind) and therefore untreated. The medication which most men did, and do, reach for is alcohol – which takes the immediate edge off the terror but only depresses the body's nervous system further.

Many people now agree that John was displaying the symptoms – and those symptoms were rooted in a distinct cause, and every cause has an effect – but they went unrecognised and untreated. No-one helped, and in the long run that was in no-one's best interest.

Andy Bown doesn't sound very sympathetic when he says 'In a band, on the road, everything is magnified, and you have a choice – you can shut up and get on with it, or you can get out.'

Keith Altham sees it differently though; 'Just because someone makes waves within a band it's not a good reason to get them out. People who make waves can be more important than those that don't. John *was* fractious. He irritated Rossi and Parfitt – and maybe Alan Lancaster as well – but it was a bad mistake to think that everyone has to go along with everything. You need people testing the temperature of the water and saying 'I don't agree with that.

'When he had his tantrum it was handbags at ten paces sort of stuff. I think he thought that they'd all make it up in the morning. But it didn't, and that was very sad, but by then a petulant streak had come to the surface within the band. The feeling was 'Well, if you don't want to play with us then we don't want to play with you – I'm going to take my guitar and go home.' Rossi and Parfitt could have solved the problem, but for whatever reason they obviously decided not to.'

Phil May, who was close to John, thinks it was close to professional suicide; 'When you think you're going to get pushed you sometimes decide you're going to jump. For the sake of your own dignity.'

'If it had happened in London, or if he hadn't been allowed to get on a plane, they would had sorted it out the next day - when they were sober or not stoned or whatever', Gillie says. 'They let him go, presumably because they wanted him to go – or nobody was prepared to go and get him back. They may well have wanted him to go at that moment in time, whether or not that was the long-time plan, I don't know. It was all pride and God-knows-what, but there was nothing I could do to help because I simply wasn't part of it.

'Alan has often said that he feels bad about it now. John thought it was the best thing at the time; because he thinks the stress would have killed him if he'd stayed.'

'It was crazy really', Colin says, 'The reasons weren't good enough for him to have gone like that. But then if someone's that unreasonable you can't sit down with them and work it out.' Colin's reasoning is that there was one member of the band that was causing all the problems, ruining both the atmosphere and the recording session, and the only viable solution was to get rid of that one person. Almost no matter the cost.

Bob Young regrets that he wasn't at the Montreux session; he thinks that with his diplomatic skills he might have been able to sort things out; 'On the road I'd always been there to sort him out, but I wasn't there.' He agrees that no-one tried to sort the problem out or repair the damage. He insists though that there was no plan to get rid of John; no conspiracy to make the most of one of his tantrums; 'Pete Kircher wasn't sitting at home or at an airport or something, waiting for a call'.

Alan agrees that Bob could have sorted things out; 'He would have smoothed things over.'

Bob puts the responsibility very firmly in John's court though, and says that he'd threatened to leave innumerable times previously. But when he did finally get on a plane, no-one was in any mood to try and talk him out of his decision'.

As a good friend, Trevor Baines now thinks that John leaving Quo had been on the cards for the some time, but describes it as 'a disaster; bad, really bad'.

Just before John's departure the band had been re-united with Jess Jaworski, by then a successful businessman. He joined them at a gig at The Hammersmith Odeon, where the band was celebrating its twentieth anniversary. Jess says he was very surprised to hear that John had left; 'I expected Alan to go first. He was always a bit of an abrasive character; always the 'I am', just difficult. John was much more easy-going. He used to just go with the flow. I was really surprised. I didn't think he'd have gone before Alan.'

It is suggested that as John was a quarter of the band he was paid accordingly, and if he was replaced by a hired hand, a journeyman, a considerable amount of money could be diverted to the remaining three members.

At no point did John decide that he wanted to get back into the band, or make any contact with them at all. The Quo management was in touch with him over administrative matters, and a pay-off was negotiated, but at no point did John make any sort of approach to the other guys.

Nor did the members of Status Quo make any approach to him. They had each others' phone numbers but nobody called. 'Francis Rossi was the lynch-pin, and he was happy with Pete Kircher', says Colin. Bob Young reinforces the point; 'John never phoned the band and no-one from the band phoned him. That was it.'

No-one needed the aggravation and the consensus within the band was unanimous. Anyway, they were contracted to produce a studio album and everything was set up, costs were being incurred and there was no reason not to get on with it.

However, as Alan Lancaster says, 'When John Coghlan left Status Quo the whole sound changed. The chemistry changed. It was never the same again.'

Colin Johnson agrees. He says that he began to get frustrated with the band when they 'softened up a bit' and became more poppy; 'After about '82, Andy Bown was more influential with the keyboards, but that was the wrong sound. It was too sweet, too nice. The aggression had gone.

'The difference was that, on the one hand the original rhythm section had left the band, and on the other, Francis Rossi had control – his ideas of what Quo should be had moved on. I don't know what he wanted, but it was far more poppy. His solo album was basically Quo but without Parfitt, and it was very pop-orientated. That was a benchmark for what he was going to do with Quo later.

'Rossi and Parfitt had became a comedy duo on stage and that certainly didn't fit with the image.'

18

The 'Never Too Late' album wasn't delivered late; it was released on time and went to number two in the UK album charts. Quo had been doing exceptionally well with their album sales, despite not being 'an album band'. After 'Live!' Went to number three in '77, and 'Rockin' All Over The World' peaked at number five the same year, 'If You Can't Stand The Heat' in '78, 'Whatever You Want' the following year, and the hit compilation '12 Gold Bars' (which stayed in the charts for most of the year) in 1980 all went to number three. The first album on which John played no part at all, '1+9+8+2', released in early '82, was their first number one album – and the only one to date.

Quo's new drummer, Pete Kirsher, had been in one-hit wonders Honeybus, whose UK number 8 of 1968, *I Can't Let Maggie Go* was one of the very first examples of a pop tune being used in a TV commercial (for Nimble sliced bread). He was very much thrown in at the deep end. Very soon after the recording session finished he started played live gigs with the band. His first was on April 15 at City Hall in Cork – the first of four dates in the Republic of Ireland, followed immediately by two nights at the Antrim Forum in Northern Ireland. They then embarked on a lengthy UK tour and Pete was introduced to the rigours of life on the road with Quo.

Pete's role wasn't an innovative one. It wasn't for him to alter the drum parts that John had created; that would have changed the whole sound of the band, and what was needed was continuity, not creativity. He was required to play the way had John had, note for note; so perhaps he had been replaced by a drum machine – albeit a human one.

The problem for Quo fans was that Pete Kircher didn't look like John Coghlan; he didn't have the attitude or the heavily-lidded eyes. He didn't look like a full-tilt rocker. On fans' discussion boards even today there's talk of John being missed because he looked right, or fitted the band's then-image. Perhaps a little cruelly, Pete has been described as nothing more than a metronome, who was unable to replicate John's high speed shuffles. Other fans equate John's Quo drumming with the work of Keith Moon or John Bonham in that he rarely played any given song exactly the same way twice.

In 1986 Pete left the band and was replaced by Jeff Rich. Pete seems to be the least popular Quo drummer with their fans. Jeff Rich was replaced by Matthew Letley in 2000 - which means that in its forty years Status Quo has had two bass players, and three keyboards players - but four drummers.

Some fans have described Jeff Rich as having 'more personality' as a drummer than Kircher, but criticised him for being 'a bit too perfect'. One fan incisively criticised John's successors, saying that they are 'without any highlights in their technique'.

Matt Letley has been praised by fans for taking Quo's drum sound back as closely as possible to that of the early days; he seems to be second most popular Status Quo drummer after John.

Kenney Jones considered John to be 'An excellent drummer, who's very good at what he does. He set down a specific style for Quo, and he gave them a unique sound. Whereas the rest of us were trying to play behind the beat, John was slightly ahead of it. His playing was exciting – and he had to be fit and energetic to play the way he did.

'John and Alan played very well together, and that changed when they became half Quo and half something else.'

When the 'Never Too Late' album was launched at a press conference in London, Pete Kircher and Andy Bown were included as members of the band – to Alan Lancaster's surprise, he insists. He adds that the 'hard rock boogie' he championed was now on the way out, and 'Rossi's country rock' was to be Quo's future 'I was very uncomfortable playing that stuff. I thought we were turning into a laughing stock.'

In 1986 Alan followed John and departed the band, leaving just Francis from the original line-up who had recorded *Pictures of Matchstick Men*. He was replaced by John Edwards – universally known as Rhino – who, like Jeff Rich, had been in the very well respected and hugely hard-working Climax Blues Band.

Alan had lived in Australia for several years by then, which was far from ideal, and this made him seem very much semi-detached from the band. It's difficult to know what the others were supposed to think when one of their colleagues lived halfway round the globe; as far away from the action as you can get without actually leaving the planet.

'It felt like a different band after John left', Alan says, 'The ideology behind the band had changed. John leaving was a tragedy.'

Paul Brett says of the post-'86 Quo, 'Rick and Francis have always played to their limitations; Rhino and Jeff as musicians were far superior to the music they were playing. They could play anything, be in any band.'

Shortly after John left the band, Status Quo were awarded an Ivor Novello 'for their outstanding contribution to the music industry', at a reception in London. The Ivor Novellos are almost like the Oscars of the music business, and what should have been John's - as it was in recognition of his part in their work over the last twenty years – was presented to, and accepted by, someone else. Someone who had only been with the band for a matter of weeks. Not good at all.

So far as Quo were concerned it was almost as if John had become a non-person. It wasn't that he was air-brushed from history – there was far too much documented history – but he was very definitely old news. After the trauma the band had endured, they were perhaps right to put the past behind them and forge ahead with the new line-up. There was no question but that they were moving on. It's what Francis wanted, and that's what happened. However, for John it was very cruel.

He didn't touch a drum kit for about a year; 'I'd fallen out with the band, but in a way that meant that I'd fallen out with drumming as well. I sat at the kit once, and realised that I wasn't enjoying it. So I just decided to let my body have a rest. I think that rock 'n roll had taken quite a toll, so we went on holiday a couple of times and I worked hard at doing nothing.'

'We went on holiday a *lot*', Gillie says, 'Which my mother was worried sick about. We were young and stupid, so we didn't worry at all about the future.

'To be honest, we'd been told by the management that the future was, quote, unquote, 'taken care of'. We assumed, fairly naturally, that meant that pensions were in place. And they weren't.'

At this point, with his name still in the headlines, his aura as a top-flight rock star still intact and his contacts in the industry still in all the right places, John should have been hustling.

Given that working as a session drummer – even a highly thought of and well paid one – was definitely not for him, he could have gone one of two ways: There was any number of rock, harder rock, or even heavy metal bands that would have welcomed him with open arms and cheque books. Line-ups change, drummers fall off their stools. After a break to take stock and get his breath back John could have walked into a respected and successful band – perhaps at a slightly lower level than Quo, where, as trade-off, his influence would have been greater – and the change might have done him the world of good.

The harder route was to inject new life into The Diesel Band and turn that band into a full-time class act. That would have been more difficult for anyone, and especially for John, who isn't one of life's organisers or team leaders.

The problem is that John did neither. He and Gillie socialised on the Isle of Man and took holidays; he went off road racing with his Range Rovers and looned about in his military vehicles. Sure, after twenty years with first The Spectres and then Quo he was due a little R&R, but this stretched and stretched.

Trevor Baines had a plan. He owned a show business agency, and he wanted John to *actively* do nothing, and his agency would promote him as 'The world's best rock 'n roll drummer', and every now and again he would play a top-flight gig, carefully planned and promoted. Trevor says, 'Id have reverse sold it. I'd have said that John left Quo because he is too good for them, and he's too constrained playing what is very basic rock 'n roll; he's moving on'.

As part of the settlement for leaving Quo however he wasn't supposed to do anything unless the old management promoted it. The Quo management were telling John that they had big plans for him and everything would be revealed soon. That didn't happen.

Even guesting with friendly bands would have kept his profile up; kept his photo in the rock press, but John simply didn't hustle. He didn't hit the phone, he didn't keep up his contacts, he didn't stay in touch with his friends in the music business. Instead, he stayed on the island and messed about; not making the connection between, on the one hand, money still going out, and on the other, almost nothing coming in.

He says, 'I had always been in the position where people rang *me*. I didn't ring them. Gillie would say 'Why don't you ring up so-and-so, see how they are?' But I wouldn't. I just wouldn't. For all those years I'd had a manager and an agent who had done all that for me. I was too proud to

4 MANX STAR, Friday, 12th March, 1982

Fenella's Roundabout

John and Gillie name the day

ISLE of Man residents for six years, John Coghlan and his attractive girl-friend Gillie West have been telling friends they have fixed the date to tie the matrimonial knot in London on May 7th.

It has come as some surprise to their wide circle of friends as the former Status Quo drummer and his vivacious companion seemed happy to be what is popularly known as a live-in couple.

But it came as the greatest surprise of all to Gillie when John proposed out of the blue whilst enjoying a quiet evening at home. It was St. Valentine's Day.

Gillie said: "Since then we've been to London and arranged for the wedding at Marylebone Registry Office and the reception at the Savoy Hotel. We are going to spend the night there before going off on our honeymoon to some quiet and pretty place in the sun — probably Bermuda".

Why have they waited so long for marriage? "We have not really felt the need. It wasn't because John couldn't he's been divorced for years, but suddenly the time is right. I'm thrilled and so is my mother and John's parents."

Gillie West will be 28 this month and she was involved in the music world's management side. She was once personal assistant to Tito Burns and then worked for NEMS, Bron, and for three years with MAM. Thirty-five-year-old John Coghlan has been a drummer for 20 years. He made headlines at Christmas when he broke away from Status Quo who have had so many hits in Britain and Europe.

Now he is forming his own group, no name has been chosen yet, and this past weekend he has been rehearsing at home with John Fiddler of Medicine Head, Terry Uttley of Smokie — who lived in the Island for six months — and Ray Majors of Mott the Hoople. "But nothing is signed up yet," says John, whose collection of four military vehicles is a familiar sight around Manx roads. He is a great supporter of Island sports, particularly boxing, and local charities. He and Gillie, who both come from South London, are well-known in the Island. They lived first on the coast at Ballaugh and latterly in the centre of Ballasalla village where Gillie West has restored an old house with artistic flair. Now she has bought a piano in a local auction and plans to learn to play during the next year, "but I'll have to find someone to teach me."

Her wedding gown has been bought from Belville Sassoon. "It's a secret, but it's very unusual."

John Coghlan and Gillie pictured yesterday.

Manx Samaritan

A Manx friend found herself in dire trouble at Nottingham's busiest crossroads when her car packed up whilst she was in a three lane stream of traffic. Absolute consternation for my friend until a tap at the window revealed a Good Samaritan — and a Manxman. Geoffrey Lane, son of Mrs Lane of Saddle Road, Braddan, was himself in a hurry from his Warwick base but he had spotted the Manx registration from some distance, negotiated the heavy traffic on foot to see if he could help. He could and did.

A Manx Samaritan indeed — my chum is so grateful and still amazed by the coincidence.

A birthd

9

"figh

APPROPRIATELY Irish-born Mrs Minnie Quayle celebrates her birthday on St. Patrick's Day. She will be 96 next week and at her side, as always, will be her 90-year-old husband Tommy.

Ask their family how they are and the answer, inevitably, is "fighting fit — and fighting is the operative word." The Quayles have come through 64 years of married life — enjoying a jolly good argument most of the time, but utterly devoted to each other, though neither would

John and Gillie's marriage announcement in the Manx Star, 12th March 1982.

ring people up and tell them that I needed work. I knew that it was what I should be doing, but I didn't want them thinking 'Oh, he needs the money' even it was true.

'A lot of the time I was thinking 'I'm happy and healthy; why would I want to be embarking on a big tour?' Then you realise that the phone isn't ringing.

'There was a big hole in my life. A big void. That's when you find out who your friends are. You think you can get some musicians together and go out and get a record contract. But it's not like that. People don't want to know.

'Gillie was a great strength. A great strength. She stuck with me through all the bad times. I finally started playing again but I didn't want to do it on that scale. Well, to be honest the chances of that were very slim.'

Gillie says; 'John has never had to think for himself. He was sixteen years old when he joined the band, and from then on everything was done for him. He never needed to think. John's support was his mother, then the band, then me. That was the problem. John has never been pro-active in anything in his life. That sounds unkind, but if you tell him to turn up somewhere he'll do it. He'll never do it on his own unless it's something he really wants to do.

'But there's only so much pushing you can do. *He* had to do it.

'For years we lived down the road from John Entwhistle of The Who, who had been a mate, and who lived at Stow-on-the-Wold. I kept telling John to go and see him, buy him a drink, try and get back into the *milieu* a bit. He loved the idea of that but he was never going to make the first move.'

There was one landmark in this period though. John decided, and it was his decision, not Gillie's, that they should get married. 'I wasn't bothered about getting married', Gillie says, 'I didn't make the decision. He did. He had always said that he had done it once and was never going to do it again. I knew that I didn't want children and I wasn't keen on being Mrs Someone-or-Other.'

John's motivation, Gillie is certain, was comfort. He had left the security of the band, which for nearly twenty years had been wrapped around him like a warm overcoat on a cold day – his insulation from the outside world – and marriage was, in its way, the next best thing. Gillie's mother was uncertain about the match, but after some thought Gillie herself decided that, after living with him for six years, she was sure enough to go ahead, and said 'yes'.

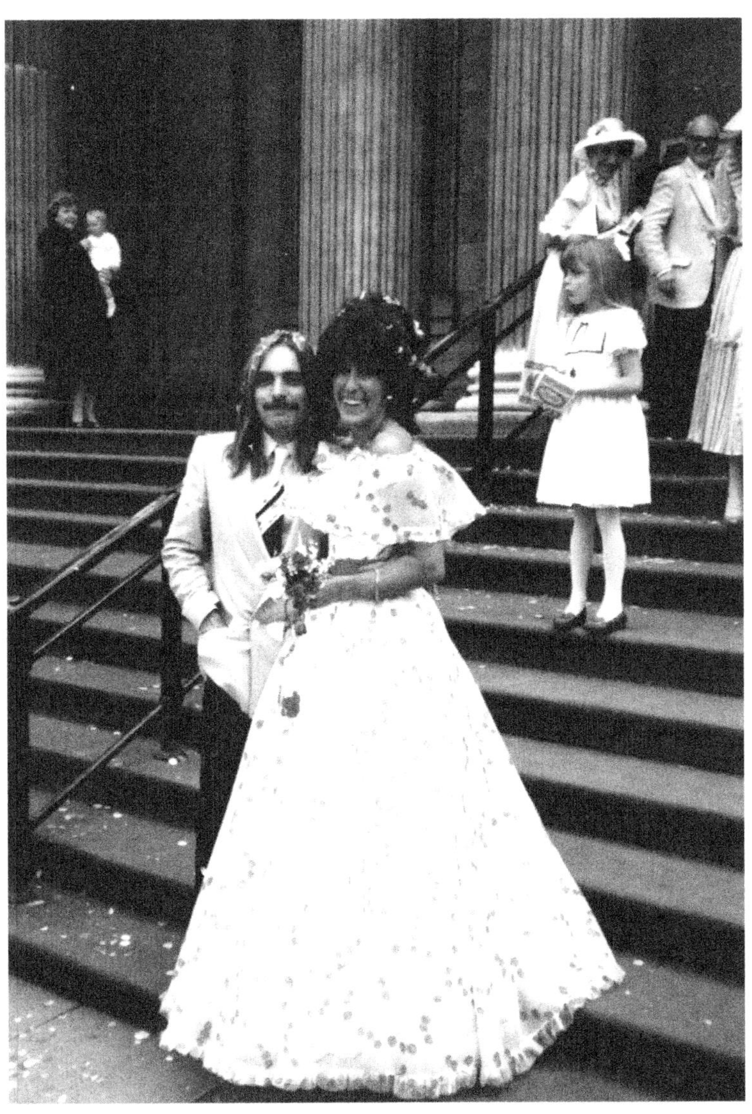

John and Gillie on the steps of Marylebone Registry Office after their wedding in May 1982.

The announcement of their marriage merited a big spread in the Manx newspaper, and the wedding itself was 100% rock 'n roll. The ceremony was at the registry office in Marylebone Road – Gillie insisted on London; all her friends were there. The nuptials took place on Friday May 7 1982.

John asked Richard Beddall to be his best man, because – Richard suggests – he was an ally and a safe pair of hands, and was used to making speeches. He could be relied on to keep everyone in order, run the reception to schedule, and keep the speeches decent.

The bridegroom, not the bride – as is more traditional - turned up late. Richard had taken him to Claridge's for lunch, and one bottle of champagne followed another just as one course followed another. Driven in their Rolls by Quo's chauffeur, Gillie went round and round the one-way system until John deigned to roll up.

To say they were in their finery is an understatement. Gillie describes her wedding outfit as 'The full Princess Diana-Scarlett O'Hara frock'. They were going to have a rock star wedding, no matter what.

The reception, for eighty, was held at The Savoy in the Art Deco room, facing the river. An elderly pianist played a selection from Cole Porter on a full-size grand piano – until someone produced the sheet music for a selection of Status Quo songs and persuaded the bemused old gentleman to have a crack at those instead.

The guests included members of both The Nolans and Roxy Music, which must have been a curious mix. Despite being invited, no members of Status Quo attended, though the manager, Colin Johnson, did. Photos of the wedding appeared in most of the tabloid papers.

The party continued at Tokyo Joe's, running on into the small hours. The actor Geoff Hughes, then very famously starring in Coronation Street as layabout Eddie Yates, was called upon at four in the morning to help carry John to bed.

The couple stayed on at The Savoy for the weekend, in a suite with fabulous views along the Thames, and on the Sunday morning the London Marathon went by; they waved at Jimmy Savile and he waved back.

For a week they toured the very best country hotels of England; The Chewton Glen in The New Forest, The Lygon Arms in Broadway, and The Bibury Court near where they live now. It was four-poster beds and jacuzzis at every stop. The Coghlans then flew to Bermuda for a further fortnight's honeymoon.

19

From a legal point of view, as a long-time member of Status Quo John was a partner in an established business, and Quarry needed to sort that out. He had ownership of 25% of the name and the intellectual rights that went with it.

The negotiations were protracted, and technically John didn't actually leave Quo until May 1984. By this point the band was splitting up, and were underway with their farewell End Of The Road tour. It wasn't to be the end of the band of course, but that was the intention at the time and the atmosphere was accordingly strained. Just about everyone, band members and management alike, was coked up to the eyeballs, and no-one seemed to be speaking directly to anyone else.

On July 13 1985 – ironically just a few weeks after John had legally left the band - Bob Geldof invited Status Quo to play Live Aid at Wembley Stadium. It was an unknown quantity but they accepted, and it turned out to be a massive boost to the band's career – and possibly saved them from extinction.

They opened the UK half of the show at exactly one minute past noon with *Rockin' All Over The World* (followed by *Caroline* and *Don't Waste My Time*). They were playing to about 65,000 people in the stadium, and hundreds of millions watching their TVs around the world.

Alan Lancaster flew back from Australia to play Live Aid, but John wasn't asked to re-join the band, even for that momentous one-off gig. 'I watched Live Aid on TV and it was a very strange feeling for me' says John. 'It was wrong, me not being there.'

While John would doubtless have enjoyed the gig and the massive spotlight it threw on the band, it's unlikely that he would have enjoyed the company of the other members of the group: Talking to 'Q' magazine, Francis said, 'We were the first band on and we were already as high as kites by midday. After we finished playing we spent most of the time doing cocaine in the toilets. We didn't spend much time thinking about the starving in Ethiopia.'

The valedictory deal was finally completed in July 1987, and the legal and accountancy fees left a large hole in the final settlement. The presentation of John's case hadn't been helped by the fact that he had used a solicitor who was more used to divorce cases, and knew nothing about the music industry.

Back in 1976 John had put together a fairly *ad hoc* group called John Coghlan's Diesel Band (the name having been suggested by Jackie Lynton). When John left Quo the story for the fans and the press was that John was going to do a lot more work with Diesel, and the difficulties that had precipitated his departure were either played down or denied.

Bob Young was involved in the logistics from the start, and remembers the band as being great fun. In an interview with the Quo fanzine 'Backwater', John said, 'It was created as a loon band. It wasn't me trying to express myself or any of that crap, I just felt I had the energy to do it.'

That year the band appeared at The Marquee, and played for over three hours – despite having only rehearsed a one and a half hour set.

Diesel was always more of a gigging, pick-up band and didn't have the obvious recording potential. The band would disappear for a while and then re-surface in a flurry of energy and beer-drinking. They placed many gigs in the UK and toured the continent on a few, rare occasions – where they were always extremely well received.

Over the years The Diesel Band's line-up included any number of musicians, including Phil May, Ray Minhinnett (who had played with Alan Price, Georgie Fame and Frankie Miller), Andy Bown, John Verity, Jackie Lynton, Charlie McCracken, Mike Simmonds, Bob Young and Mickey Moody.

On July 9 1985, just a few days before Live Aid, the Quo fans in the audience at a Diesel gig – back at The Marquee – were astonished and delighted when Francis and Alan joined the band on stage, and they ripped through three Status Quo favourites – *Roadhouse Blues*, *A Mess Of Blues* and *Caroline*. It was great fun but it was a one-off. The Diesel gigs started to become far less frequent in the years that followed.

A new group, Freeway, emerged in the middle of 1984, but was rapidly re-named Partners In Crime (one of many bands to have used that name over the years) – which may or may not have been a quote from the Rolling Stones' song *Tumblin' Dice*. The line-up included guitarist Ray Majors, Mac McCaffrey on bass, keyboards player Mark Vanchque, vocalist Noel McCalla – and John on drums. A contract was signed with Epic and things were looking good.

Two singles, *Hold On* and *Miracles*, were released in '84, and the album 'Organised Crime' was released in '85, followed by another single, *Hollywood Dreams*.

The band only played live a couple of times, including once at The Marquee in November 1984. In January 1985 the band played a set for BBC radio – six numbers from the 'Organised Crime' album - recorded at their Paris Studios in London.

They were offered a tour supporting a heavy metal group, which would hardly have been right for a fairly 'soft rock' band. John doubts that enough promotion was put behind their efforts and after making some initial impact the band dissolved in '85. Its collapse was a substantial blow; 'It was a big let-down; I was pretty upset by all that. I was starting to lose respect. I simply lost heart.'

By the mid-Eighties the music industry had moved on, and the A&R men were looking for solo singers to promote. Apart from the honourable exception of Dire Straits, no-one was becoming well known for playing an instrument; not even guitarists were rated any more. Apart from Phil Collins – famous for his vocals rather than his drumming - no teenage music fans knew the names of any drummers. The days when young music-lovers knew of, and admired the work of, Keith Moon, John Bonham, Ginger Baker and John Coghlan were gone forever.

Be they male or female, the entire industry was geared to turning out solo singers who could provide a short run of rapid hits. Solo artists are easier to manage, easier to move about, and cost less. The industry wanted Boy George, Kylie Minogue, Rick Astley, Howard Jones and even, god help us all, Marilyn. The fans had no idea who had played the musical instruments on their records. If you had asked someone who had just bought a copy of *I Think We're Alone Now* by Tiffany who had played the drums on the recording session, you'd have received an exceptionally blank look.

Pop and rock music had become a commercial enterprise like any other, and businessmen created a saleable commodity for an identifiable market and put far more investment into the promotion than into the creation. They didn't make records; they generated 'product'. Like all businessmen they wanted the maximum return for the minimum investment – and in the shortest possible time.

In 1990 John toured Australia with Alan Lancaster and his band The Bombers. After a band called The Party Boys, Alan had formed The Bombers in '88 – with the lead guitarist from The Party Boys, John Brewster (not to be confused with ex-Blodwyn Pig Jack Lancaster's early-1970s band Lancaster's Bombers!).

Having made money on property development projects in Australia, Alan put a lot of his own cash into the band, and financed the recording session for what would be the album 'Aim High'.

John was to play drums, but problems soon emerged. Alan says, 'John thought he was still the big rock star. He thought my band was a big time thing, and really it wasn't. There had to be a lot of discipline; we had to do things for ourselves. We had to do production and management ourselves; there wasn't the money to pay other people.

'John became a bit of a handful. He didn't have roadies to wait on him. He was getting edgy because he was away from home, and Gillie, who was there, wanted to go back to London. They didn't appreciate that it was like starting a new business. I couldn't work in that environment. I had to ask John to leave. I hated doing that but I had too much money on the line.'

But still John wasn't hitting the phone, wasn't networking, wasn't out there hustling for work. He wasn't going after session work, or pushing himself forward to join the increasingly large and big-selling Sixties revival packages – which would have suited his playing style and pleased old Quo fans.

John re-formed The Diesel Band in 1991, with Bob Young's help, and they played fourteen Swedish venues in as many nights in the October and November of that year. Bob Young remembers the tour as great fun, and it was at that point that the decision to cut a Diesel record was made.

In 1992 Diesel recorded a full-length album in the Tuff studio in Gothenburg. The session lasted from January into March, though the band also played some gigs in Sweden while recording. Most of the tracks were original songs, written by Bob Young, Phil May and other members of the band. They recorded two old Quo numbers, *Mean Girl*, which wasn't on the final track list, and *Living On An Island*, which was. Another song, *One Way To Roll*, had been written for Quo by Bob Young and Mickey Moody but had not been used by them. The album was to be called 'Flexible Friends'.

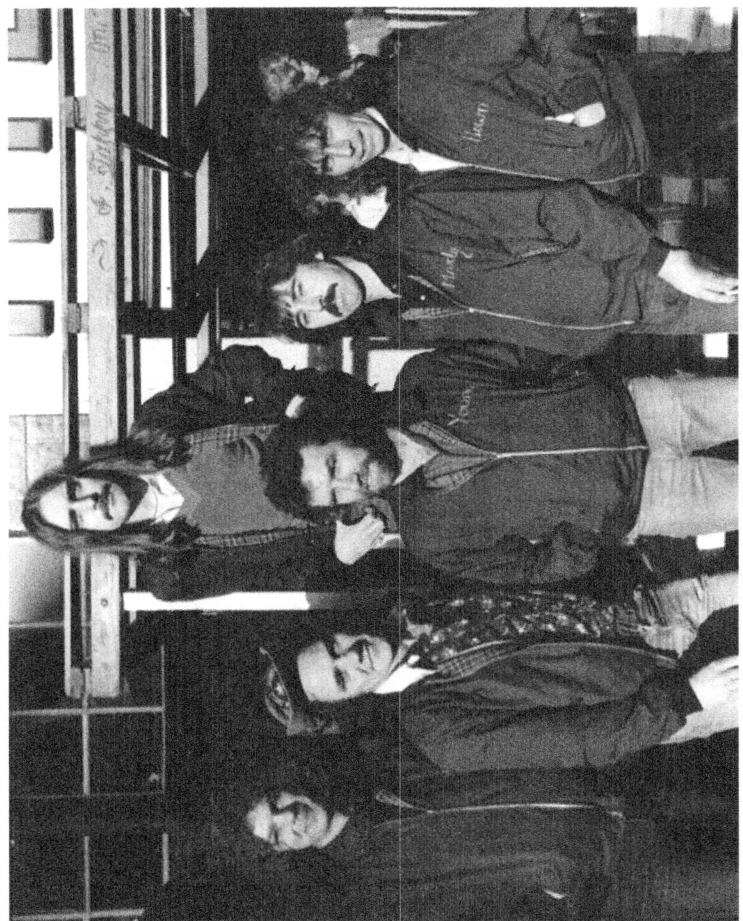

The Diesel Band in Sweden in 1992 - wearing their personalised jackets with the nice tartan linings. Below John from left: Neil Murray, Jackie Lynton, Bob Young, Mickey Moody and Andy Bown.

A single taken from the album was mooted – *River Of Tears* backed by *No Moon Shines* – with Phil May singing and Ray Minhinnett playing forceful guitar. Those two tracks sounded vaguely American in style, and were perhaps too soft, too MoR, and the lyrics were too wordy and lacked impact. *No Moon Shines* was perhaps the stronger of the two tracks, with more than a hint of The Stones to it, especially around the chorus.

Phil May particularly enjoyed playing with Diesel because he got to play guitar as well as sing, but he says, 'It was a collection of a lot of different things. I don't think that anybody knew what they were going to get out of it, and no-one got what they thought they were going to get. It didn't have an identity.

'The studio in Sweden where we made the album was very clinical. It wasn't a great rock 'n roll studio. It wasn't a good vibe – it doesn't have to be a happy vibe to make music, but it was very negative there. I found it quite tough. After making that album I decided that if I never saw Sweden again I don't care. The best thing they had at the studio was the pornography. They had an incredible collection of porn.'

Bob thought the session had gone well and that the album was very strong – though he says that John should have put that album together in the late Seventies, when he was with Quo. He admits that's with the benefit of hindsight though ...

The album had been slated for release as early as April, but that was rescheduled for August. A Scandinavian tour was supposed to follow release, with additional gigs in the UK. It simply didn't happen. Diesel supported Santana in Gothenburg in late April, but everything then went quiet. Large numbers of bootlegged copies are known to exist but the album was never released, and to this day there's uncertainty as to where the master tapes are.

The tragedy of the Diesel album was that it was funded completely by the Coghlans; 'I've never seen a penny back from that. To give him his due, I know that John feels really bad about that. I paid for that year in Sweden, and making the album. Great album but nothing ever happened. More fool me.'

Things were far from good. John was in his mid-forties and everything seemed to be stopping. The failure of both Partners In Crime and the Diesel project was both sobering and depressing. John could have made a lot more of The Diesel Band, in Bob Young's opinion, but no-one pushed. There was no money around and no apparent way forward. After Live Aid, Quo had been revitalised and seemed to be going from strength to strength once more. John was no part of it though.

The notion of walking out of the marriage, of leaving the downward spiral never occurred to Gillie; 'I was part of it all. I never thought of leaving him; he was my other half, for better or for worse. It was part of the deal.

'I've often been thoroughly pissed off about the whole thing, of course I have – but I've never considered taking off.' Saying this, Gillie realises that it doesn't sound rock 'n roll enough, and adds, perhaps mischievously, 'If there'd been a better offer I might have done, but there wasn't, so I didn't.'

It's something that has occurred to John too; he is slightly awed by Gillie's faith in him; 'Rock 'n roll is the sort of business where people are around you when you're famous, when you're doing well – but as soon as the apple cart turns over they're out the door.'

He says that he once plucked up the courage to ask her why she had stayed with him, despite everything. The answer was simple. She said that it was because she loved him, and that rather put an end to that strand of conversation. It helps, John says, that Gillie is passionate about tennis – which leaves him cold – and his delight in military vehicles isn't something that Gillie might not otherwise have considered to be lady's preoccupation. The fact that they currently see each other only at weekends is good too, John thinks; 'That's healthy. She's got her friends and I've got mine. Sometimes, if she's been away for a couple of weeks, it's as if we've just met again, and it's fabulous. I love her enormously, and as importantly, we get on really well.

'Most musicians are temperamental, and for anyone to settle down with a musician is a great challenge. She understands the music business though, and she's a very positive woman; she's the one if you want to get the job done. I think that stems from her boarding school days. She's very smart, and very good at getting the best deal.

'The fact that she didn't want kids was great. I had Charlotte when Gillie and I met, and that was fine. Neither of us wanted more children. That would have been impossible for us. I couldn't imagine myself driving a people carrier ...'

'I couldn't have coped on my own though. I do love my own company but I could never have lived on my own.'

In 2002 Gillie was a contestant on the TV quiz The Weakest Link, and, very clever woman that she is, she stomped through to win. She was popular with the studio audience; she was there to entertain, to make the most of the appearance, and not just go all gooey like 'the civilians' do. When Ann Robinson bullied her to reveal her age, Gillie won an admiring round of applause.

John had offered to go to the studio with her for the recording, but she told him, 'No, I need to win this. I'll go on my own so that I can concentrate'. For her it wasn't fun, it wasn't an outing. She was there to win. The loser, in her brief aside to camera just ahead of the end credits, muttered with unpleasant bitterness that it was obvious that Gillie didn't really need the money …

Richard Beddall, who knows them both very well says that Gillie was a very good influence on John, and that despite the roller-coaster nature of their time together, he thinks they have been very happy together; 'She's very caring, and she knows John very well indeed. And he really appreciates what she has done for him.'

Gillie has thought of giving up work to be John's manager, but admits that all her industry contacts are now stone cold, and in reality they couldn't afford to take the risk of losing the one steady income in the hope that John's earnings might pick up. Also, John would want to have absolutely everything done for him – every little detail, *everything* - and it wouldn't be too long before Gillie was going for him with the letter opener. 'He's a musician, an artiste, so you have to make allowances', Gillie adds, rolling her eyes.

'The bands in those days weren't like bands now. They didn't have a handle on business managers', Gillie says, 'Nowadays they know about business from nine years old. In those days bands weren't encouraged to know what was going on; the management looked after everything - and we were encouraged to trust them. It sounds pretty stupid, but yes, we trusted them.

'We got screwed. I suppose we all got screwed, but it's water under the bridge now. No-one ever told us to put some money into a pension fund. Kids in the pop world nowadays aren't kids; they have pensions from the age of nineteen. We assumed that investments were being made, and they weren't. We were young and we did have fun, and I don't regret that for a minute.'

A lot of the money, as Gillie and John well understand, was simply frittered away. It got spent. Be it houses, holidays, parties, vehicles, drink, clothes, whatever …

Soon after John and Gillie moved to the Isle of Man Trevor Baines suggested that they buy a hotel. Not to run, simply as an investment. There was one in particular, in Ramsey, which was for sale for £60,000, and would now be worth millions. He says that Gillie was against the idea, but that, overall, neither John nor Gillie was at all interested in financial planning.

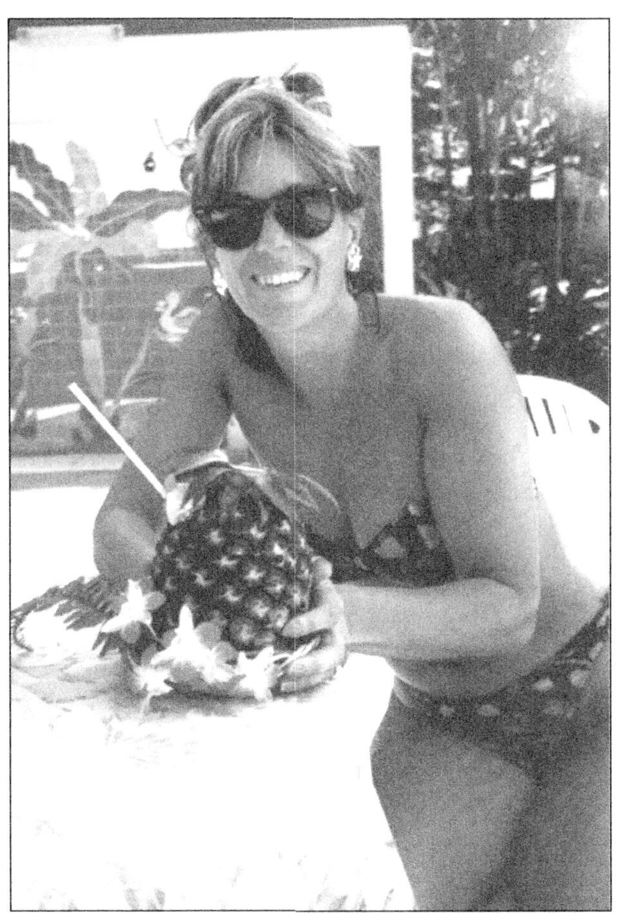

The notion of walking out of the marriage, of leaving the downward spiral never occurred to Gillie; 'I was part of it all. I never thought of leaving him; he was my other half, for better or for worse. It was part of the deal.'

Trevor, who knows more than most about both money and the entertainment industry, says, 'They were screwing John. There's no question about that. When he left he did get a lump sum, but it was spread over ten years. It wasn't fair.

'It suddenly appeared that they were *all* broke, but they sold millions of records and had enjoyed hugely successful tours. Something was going wrong, a lot of money was going missing.'

Trevor's understanding is that in those days the bands never actually saw any cash. The management told them to let they know what they wanted, and they'd sort it out for them. It was a great advantage for the musicians to be utterly dependent on them, and of course – as creative artistes – they loved being molly-coddled and having anything at all worldly kept at arm's length. What this meant though was the cash stayed in management bank accounts, not in the individual musician's. That gave the managers a lot of power, and a lot of freedom to move money around as they wished and account for it accordingly.

The exceptions, Trevor says, were people like Mick Jagger, 'I'm not being unkind, but he came from a different background – a better-educated background – and they knew about the importance of getting a decent accountant, and knew how to manage money.

'John trusted everybody, which isn't a bad way to lead your life – until you're proved wrong.'

Bob Young says that most bands in the Seventies were incredibly naïve, especially compared with attitudes nowadays; 'There were a lot of opportunities for people to take advantage of musicians then. We weren't interested in looking at the books, to be honest, and for a lot of us the drugs accounted for a lot of money, to be honest. And if you're taking drugs, or busy getting drunk, you're not taking care of business.' Alan reckons that in all their years together no-one in the band ever got a royalty statement telling them exactly what they had earned.

John and Gillie did their share of spending of course, and all the limos and private planes were carefully re-charged to them – accountancy which they didn't see until long after it had happened. And undoing the labyrinthine accounts of management, publishers, record companies *et al* was virtually impossible, as many, many rock and pop musicians found.

In 1986 John and Gillie returned to England and bought the house they still live in. It's the very last cottage in a pretty, typically English Cotswolds village. Many of the houses are large, sit comfortably in their own grounds and are frighteningly expensive. The cars outside the village pub are

BMWs, Audis, Range Rovers and Jaguars – not many more than a year or two old. John's ancient hatchback is probably the oldest car in the parish.

The day had come in 1984 when the bank said that enough was enough. John was away and Gillie was at home alone at Walton House. The bank manager had written: 'We were with William's & Glyn's, and they got taken over by The Royal Bank Of Scotland', Gillie says. 'So our lovely old bank manager – who came to dinner in the good times and was a fan of the band – got moved, and was replaced by a little beady-eyed Scotsman. I've never forgotten him ...'

The letter was to say that he was shutting the accounts and calling in the overdraft, which at that point stood at £75,000. Gillie phoned him and pointed out that monies owed to them were due – in fact were over-due – but he was, unsurprisingly, unmoved. The plug was pulled. As Gillie says, 'That was my last moment of complacency. I've never stopped worrying about money ever since.'

Trevor doubts that it ever occurred to John that the money had stopped coming in; 'He had no understanding of money at all. Someone had always paid the bills, so he thought someone would go on paying the bills. Mind you, they had both been told that there was plenty of money – so why should they stop having fun?' He says it was Gillie who first realised how things were, and that things were never going to be the same again.

Another effect was that Charlotte had to leave the private prep school at which she was being educated, and was enrolled at a state school.

Gillie started working, but that meant being in London. She got work modelling and doing promotional activity, but none of that was on the Isle of Man. Nor would she, or John, have wanted it to be – for obvious reasons. Over there they were still celebrities. Few people knew that they were broke celebrities.

The island's usefulness as a tax haven had been greatly reduced when Margaret Thatcher sliced the higher rates of income tax. The rich migrated back to the mainland, and unfortunately for the Coghlans this meant that the value of large property on the island plummeted. For a long time their home was unsaleable; people who could afford houses of that size were moving out, not in. It was just about their only saleable asset. It stood empty – fully furnished, empty, and increasingly damp - for a year before a buyer was finally found, and the price was not what they had hoped for. More than half of it went in paying off debts.

In the meantime the two of them camped out in a friend's spare room in west London, living out of suitcases. They were there for two years.

Gillie worked as much as she could and John gigged when he could. Soon he started delivery driving on a casual basis. The cars had gone. The military vehicles had gone. The halcyon days were gone.

Quite apart from the economic necessities, the Coghlans had pretty much 'done' the Isle of Man, they say, and because the rich, well-connected, party-goers were leaving, the social scene there was not what it had once been.

Gillie says that the Quo organisation actually discouraged wives and girlfriends from asking too many questions about the financial position, as she says that she was indeed in blissful ignorance. They had all had first wives, had all had expensive divorces, and 'the office' saw it as part of their duties to actively keep information away from second wives in case they became second ex-wives.

With Walton House sold there was cash available to buy a house, but it was going to be something fairly modest. Gillie retained a fondness for Cotswolds from her time at Westonbirt School, and John the south London lad was now much more the countryman. Pam Ayres, who had also moved to the Isle of Man (the only known case of a poet needing tax exile status), had returned to her native Oxfordshire, and invited the Coghlans to stay with her and her family while they house-hunted.

Gillie decided that they needed somewhere easy for both London and Heathrow; 'I didn't want Essex because John had done Essex with the first wife. If you go to Kent you have to get through east London to get anywhere else. Surrey we couldn't afford. Cornwall, Dorset and Devon were too far from London. The M4 - M40 corridor seemed obvious.

'To be honest, I'm the one that has to be near London. John says he wants to come to London, but when he does, he hates it. He loves the countryside, the walks with the dog, and the life in the village.'

One further deciding factor in ending up where they did, was Pam Ayres' GP. Gillie says, 'I danced with this lovely man at Pam's fortieth birthday party, and he told me that he had delivered both of her babies and I fell in love with him there and then. Beautiful man. He climbs mountains for a hobby, and goes on expeditions. I decided that I wanted him as my GP.'

John and Gillie are very much at the heart of village life, different though they might be from everyone else (Gillie makes the short walk to the pub dressed as though she was going for dinner at The Ivy, or as if she's expecting the paparazzi to burst from a parked Range Rover, while everyone else is in Barbour jackets or ancient Aquascutum tweed). They are still treated like celebs, and on occasion John will bring in a few mates and put together a scratch band to play in the field behind the pub. They still make a huge thing of Christmas, with parties just about every night. The Saturday before Christmas is always their bash, and the tiny cottage will be crammed with local worthies, elbow to elbow, barely able to raise their glasses to their lips.

A house in France, in addition to a larger one in the middle of their village, features on Gillie's day-dream wish list; 'It would have to be hot and sunny and close to great restaurants and the best beaches'. John adds, 'I could live very happily in the South of France; I love the food, the wine, the weather and just the French way of life.'

Doing what he does best; playing thunderous drums for Status Quo.

20

A curious phenomenon in pop and rock music over the past twenty years has been the inexorable rise of the tribute band; where the sound, the look and in many cases the tiniest mannerisms of famous groups are meticulously re-created by other, often younger, often less talented, and certainly less fortunate musicians.

The best of them – such as The Bootleg Beatles – are unnervingly good, and in one non-stop show they canter through the band's development over several years, complete with changes in clothing, wigs and instruments: All correct to the smallest detail. The Bootleg Beatles actually appear on stage with a small choir and a string section, and perform songs such as *A Day In The Life* and *Strawberry Fields Forever*, which The Beatles themselves only ever played in the recording studio, and certainly never played live.

Tribute bands are now a sizeable part of the live music scene, and they give fans the opportunity to both hear a favourite band's songs in the back room of their local pub or wherever, and get – to a greater or lesser degree - some feel for the original performance. Members of some of these groups are more like actors than musicians; but playing the same character every night of their professional lives. Some of them play musicians who are long dead, and who they probably never saw or heard playing live. How many Jimi Hendrix Experience tribute bands saw him play live? And how the guys who 'play' George Harrison in Beatles tribute bands felt when the real George died can only be guessed at.

Every year around a hundred and fifty Beatles tribute bands play at the Matthews Street Festival in Liverpool – from all over the world. Not so long ago The Bootleg Beatles and The Counterfeit Stones sold out the Budokan stadium in Japan.

The original musicians often seem to be flattered by having a look-a-like band aping their work; it means you've moved on to a certain level of fame, and is only one rung down from appearing on *Later* or being invited onto *Desert Island Discs*. Some are slightly awed by their *doppelgangers*, and will admit in private that their alter egos actually play better than they do themselves. Others, with several tribute bands trailing their coat tails, can rate their impersonators and will tell you who they think 'do them' best. How would the front man with a Led Zep tribute band feel if he saw the real Robert Plant standing looking at him from the front row, arms folded and a slight smile on his lips?

At the same time, it must be said, tribute bands can be seen as simply naff. The obvious question is 'Why don't you get some original material and start a real band?' One answer is that for the vast majority of musicians, with the music industry focussed utterly on formulaic output, the chances of any sort of breakthrough, let alone worthwhile success, are tiny. At least there's a demand for tribute bands and that allows a lot of people an opportunity to play, for money, in front of an audience – which might not otherwise be the case.

It's hard to say how many Status Quo tribute bands there are in total. It's also impossible to say which real rock bands have inspired the largest number of impersonators, but Quo must be in the top three alongside Led Zeppelin and The Doors.

John Coghlan is one of the very small number of musicians who play in these bands – which means that in the line-up three guys are pretending to be other musicians but he's appearing as himself, like having a cameo role in a movie: They're called State Of Quo when John's not with them, and John Coghlan's Quo when he is.

State Of Quo came into being in October 1996, and the line-up they replicate is the four-piece Seventies band. They are Paul Carr (Rick Parfitt), Mike Grady (Francis Rossi), Graham Peters (Alan Lancaster), and Dave Owen who is, sort of, John Coghlan when John Coghlan's not there.

State Of Quo play pubs, clubs (there are many live music clubs round the UK which are well-established arenas for tribute bands), corporate events and private functions. The real fans are to be found in the clubs; men more than women, and, predominantly but not exclusively, in their thirties and forties. They are the guys who got into Quo's bloke-rock as teenagers and are never so happy as when they're jiggling their skulls to *Down Down*.

The atmosphere at these gigs is often utterly joyous, and though the lyrics of Quo songs were never of the greatest importance, everyone know the words to all the songs. Middle-aged men drape their arms around each other's shoulders in a most un-British way and shout the lyrics to each other, united in their beery delight. Licensing laws allowing, they're family occasions too, with the now-married, be-mortgaged, Vauxhall-driving, slightly balding fans introducing their youngsters to the delights of British boogie.

The guys in State Of Quo regard John's presence as a huge plus, not just for his musicianship but also for the prestige, needless to say. They've very definitely got something that no other tribute band has got. They also regard him, it must be said, with some awe – and they admit that they work harder and play better when he's behind the drum kit.

Paul says that they all got into Quo when they were at school, and they've never really grown up – or grown out of their love for the band; 'We followed them all over Europe – all over the world in fact. And no other British band has done what Quo has done. They've stuck to their guns and got on with it. They've been enormously successful by anyone's standards.

'We do what we do because we're fans of the music. Not so much fans of the act. We're not into the Stars In Their Eyes thing; we take great pride in playing the music really well.

'There's times when we're on stage and I look round and there's John Coghlan – *the John Coghlan* – on drums, and I think 'We are not worthy'. In the late Seventies we were always in the front row at Quo gigs. They were our idols, and to actually be playing in the band with him is amazing'.

Mike adds that if, twenty years ago, someone had told him that he'd be playing in a band with John Coghlan he'd have laughed in their face.

The band vigorously deny that Quo music is easy to reproduce; for years there was a joke about them only knowing three chords, but simply listening to their music explodes that myth. Paul says, 'A lot of people can play Quo songs to a certain standard, but to get them sounding right, get them sounding like the recordings takes an awful lot of work.'

However Andy Bown says, 'The cover bands play the same chords, they copy things note for note, but none of them get anywhere near the chemistry. They don't get it.'

John is happy to play with Paul, Mike and Graham because, he says, as musicians they are as good as the original Quo ever were. He also says that he's tried to play Quo numbers with other musicians, who perhaps weren't primarily into that music, but somehow it's never worked.

If State Of Quo hadn't come up to that standard he might have sat in at a gig or two but would never have put his name to their gigs. 'These lads do deliver the goods', John says, 'At our gigs, even in small venues, fans come up to me and say 'I just have to shut my eyes and I'm back at a Status Quo concert'. I've seen other Quo tribute bands, and they were okay - but they didn't have the edge; I didn't get the buzz'.

The band insist that John's playing generates great discipline, and that once they've hit the beat he doesn't allow them to speed up or slow down. 'As a drummer he's utterly solid and he never flinches. If the guitar starts too fast he'll bring it down to what it should be.

'He's never lost it', Graham says. 'Playing bass to his drumming sends shivers down my spine.'

'John is a phenomenal drummer' Mike adds. 'He's rock solid, and has a drum beat for every occasion. No-one can play that four-to-the-bar shuffle like he can. Rock solid, that's John.

'I also think that John really enjoys playing with us. I'll look at him and there'll be that bit of invisible contact. I'll know that he's doing a fancy bit on the drums, and he knows that I know!'

Paul chips in, 'In all the time I saw John playing with Quo I never saw him smile. There are very few photos of him smiling from the Seventies and Eighties. Watch John with us though and he's grinning from ear to ear. It might only be an audience of three hundred or so at one of our gigs but he obviously loves it.

'There's a certain point in *Railroad* where it goes from fast to slow, and we turn round to John for a cue – and you can guarantee that you'll get a smile out of him at that point. Then he shuts his eyes and gets into it. Does his shuffle. That's what got me into Quo in the first place: That's what makes it my favourite Quo song to play.'

It's a bit tough on drummer Dave that he has to either sit on the side of the stage or stay home when John's with the band. They play a different set though, to suit either drummer. With John they play all the hits, but when Dave is playing they perform album tracks a lot more and allow themselves more guitar solos.

Bass player Graham's ambition is to also stand to one side, to watch John and Alan Lancaster perform with Paul and Mike; 'That would be terrific – Quo versus Quo. It ought to happen. And my nose wouldn't be put out of joint because I idolise Alan Lancaster as a bass player and always have done. I've never had the opportunity to have a chat with him. I'd give up my place in this band just for that opportunity.' Which rather sums up the dedication of the average Quo fan.

It ought to be sad and pitiful that John Coghlan plays drums with a Status Quo tribute band, and there are those in the music industry who couldn't see it any other way: 'It's not something I would choose to do', Andy Bown says.

Bob Young – who admits to being a fan of Bjorn Again - sees it differently; 'I say good luck to him. If that's how he can get an audience, if he's having fun and he's playing the music he was associated with, good luck to him. I saw him drumming with them, and they were great.'

Here's a man who was a co-founder of a massively famous band and was its backbone for a decade and a half - but who now trots out the old hits for tiny audiences and earns a pittance doing so. And there's no question but that the money, little though it is, comes in very useful.

In May 1998 John was part of the identity parade in the BBC2 television programme *Never Mind The Buzzcocks*. This hugely jokey pop and rock quiz has seen fourteen seasons in the UK, and there is now an American edition. One regular feature sees five people walk on to the set – four actors and one person who was once in a rock band – and the six contestants, arranged in two teams, have to guess which is the musician (or ex-musician). A short clip of the mystery guest in his or her heyday is screened for viewers first.

Any music fan of a delicate temperament tends to watch this section of the show through their fingers, or at worst, from behind the sofa. The wise guys on the panel often go to great lengths to humiliate, and it's a constant surprise that none of them has ever been punched by an overly-demeaned member of the line-up. Some ex-stars appear for a joke, or because they simply don't care – or maybe because it's a last, desperate chance to stand in a spotlight (though they're not supposed to speak or move, so their involvement is limited). Others do it for the fee.

John's appearance was preceded by a short clip from a 1978 Top Of The Pops performance of *Down Down*, and fortunately for him one of the teams included Motorhead's front man Lemmy. He and John have known each other for many years, so a correct identification wasn't a problem. To appear in the line-up of *Buzzcocks* and not be recognised must be deathly, even if you were, say, only the bass player in Unit 4 + 2 or the keyboards player in Chicory Tip.

'An agent asked me to go on *Buzzcocks*, and I wondered if it was a good idea or not. I'd watched it many times, and what worried me was that you can't go on there and wear what you want to wear. They tell you what to wear. I was given horrible baggy trousers and a funny shirt …

'None of the other characters in the line-up looked like me, and you'd have had to be completely smashed out of your head not to know it was me. Unlike a lot of other people who did it, I had had a very high profile. I stood out like a sore thumb, and even if you weren't a musician you'd have known it was me.

'I went to the bars and had a few beers, and thought I'd approach it as a complete laugh. I thought it was tongue in cheek. Afterwards I thought 'Did I really need to do that?', and to be honest, I don't think it did me any good at all. I don't think I'd do it again …'

Around that time John played some two dozen or so gigs with bass player Noel Redding, who had famously provided the backbone for The Jimi Hendrix Experience. They usually worked with Eric Bell, who played guitar with Thin Lizzy – so for music fans of a certain age it was a dream line-up. Noel had been a chum for many years.

Noel guested once with Quo at a gig in his home town of Folkestone, and hadn't been on stage long before the police arrived alongside John's drum riser. They informed him that they were playing beyond their allotted time and there had been complaints from local residents. They ordered John to stop playing, which he refused to do. They were in the middle of *Bye Bye Johnny*, he remembers, and he shouted at the police that they'd need to have a word with Mr Parfitt at the front there. This meant that they had to walk to the front of the stage and challenge three thrashing guitarists. The crowd roared their disapproval, and unable to identify which one was Mr Parfitt, they undertook a tactical withdrawal. Later they tried to ban the local boy from guesting with visiting bands.

John, Noel and Eric played mostly blues material, with a few old hits from their respective backgrounds; 'Noel always said before a show that he didn't want to play *Hey Joe*, but we could usually get him to do it once he was on stage. It was always a bit off the wall, playing with Noel', John remembers.

Noel was becoming increasingly frail by the late Nineties though, and John usually had to go to him; they often played County Cork, near Noel's home. Famously Noel played most Friday nights at De Barra's Bar in Clonakility; 'It's one of the most fabulous venues I've ever played in. It's like the early Marquee Club', John says.

Noel died in the spring of 2003, still trying to sue Jimi Hendrix's estate for royalties.

In May 2004 Maartin Allcock – best known as a member of Fairport Convention - released a new CD, 'Serving Suggestion'. John played drums on four tracks on the album, which was recorded in Banbury in Oxfordshire late in 2003. It's a very eclectic album, which influences ranging from Romanian folk tunes to Irish reels and polkas – via some distinctly rock 'n roll touches.

Although they seem to come from different ends of the musical spectrum, Maart says that John was a natural choice to play drums on the album. Tracks such as *Everything Changes* and *New Breton* are fairly straight rockers from a drumming point of view, and very much John's sort of thing. However *Ardal Gymraeg* and *Hornpipes* come much more from the folk tradition and must have been something of a change for John. And boy, can Maartin Allcock play rock-god guitar when he wants to ...

Maart says, 'I met John at the recording of Geoffrey Hughes' This Is Your Life, and I liked him very much. He struck me as very much a real person, and when some particularly rocky tunes came to me for 'Serving Suggestion' it seemed obvious to ask him if he'd come and play.' On the sleeve notes Maart has written, a little mischievously, 'John Coghlan was the original drummer with Status Quo, before they became a cabaret act.'

John with his all-time drumming hero, Buddy Rich, sitting at Buddy's kit after a gig in Preston.

21

John says that he has often thought of putting his drum sticks down forever and doing something else for a living, but has no idea what. Several friends have expected him to give up rock music completely – but, it has to be said, he has no other qualifications. He admits that if he tried to run a guest house he'd make Basil Fawlty look kindly and welcoming. When he does play, the buzz is still there – but the drumming work is too infrequent and simply doesn't pay the bills; 'I'll play a gig and really enjoy it, and be looking forward to the next – but that next gig might be weeks away.'

He doesn't own a big collection of records or CDs, and goes to live gigs very rarely. Once there, unless he's completely absorbed in the music, he soon gets restless and disruptive. There are very few bands he would turn up for: 'To be honest, I don't like being part of an audience. I don't like just being part of the crowd. I always think that my place is up on stage. But I would go anywhere now to watch The Stones playing.

He describes The Stones as 'Probably the greatest band of all time. I saw them at Wembley recently and they were just great. They put on such a show. I can't think of anyone else who can keep up with them.

'We played at a poll-winners show in London and Jimi Hendrix was supposed to be on last. For some reason he couldn't make it and they put The Rolling Stones on instead. They hadn't told the audience though! When they came on stage the place just erupted; everything was thrown in the air – hats, coats, chairs. They went wild. It was great just to be there, just to watch them playing.

'Apart from them, I've always admired bands like Led Zeppelin and Pink Floyd. We did a gig in a ballroom in Bournemouth supporting Pink Floyd and I couldn't believe their light show. I thought it was really weird music at first; we said to each other 'What was all that about?' Honestly … a ballroom in Bournemouth! That's not very rock 'n roll, is it? Later on I saw them in London on the Brick In The Wall tour and just loved it.

'When it comes to playing CDs at home, first choice is still Led Zep or The Stones. They're just fantastic bands. People say that The Stones shouldn't still be touring because they're old, but they'll keep playing until they fall off the perch – and why shouldn't they? The fans are still turning up for their gigs so they're doing something right.

'I simply couldn't believe it when John Bonham died. That really upset me in a big way. I loved the way he played, and I *would* say this, but he made Led Zeppelin for me. I met him before he was with Zeppelin; he was playing with Tim Rose's band, and I was with Mick Avery from The Kinks at a BBC radio session near Piccadilly. Mick and I went to watch Tim Rose's drummer, and we just thought 'Fucking hell, who's he?'. There was so much power in his playing. He came up to Mick and me afterwards and said 'Tim's going back to America. Can I give you my number? I really need some work.' Next time I saw him he was with Led Zeppelin and they were the biggest band on the planet.

'I loved meeting other bands and having a drink with them; groups like The Kinks, and Fleetwood Mac. I've always loved Fleetwood Mac. Always enjoyed Mick Fleetwood's drumming. On one American tour we were with a band who called themselves Fleetwood Mac, but weren't. They were impostors. I don't know how they thought they could go on stage when there wasn't a single member of Fleetwood Mac in the line-up. There was a hell of a lot of shit over that. They got themselves sued rotten. The tour was cancelled and we all came home.

'Queen were good mates too; I remember they came to see us *en masse* once at the Hammersmith Odeon. We always got on well with The Pretty Things and The Who. Slade were always great fun. We did a gig once in a barn in the West Country. There was Quo, Slade and Kenny Ball's Jazzmen – which was an interesting line-up! When we turned up we realised that we had another gig that night – so we set up and played before the audience came in. It was really stupid. As the audience was arriving we were driving out. And we got paid! Noddy Holder has never let me forget that.

'Rick Parfitt was always a good friend of Cliff Richard, which sounds unlikely, but I got on with Cliff really well. Rick used to bring him to gigs; he was a really nice guy. We'd be boozing away and he would just have the occasional glass of wine.

'A while ago Hank Marvin was looking for a drummer for The Shadows. I did nothing about it. I don't know why not. Playing for them would be great. I'd like to play with The Hollies too – they have some great songs – but their drummer, Bobby Elliott, fits the band like a glove.

John's first – and to this day, greatest – drumming hero was Buddy Rich: 'I spent an hour with Buddy Rich once – incredibly, at Preston Guildhall. We were playing a gig in Preston and a guy called Eddie Haynes who was a rep for a drum company said 'Buddy's in town and I'm going to see him. Do you want to come?' You bet!

'I went along with Eddie and met him. I've got a photo of me sitting at Buddy Rich's drum kit, with him stood behind me. That's a real treasure. He was a lovely guy, so nice. He asked me to play for him and I just wanted the floor to open up and swallow me. How do you play for someone that great? I thought he was bound to pick a fault, but after I'd done my very best he said 'I never realised the drums could sound so good'!

'He was great with me. I think he was having a good day because I've been told that he could be incredibly nice or he'd be a complete bastard ... but I suppose we can all be like that.'

Apart from Buddy Rich, John singles out the Englishman Simon Phillips, who has played with Jeff Beck, Jack Bruce, Brian Eno, Frank Zappa, Toyah Wilcox and The Who as one of the drummers he most admires. Also from London, Simon's father was Sid Phillips, the leader of a big band – where he started his career at the age of 12 as the youngest band member by some fifty years or so.

'The drummers I really admire *play* the song. They make it swing. There is a broad range of technicians, as you might say. I've admired Charlie Watts for years; I think he's the only drummer alive who could ever work with The Stones. He's brilliant.

'I met Keith Moon a few times. He was just a great guy and an unbelievable drummer. I thought his drumming was fantastic. I would say this, but he *made* The Who.'

Andy Bown describes John, as a drummer, as 'brilliant, magical'. A lot of the success of Quo's sound, he says, was down to John. 'And even he doesn't realise that'. He says that John's drumming shows terrific wrist action, and 'He has more technique under his belt than the drummers in

95% of the rock bands these days'. The question, Andy adds, is whether or not he chooses to use it.

Keith Altham describes John and Alan Lancaster as absolutely essential to the identity of Quo in its heyday; 'John isn't a great technical drummer, but he is a very powerful, solid drummer. He put up a storm behind what Quo were doing on stage, which drove it along. That was very important, and Alan was a very sharp bass player – with a great bluesy voice too – and the two of them were a terrific team; a perfect unit, just like The Who's rhythm section.'

John Coghlan looks back on his two decades with Status Quo with, mostly, great affection. He's very proud of the band's achievements, but doesn't overstate their role in the history of pop and rock; 'We were always really good at delivering the goods. We made terrific singles and always managed to re-create the singles on stage.'

Keith Altham agrees, 'Status Quo were – are – a great band. Like all the great bands of their time they have proved that by surviving. Their success is defined by the length of time they've been around *and* have sustained commercial success. They've always drawn in the crowds, and you don't do that by simply being lucky.'

Playing Wembley – both the Stadium and the Arena - rate very highly on John's list of all-time best-ever moments. Quo played the stadium with Elton John, and John remembers that as being just about the gig of a lifetime. Playing The Royal Albert Hall was a landmark too, as was playing the huge American football stadia. Remembering smaller gigs, The Marquee in Wardour Street was always fun and gave the band a lot of kudos – as did Hammersmith Odeon. 'And Glasgow Apollo was always a fantastic gig'.

Like many of the band's fans, John contends that the band was at its greatest, at its best in the sense that it was most raw and heaviest when it was Rick, Francis, Alan and himself; 'It's a bit lighter now. I don't like things like *Marguerita Time*; that's not what Quo is about. Mind you, a lot of fans have said to me that they don't like *In The Army Now*, but I thought that was a great song.

'Overall, the band was about having a good time' John says. 'Hey, it's party time! We were saying 'Come into this building and you'll have a really good time'; the bar's open, come and have a drink and just wait until the band hits the stage! We were a beer band, a five pints of best bitter band. We were never a 'two white wine and sodas, thank you very much' band.

'Some times I was most friendly with Alan, then with Rick, then with

Francis. There was no one guy in the band who was my personal mate, my favourite. Other times no-one would be talking to anyone. Usually because we were too knackered.

'In fact, Alan and I used to row a lot. It never came to a fight, but people were always shouting 'Ah, fuck it' and were kicking things over. It was all very well though to say 'Yeah, let's do a world tour' but it was simply too much in too short a space of time. You're only human and you can only do so much. I don't care what anyone says, you can't come off stage, go back to your hotel and go straight to bed. It doesn't happen like that. It takes ages to wind down.

'Between the band and the road crew there was always someone having a bit of a party; 'You think you'll just go for an hour or so, but you end up watching the sunrise. Then you go to bed and only get four hours sleep before the whole cycle starts all over again. The old merry-go-round. You don't *have* to go to the party – but you do.

'I remember one gig in Belgium, at the end of a long, long European tour. And I remember sitting outside thinking 'Thank fuck that's over!' Which is not how I ever expected to feel about it all.

'But we were a very tight little unit when we had to be. We could be very supportive of each other. Francis, Rick and Alan were thrown into jail in Austria after a bit of a fight at the security desk at the airport. I wasn't there because I had my Range Rover and I had decided to drive to the next gig. They were put in three separate cells with all these criminals, and when they finally arrived for the next gig they looked absolutely terrible. I told them we ought to cancel the gig, but Francis said 'No, we don't do that. We'll go on'. And he was quite right; all these fans had paid for their tickets and taken the trouble to come and see us. We had to make the effort.

'You've got to be a special type of person to be in the music business. You've got to be very strong. It's not a business for the weak, or the weak-willed. The pressure is incredible. I responded to it by drinking too much. Other people around me responded by taking too many drugs. When we were together we got on really well on a one-to-one basis, but collectively we all seemed to change. You're bound to get the times when there's a bit of a downer.

'Whenever Quo has had a change of drummer so many people have said to me 'They didn't phone up then? Didn't try to get you back?' But they've never phoned me and I've never rung them. But then I couldn't imagine myself back in the band on a permanent basis, but I think we should do a reunion gig or two for the fans' sake.

'The band has had some good drummers since me, but I set the drumming style for Quo, and they're rather stuck with it. Jeff Rich was possibly better than me from a technical point of view, but a lot of drummers can't do the fast shuffle that I do. A lot of the songs miss that shuffle, but I can do that – I learned how to relax to do that.'

Colin Johnson agrees, 'As a drummer John was very good for Quo. He was very solid. He would be the first to admit that he's not a technical drummer. There are better drummers that are not successful and there are worse drummers who are successful, but he worked very well with Alan Lancaster in that important bass/drums combination. There were times when his concentration lapsed on stage, and the timing would go or the ending would be messed up. But, once you lose a main, long-standing member, something goes. The drummers after John were too pure for Quo. It was a rough-edged band, and John suited that.'

'You can say of all the guys in Quo that there were always better players around, but John was the right drummer for Status Quo at that time,' Bob says, 'John was part and parcel of that Quo sound.'

It's difficult to say what John does these days. Gillie works in London during the week and John stays in Oxfordshire. He has just started working on drum clinics for percussion specialists Drumwright in Reading – along with Jeff Rich, which has a nice symmetry to it. For percussion anoraks: Nowadays John uses Yamaha 9000 series drums, Avedis Zildjian cymbals and Vater Session hand-selected hickory drums sticks.

Drinking tea in the kitchen of their thick-walled cottage, overshadowed by higher ground immediately to the north and west, he can seem Hobbit-like – or like a character out of *Wind In The Willows* in a riverside burrow.

His constant companion is their West Highland terrier, and John seems to be entirely content meandering round the village with the dog, chatting to neighbours and flirting with the local ladies in their twin set-and-pearls. If you were to see him sitting by the fire in the front room of the local pub, a pint of Best in one hand and a military vehicle magazine in the other you'd be well advised not to disturb him.

He still has a very rock 'n roll quality to him – particularly when he wants to have – but he's also very conservative, and enormously English. He is an unashamed, unapologetic monarchist and traditionalist, and a passionate supporter of the British armed forces. Many airmen from the local bases live locally and he will talk to them for hours, fascinated by their experiences and knowledgeable about the aircraft they might be talking about. For people like that he has boundless respect.

John with family and friends - August 2003

John is proud of his country, of its rural landscape, and of its traditions. He has an unshakeable faith in real ale, roast beef - and spicy curries. He likes the company of people he knows well, and is a welcoming and conscientious host - but is still far from comfortable with new people, or those who he thinks are invading his privacy or presuming upon him.

The worst thing that anyone can do is bounce up to him and ask if they know him from somewhere, or say something like 'Didn't you used to be John Coghlan?' His life has split into two halves; the first half with the band and the second half - now the longer period - being life after Quo. He's happy to talk about Status Quo with the right people or under the right circumstances, but if the time or the mood or wrong then the shutters will snap down.

Overall, it's probably not something that he thinks about a huge amount, and doubtless doesn't dwell on. The way he has shrugged off the disappointment and the difficulties is remarkable. He is genuinely sanguine about his situation, and completely free of rancour. He never has a bad word to say about his ex-band-mates, and though he undoubtedly misses the band and everything else that went with it, more than anything he regrets not being part of the team; not belonging to that small, tightly-focussed band of guys who were determined to conquer the world at all costs - and on their terms.

If any of the other guys ever chanced into his local John would be

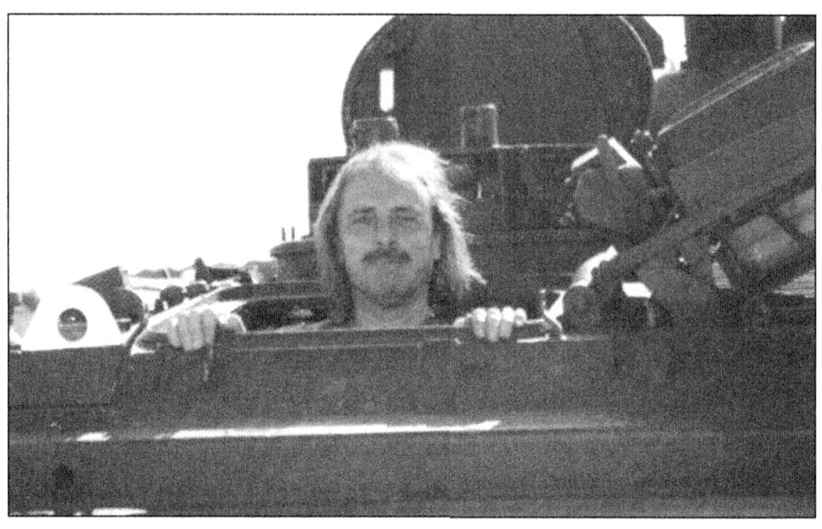

Summer 2003; John at his happiest - in the driving seat of a tank at a Military Vehicle Trust meeting.

beside himself with genuine delight – and he very much wants to be able to feel that they now don't think too badly of him: 'I don't know how Francis feels about me', John muses. 'I saw an interview on TV where he said 'John's a really nice guy' – I think those were his exact words. Maybe all is not lost.

'I've seen the band a couple of times recently. Rick invited Gillie and me to go and see them at the Oxford Apollo on the tour before last. It was good. It was alright. Francis didn't know I was coming but he gave me a bit of hug and asked how I was.

'Deep Purple got back together again; The Eagles got back together again – despite saying that hell would freeze over first! We always had the most loyal fans and I think they'd like it, and I think they deserve it. It would work – fan-wise and box office-wise.'

John does seem to be completely free of any bitterness or anger about the past – unlike Alan, to whom both of those adjectives can probably be applied. 'It's been a long time since I left, and time heals. I don't hold any grudges. None at all', John says, hinting that others might well do so.

Certainly, if someone from the Quo office called him and invited to play even a single gig with the band again, he'd be there. He'd take no emotional baggage to the event, and once he got behind his drum kit he'd be as happy as can be – and would work like a demon.

Alan has said that he would never ever play on stage with Francis Rossi again, but has then qualified that apparent absolute by saying that while money wouldn't get him, a really good cause, a truly worthwhile occasion might.

Rick's take is that 'the numbers would have to be right', and that if a reunion gig or tour was offered with the right pay-packet he would turn up. Francis though is more definite; There's no way it could happen. It would be an explosion. Something would go terribly, terribly wrong. It couldn't happen in a million years.'

'You can always have Status Quo if you've got Parfitt and Rossi because they were the musical identity of the band, but Status Quo were never as good as when it was Parfitt, Rossi, Lancaster and Coghlan,' says Keith Altham. Huge numbers of fans seem to agree, and they cite that four-piece line-up as being a essential, unequalled hard-rockin' Quo. Anything else is a lot less. Status Quo conventions echo with speculation about that line-up appearing on stage together once more, and thousands of words are typed into forums on web sites on the same subject.

'If they got John and Alan back for a tour, they would double their current takings', says Trevor Baines, 'Of that there's absolutely no question. They need to chuck away the past and say 'Hey, come on boys', but there's none so blind as those that will not see ...'

A few years ago John played at Richard Beddall's fiftieth birthday party, and Richard describes the performance as 'absolutely stunning'. He says, 'He did put everything he'd got into his playing. When he was playing drums with Quo he was pumped right up. It was pure adrenalin, and yes, when he came off stage he could be very stroppy, very difficult and argumentative. I'm quite sure it was a defence mechanism though. When he was playing he was a different person.'

Bob Young says that John hasn't actually, essentially changed over the years; 'He's less mad than he was. He's a very interesting character, slightly unpredictable, slightly mad, a bit off the wall – but harmless.' Bob insists that Rick and Francis hold no hard feelings towards John. It's water under the bridge, he says, and John left the band more than twenty years ago – which is a very long time, especially in the music business.

'Rick and Francis are a parody of themselves nowadays', Gillie says, 'I get upset seeing them; I find it hard to deal with and I hate seeing the other drummers. I love Francis and Rick, and Rhino the new bass player – he's a lovely guy – but Rick and Francis are caricatures. They're like actors, just playing a part.'

'John was a bad boy in some ways, but that's rock 'n roll', Trevor Baines says, 'That's the nature of the game. But he was a brilliant drummer, a powerhouse – he was born to it - and the band have never had it as good since he left.'

'John was always the odd one out', Colin Johnson thinks, 'We got up to a lot of crazy things but he wasn't really part of it. When everyone else was taking drugs he just wasn't interested. He was happy on his own, looking through a drum magazine. I don't know what he ever thought he was going to do after leaving. He probably *didn't* think. He could only ever be a drummer.'

'I would really, really like John to be happy and successful in a band again', Gillie says, 'That would just make it – for both of us. For him to be doing what he loves and to be appreciated doing it. Not having to fight for every gig and end up going to shitty places. He's still good enough.'

'Mind you, I never went for all the shit about the pressure. Five star hotels and private jets isn't pressure. Working down the mines is pressure. He says 'You weren't there!', but give me a break - how many boys of twenty-five would give their eye-teeth to be touring with a successful rock band? It was work but it wasn't exactly tough; everything was laid on, everything was on the itinerary. All John had to do was turn up. I wish he was back with that sort of 'pressure'.'

Phil May says, 'If you step away from the music business for six months everything's changed. All the contacts John had, all the people who were important, they'd all gone.

'John didn't bite the bullet. There was undoubtedly a false sense of security – and then the money ran out. John and Gillie were very comfortable on the Isle of Man, and with his collection of military vehicles and everything – and it was almost too much of a distraction. If he'd just been left with the hunger he'd have climbed back.'

Andy Bown adds, 'John was a lucky bastard, like we all are in the music business. I don't know how long it took him to realise that there weren't cheques coming in all the time, and that it had all gone and it was all his own fault. It's a difficult one to swallow.'

Index

Printed in Great Britain
by Amazon